LIFE OUTSIDE

Also by Michelangelo Signorile

Queer in America: Sex, the Media, and the Closets of Power
*Outing Yourself: How to Come Out as Lesbian or Gay to Your Family, Your
   Friends, and Your Coworkers*

LIFE

OUTSIDE

The Signorile Report
on Gay Men:
Sex, Drugs,
Muscles, and
the Passages
of Life

MICHELANGELO SIGNORILE

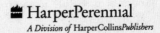
HarperPerennial
A Division of HarperCollins*Publishers*

Designed by Joseph Rutt

The Library of Congress has catalogued the hardcover edition as follows:

Signorile, Michelangelo, 1960–
     Life outside : the Signorile report on gay men : sex, drugs, muscles,
and the passages of life / Michelangelo Signorile. — 1st ed.
          p.   cm.
     ISBN 0-06-018761-1
     1. Gay men—United States. 2. Homosexuality—United States.
3. Masculinity—United States. 4. Gay men—United States—Social
conditions. I. Title.
HQ76.2.U5S54   1997
306.76'6'0973—dc21
                                                                    97-1946

ISBN 0-06-092904-9 (pbk.)

98 99 00 01 02 ❖/RRD 10 9 8 7 6 5 4 3 2 1

FOR DAVID

CONTENTS

ACKNOWLEDGMENTS

I owe an enormous debt of gratitude to the hundreds of gay men who either filled out lengthy surveys about their lives for this book, or whom I formally and informally interviewed. Without their thoughts, insights, observations, and descriptions about their lives, this book would not be possible.

The idea for this book was born from my columns in *Out* magazine, in particular those columns in which I explored personal issues affecting gay men. Many of those columns would not have come to fruition had it not been for *Out*'s founder and former editor-in-chief, Michael Goff, a man I am also proud to call a close personal friend. He often pushed me hard, and challenged me to dig deeper. For that, I am deeply grateful. Similarly, *Out*'s extremely talented executive editor, Bruce Steele, has been instrumental in getting me to say what I want to say.

Sarah Pettit, *Out*'s current editor-in-chief and an old comrade of mine from when we worked side by side in the late 1980s as editors at the now defunct *Outweek* magazine, lent her always keen observations and sharp editorial skills to this project, reading an early draft of the work. I owe her much thanks for that, as well as for her friendship and support. I also want to thank my former editor-in-chief at *Outweek*, Gabriel Rotello, also a close friend, with whom I often discussed many of the ideas in this book and who also read an early draft. I'm thankful to Larry Kramer for reading the work early on, too, and for offering valuable suggestions that made a difference.

Another good friend, Andrew Beaver, also gave me a lot of thoughful input. Many thanks, too, to Ann Northrop for supplying me with much needed diversions throughout this project, and to Troy Masters and Alan Klein for their support and help as well. Thanks also to Alan Brown, who was my guide in some of my field research on the party circuit.

Many of the ideas in this book were formulated with the help of a great many lesbian and gay mental health professionals, either from interviews I did with them or from their published works. In particular I'd like to extend my appreciation to James D. Babl, Betty Berzon, Rosemary Caggiano, Richard Isay, Duane McWaine, Tom Moon, Walt Odets, Michael Shernoff, Charles Silverstein, and Ron Winchel for their insights.

I don't have enough space to describe the many ways that my truly talented editor Mitchell Ivers was invaluable to this project. Our six-year professional relationship, as well as our friendship, has been an enormous learning experience for me. I am proud that we have worked on three books together. And I'm very thankful, as always, for his extraordinary input. Similarly, my agent and dear friend Jed Mattes, one of the bright lights in the world of literary agents, was quite valuable to this project, as usual providing his sharp observations.

Lastly, my relationship with David Gerstner for the past two years was a source of inspiration while I worked on this project. His love and support kept me going. He was there for the highs, and, more importantly, he was there for me for the lows. And somehow, he puts up with me even when we disagree.

INTRODUCTION

Somewhere between the gays-in-the-military issue and the first discussions in the halls of Congress of same-sex marriage in early 1996, I began to receive hundreds of letters and E-mails from gay men seeking advice—or just sharing their sorrows—about problems confronting them, issues for which the president or Congress could be of little to no avail.

I received a fair number of letters from gay men, lesbians, bisexual men and women, and transgendered individuals when I wrote on hot-button political issues of the day for my monthly column for *Out* magazine. But when I wrote from my personal experience as a gay man on matters closer to home—urgent concerns like the reported breakdown in safer sex among many gay men, or mundane but nonetheless trying topics, like the difficulties navigating relationships—I got an extraordinary response from gay men who had also been affected by these issues personally.

I began corresponding with many of the men who had written me about the heartfelt issues affecting their lives, and found that the topics I was discussing in my column were only the tip of the iceberg. Most of the gay men with whom I corresponded had in recent years been searching for answers to problems they previously might not have imagined. Many were beginning to reexamine their lives in some basic areas. In addition to sexual behavior, these areas included love and relationships, family, friendships, and growing older. These issues—similar to those confronting lesbians and heterosexuals—are complicated by the extended adolescence that many gay men experience and the awareness of the possibility of early disease and death.

Those first correspondences were the very beginning of this book. I began thoroughly researching many of the issues gay men spoke about, from looking for love and companionship to coping with midlife crisis. In travels across the country over a two-year period, I casually chatted with or more formally interviewed hundreds of gay men and observed them in various environments.

I also conducted telephone interviews about these issues with many more men of varying ages, races, classes, geographic locales, occupations, religions, and political affiliations. Still more filled out lengthy surveys I designed, which I posted in various places on the Internet. Over six hundred responses came from every corner of the country and the far reaches of the planet. I spoke with therapists who work with gay men as well as doctors, psychologists, epidemiologists, sociologists, sexologists, chemical dependency counselors, nurses, health and fitness trainers, activists, and scholars.

I wasn't simply seeking to identify the problems gay men were experiencing. I was looking for the solutions, looking to see how other people were living their lives in ways that might be instructive to those who were searching for answers.

Much of what I found in my research confirms some of my beliefs of recent years regarding gay men, their lives, and their culture. Just as much contradicts and challenges other beliefs I've had. In general, my findings shed a new light on what many gay men have wrongly and rightly believed previously about themselves and about other gay men.

LIFE INSIDE THE MAINSTREAM

Many Americans today, straight and gay, agree that gay male life is more varied and all-encompassing than ever before. Even the most homophobic and antigay heterosexuals admit—albeit with great alarm—that homosexuals are *everywhere*: Antigay zealots know all too well that there are, for example, closeted as well as openly gay teachers, doctors, ministers, and scout leaders. These zealots remain keen on exploiting those realities, hurling the old and ugly charge that homosexuals "recruit" children.

Gay men and lesbians also know—and sometimes admit with great alarm—that gays occupy every facet of American life: To the increasing dismay of gay progressives, there are gay Republican groups, gay anti-abortion groups, and gay gun-owners. To the chagrin of gay conservatives, there are gay feminists, gay sex radicals, and gay Marxists.

While these differences might on the surface reveal a disjointed and fractured group, the variety is in many ways also a measure of the gay movement's success. As more people come out of the closet, they create more choices about *how* to be gay or lesbian. A great many gay people of the youngest generations are in fact growing up without the closet at all, realizing their homosexuality at a young age, often in their early teens, and going through adolescence as openly gay individuals, out to their parents, classmates, teachers, and friends. Many are dating in high school, joining gay and lesbian youth groups, and even organizing politically. And they are perhaps constructing their lives less around the concealment of their homosexuality and more around other issues affecting them, living their lives as most other Americans do.

Gay men and lesbians of all generations are integrating

their gay lives into their biological families' lives in ways that were not acceptable before, bringing friends and lovers home for holidays and family events and inviting their biological families into their own families of gay friends. Rather than cut themselves off or accept family rejection—as many were forced to do in earlier times—they're working hard to stay close with their families, often finding the bonds even *stronger* since they've come out.

Similarly once rejected from most religious denominations, many gay people are finding themselves welcomed in an ever increasing number of Christian churches and Jewish synagogues. In many cities, some synagogues and traditional Protestant churches have congregations that are predominantly lesbian and gay. The Metropolitan Community Church, founded in 1968 by the Reverend Troy Perry specifically to include the lesbian and gay community, has experienced dramatic growth in recent years; it is today in fact the largest organization serving the gay community in the United States, with a budget of $10 million annually. An MCC church is often a center of gay life for many, both in urban centers like Dallas and San Francisco, where its largest congregations are, and in smaller cities and towns, such as Augusta, Georgia, and Biloxi, Mississippi.

The strides of gay liberation have also made it safe for lesbians and gay men to organize openly and officially in almost every major occupation, from aviation to journalism. More and more gay people are finding that, rather than lead a secretive or *heterosexualized* life at work, it is far less stressful simply to be out. More and more employers are coming to realize that this increases productivity rather than harming it.

Perhaps most profoundly, all of these changes are being recorded daily in the American media, as gays and lesbians have in recent years found our lives under a microscope for the first time. Gay life, in the urban areas as well as in the suburbs, small towns, and beyond, has been the subject of much media attention, showing straight as well as gay America that gay people can and do lead a vast array of "lifestyles" and not one particular "gay lifestyle" that, as the stereotype had pegged gay men specifically, centers around sex and hedonism. The visible choices now offered to young and older gay men and lesbians are in fact greater than they have ever been. And for many, life outside the mainstream of urban, suburban, small-town, and rural America is no longer the only option.

TWO PHENOMENA

For gay men in particular, a wide variety of social and sexual subcultures have also developed and grown over the years. In addition to the social groups that formed around specific age groups, occupations, and interests—from opera aficionados to bowling enthusiasts—there are social groups, bars, and night-clubs for African-American gay men, Latino gay men, Asian gay men, Native American gay men, and men of other racial and ethnic backgrounds, as well as for gay men of all races who wish to socialize within interracial settings. Many men have become more aware of gay sexual subcultures that offer alternatives. Gay "bears"—men who celebrate a wide variety of body types and particularly larger, hirsute men—have gained more visibility. The leather and s/m subculture within the gay world has organized and grown dramatically, some segments of which having also established themselves as more open with regard to body type, age, and class.

And yet, as all of these changes have occurred in the gay male world, and as this phenomenon of expansion has offered more choices to gay men, another phenomenon has also continued over the years, almost unabated: There is an overriding, mostly white, youth-focused, and often drug-fueled social and sexual gay male scene that is highly commercialized and demands conformity to a very specific body ideal. Its cultural influence and impact are significant, and it affects many—perhaps most—gay men, even if they think they are far removed from it, regardless of whether they belong to other subcultures or social groups within the gay world or not. Emanating from within the urban gay ghettos, this phenomenon, as we know it today, has it roots in the 1970s and indeed began in part as a reaction to the harsh homophobia of life *outside* the ghettos. Today it appears to be growing larger and more rapidly.

Part I of this book, entitled Life Inside, is a look at the inner workings of this phenomenon. That title, however, is by no means intended to represent all or even most of gay life inside the urban ghettos. Rather, Part I is a look at one particular and powerful trend that emanates from within those ghettos. It focuses specifically on how this phenomenon originated, how it has evolved over the years, where it has taken us today, what tensions and problems it creates and exacerbates for many men, and why it is more powerful than ever before. Part II of this book, entitled Life Outside, is a look at several specific aspects of another phenomenon in the gay world: the expansion of gay life outside this particular social and sexual scene.

PART I: LIFE INSIDE

The modern urban gay ghettos served in the 1970s as refuges for gay people, places where gay men could explore their newfound sexual liberation shortly after Stonewall and create the kinds of bonds with other men that were previously denied them. For a great many gay men during that time, gay life centered around bar and nightlife culture, including baths, sex clubs, and all-night dance palaces, many of which—though not all—catered to primarily white, middle-class gay men with money to spend. Recreational drug use was for many the norm, considered part of the new liberating climate and a way of overthrowing the repression of previous years. After many years of being stigmatized and stereotyped as effeminate and as less than manly, many of these white, middle-class gay men also proudly and enthusiastically conformed to an idealized version of physical manhood—muscles, mustaches, and tight jeans—that had rapidly evolved within these urban gay circles. The cultural influence of this decidedly hypermasculine "clone" aesthetic went out to the far reaches of the gay male world, beyond the urban ghetto and beyond the cities themselves.

Situated within a larger heterosexual culture that was much more ignorant of gay people than it is today, this hypermasculine, sexually charged, and drug-fueled way of life was perhaps the most visible aspect of gay male life in the 1970s. Indeed, that ignorance of any other aspect of gay life—an ignorance inspired by homophobia—contributed to the creation within the heterosexual mainstream of the unilateral "gay lifestyle" stereotype, marked by hedonism and excess.

For many gay men, the moralistic tone that accompanied this description of their lifestyle was troubling and offensive, although the description itself was not. For them, this was a liberating and celebratory way to lead their lives, a way of life they were proud of, a way that showed they had combated the sexual repression that for years made them feel shameful about sex and about their homosexuality. For others, however, it was always a potentially damaging and self-destructive lifestyle. And for many, it was perhaps a mix of both. More precisely, many men realized that it was a lifestyle that was fun for a little while but which they eventually had to break from because of its sheer intensity, which the burgeoning AIDS crisis in the early 1980s later underscored. Others realized that it was never right for them in the first place.

For many gay men, the 1970s gay urban fast life was something they fell into because it was what they first saw upon entering the ghetto. They fell into it because it was alluring and captivating and was all they knew about being gay for some time. Though there may have been other choices available just below the surface, many gay men believed that there was only one way to be gay. In many cases, they later realized that that was not true. But this was often only after a process of soul-searching and awareness had begun—for some, spurred by the AIDS crisis—a process that had them seeking out the many alternatives that rapidly emerged within the urban gay world and beyond.

Although things have changed dramatically since the 1970s, particularly but not exclusively as a result of AIDS, the same dynamic is still in place, operating for many gay men today. Despite the highly visible choices now offered to gay men in the urban ghettos and beyond, many young gay men see only one choice, the choice that is most seductive to them as they enter the gay ghettos. This new gay fast life is similar, except for three considerable factors:

- The drugs are more potent and often more destructive.

- The physical paradigms to which it demands conformity are more rigid.

- The anxieties it exploits, as well as the dangers it courts—particularly around AIDS—are greater than ever.

In interviews and surveys I conducted for this book, gay men in their twenties and thirties alternately called this urban gay fast life the gay "scene," the "hot boy party life," the "gay system," and, somewhat endearingly by one man, the "homo rocket to hell." While this book studies this phenomenon in the gay world in a very particular way, what is referred to as the urban gay "scene" should not be understood to encompass all of urban gay life. Rather "scene" refers to one predominantly white, middle-class, and often upper-middle-class segment of urban gay life that nonetheless has a significant cultural influence on much of the gay population, throughout its various racial, social, and sexual subcultures.

Although the straight world has its own somewhat similar urban sexual singles scene, it does not appear to be as influential on the whole of straight life. The straight singles scene seems to involve a far lower percentage of heterosexuals than the percentage of homosexuals who seem directly involved in the gay scene. And while there are heterosexuals in their thirties and beyond directly involved in the straight equivalent of this scene, the straight version appears to be made up primarily of younger, twenty- to thirty-year-old people who for the most part quickly outgrow it and move on. In the gay urban world, however, the scene can and often does dominate a man's life throughout his twenties and thirties, and even into his forties and beyond.

Many people, particularly older gay men, had believed—and often still believe—that the urban gay scene as they knew it had ended, or that it had at least greatly subsided. They of course knew that AIDS couldn't kill urban gay nightlife, and they knew that bars and clubs were still popular meeting places for younger as well as older gay men. But many assumed that the wild and carefree all-night extravaganzas, the competitive and highly regimented bodybuilding culture, the drugs, the orgies, and the weekend-long affairs of reckless abandon had come to a halt. These things did subside for a short time during the 1980s, but for reasons that this book explains the scene came back quite powerfully, particularly for men in their twenties and thirties, even while many gay men of all ages broadened their lives and created alternatives to it. Hence, the "scene" is thriving once again today, replete with an even more rigid physical ideal. The scene is now viewed by many gay men as an actual antidote to AIDS. These men see the scene as an escape valve that helps them cope—even though its frenetic pace and the anxieties it exacerbates and exploits, as this book explains in great detail, seem to be contributing to the pressures that have in part created a breakdown in safer sex among many men on the scene. This is particularly true among younger generations, and we are seeing the resulting serotransmissions that are contributing to the AIDS epidemic in the gay population.

That indeed is one way that this urban gay scene affects the entire gay male population, even if most gay men may be far removed from it: As Gabriel Rotello shows in his 1997 book *Sexual Ecology*, epidemiologists note that it is *core groups* within communities that can sustain an epidemic such as HIV for the entirety of a population, keeping seroprevalance high due to multiple-partner unsafe sex within the core groups. This ultimately affects everyone and anyone beyond the core group who sexually mixes with those in the core group. Thus no one in the affected population can ever slip up with regard to safer sex—not even once in a while—something that may not be humanly possible. That is not to say of course that this particular urban gay scene constitutes the only such core group in the gay population of the urban centers: There are in fact many core groups driving the epidemic in the gay population and they are not all white and middle class. The rising rates of HIV transmission among young black gay men and young Latino gay men clearly bear that out. The core group within this particular, larger urban gay scene is just one among several that are relevant to the epidemic's persistence and important to study.

Although the scene is driven at any one time by perhaps only a small portion of urban gay men, it affects a much greater number of gay men—perhaps most of us—in ways beyond the epidemiological, more than we might imagine. There are of course the men who are themselves whirling in the middle of it all, caught up in it in its entirety. It is impossible to say how many or what percentage of gay men this is—and some would say it's an extremely small minority of the greater gay male population—but it is probably representative of a large segment of young men in the twenty to thirty-five age group in the heart of dozens of America's urban gay ghettos. Then there are the many more of us, some within the same age range and others who are older, who pass through the scene, treating it as a transitional phase, or "a rite of passage," as some call it, spending a couple of years intensely involved in it and then moving on. There are others of us who go back and forth to it too, often between relationships—or during relationships—for periods of months or years throughout our lives.

And, yes, there are many who created a lifestyle that is for the most part an alternative to this specific gay scene, centered around work, relationships, families, creative endeavors, or other interests, and who access the scene only on occasion.

They may have even submerged themselves in less rigid and less taxing sexual and nonsexual subcultures within the gay world, which may or may not be highlighted by drug use. But even these men might, for example, once in a while go out to the "hot boy" club of choice or the "circuit" event of the moment, do the recreational drug that's all the rage and dance all night. Even though they barely participate in the scene, they experience its allure and its pervasive influence.

In totality then, the scene includes to varying degrees a greater number of gay men than the small group of its most loyal adherents at any one time.

Among the most prominent of the scene's cultural impacts—and one that does not require direct involvement in the scene in order to feel its influence—is the physical ideal it promotes. Chapter 2 offers a historical sketch of the physical ideal that the urban gay scene today props up, and what anxieties within us all regarding that ideal are exploited by the commercial aspects of the scene. Chapters 2 and 3 also look at why this physical ideal is more rigid than previously and how AIDS has impacted it.

The gay urban scene today encompasses what has come to be known as the "circuit," a series of large gay dance parties that occur throughout the year in cities around the country and around the world, attended by tens of thousands of gay men. The scene as a whole is much larger than the circuit itself, including other segments of gay communities in the gay ghettos, whether or not these men are also "on the circuit." Chapters 2 and 3 examine how the circuit, which some of its devotees today describe as a "movement" within the gay world, has grown and is continuing to grow, and how it has a cultural influence—in the form not only of the physical paradigms it promotes but of a value system and lifestyle it offers—that filters down to gay communities far and wide, in the urban ghettos and beyond, no matter how far removed we are from it. These chapters show how "minicircuits" in many cities have sprung up in the past couple of years that set the standard for many young gay men today on *how* to be gay—both in looks as well as in lifestyles and activities.

To study just how the values and the physical paradigms of the gay urban scene filter down to the average gay man, it is thus important to study the circuit, a powerful source of those values and paradigms. For this reason the book focuses in Chapter 3 very specifically on the circuit. Though the circuit represents a comparatively small group within the gay world, it is, as stated, one of several phenomena that indirectly affect how many of us live our lives and how we physically perceive one another. In the voices of the many gay men who appear in Chapter 3 we can perhaps all find glimmers of ourselves, even if the circuit is something with which we are hardly familiar or even something we disdain.

In that way, as this book explains throughout, even if we've left the scene far behind or even if we've never been a part of it at all, a highly commercialized gay sexual culture sells a particular physical aesthetic to us and demands that we conform to it—much in the same way that the fashion, film, and beauty industries affect the average American woman.

Describing in interviews and surveys what some gay men have called the "body thing" within the urban gay male world, as well as describing other aspects of their lives, a great many men of all ages—on the circuit as well as off—living in New York, Chicago, Los Angeles, San Francisco, Atlanta, Washington, Boston, and other urban meccas with large gay ghettos indeed used words like *rigid, trapped, stifled, suffocating, oppressive, confining,* and *pressured.* More than one gay man I interviewed even used the metaphor of being "in prison."

For some gay men, just as for some women, these feelings have led them to extremes: They're altering their bodies in dangerous ways in order to increase their worth, sexually and otherwise, because they have been led to believe that this is the only way to raise their self-esteem. Chapter 4 studies what appears to be a trend in black market and legal steroid use, as well as the use of other dangerous over-the-counter, controlled and illegal substances that promise muscular enhancement and fat reduction. This trend appears to be growing rapidly among many young gay men in the urban centers, and it promises to wreak havoc within the current young gay generation in years to come. Chapter 4 also shows how the doctor-supervised therapeutic use of testosterone and anabolic steroids, which began in the early 1990s to treat many gay men infected with HIV to fight the wasting of lean muscle tissue, is perhaps aiding in normalizing the already increasing use of black market and often dangerous steroids by many other gay men, HIV-negative and -positive, for cosmetic, not therapeutic, purposes.

The covert use of steroids and other drugs by many has narrowed the physical ideal even further. This in turn seems to be increasing anxieties in more men who are trying desperately to attain the physical ideal, but who are finding it even harder than before, often not realizing that at this point the ideal is beyond having "good genes" and working out hard: The ideal is more and more about drug enhancement. For some men, this creates enormous pressure and exacerbates low self-esteem, particularly if they are trying to compete on the scene. But even many far away from the scene who are telegraphed its physical paradigms experience these same insecurities to varying degrees.

These are the things that *The Signorile Report on Gay Men* finds happening inside the urban gay scene. Not surprisingly, outside the scene the gay world is expanding in far different ways.

PART II: LIFE OUTSIDE

As more men become caught up in the scene, others do not. They feel its powerful influence but they do not actively participate in it on a regular basis. Whether it is the young New York artist who forgoes the regimented muscle scene of Chelsea and submerges himself in the East Village creative community, or the rural Indiana man who decides not to move to the city and meets a lover and buys a farm, many gay men are breaking from the scene and are living life outside of it, realizing that it is by far not the only way to be gay.

One way of looking at this paradox in the gay world, of studying these dual phenomena, is: *The fast lane is getting faster, but the slow lane is getting wider.* Part II of this book, Life Outside, focuses on this other trend in the gay world, also growing rapidly but seemingly in a different direction.

Many gay men within the urban centers have for years been living outside the scene. They created their own alternatives and they live more in the mainstream of urban life. Part II of this book, however, focuses on this phenomenon specifically as it has played out in the past few years *outside* of the cities, where it is perhaps most dramatic and most interesting to study.

Indeed it was the explosion of gay life in the cities throughout the 1970s, and the vast alternatives offered within the cities beyond the scene—coupled with the greater tolerance of homosexuality in America in recent years, again a direct result of the political organizing that crystallized among lesbian and gay activists in the urban centers—that in many ways told gay men outside the cities that they didn't have to move to cities and join the scene in order to be gay.

Chapter 5 studies the deurbanization of homosexuality: a look at some of the many gay men who in recent years have not moved to the cities or have moved back to suburban, rural, and small-town locales after living in the cities for some time. Many of these men are not, as they often were in the past, closeted and cowering in their rural, small-town, and suburban locales anymore. They are in fact among the first generations of gay people who choose not to move to the city en masse but to live their lives openly in nonurban locales. Most realize that their ability to live outside the cities is a direct result of almost thirty years of gay organizing in the urban ghettos. Generally, they see themselves as an extension of the still-burgeoning gay movement that originated in the cities. But they've applied their small-town, suburban, and rural values to being openly gay rather than to emulating the particular gay ghetto life associated with the scene. They have refreshing and remarkable insights, and they are navigating through life in ways that may influence all gay men in the future.

Indeed, while many single gay men of all ages both inside and outside the cities are constructing their lives in various ways that break from the scene, many who are coupled are also making choices that break from the scene with regard to how they construct their relationships. In particular, many men inside and outside the cities—but perhaps more so outside the cities—appear to be eschewing the classic "open relationship" that was considered the norm within the urban scene. And yet, they're not exactly opting for a heterosexual version of love and monogamy either. Chapter 6 discusses what I have termed *postmodern monogamy*. This chapter takes a look at those couples who are emotionally and sexually monogamous on the one side—or trying to be—and those on the other side who are emotionally monogamous and are for the most part sexually monogamous, but who allow for sex outside the relationship on occasion. Though this latter group of men are actually in a form of open relationship, they don't define themselves in this sense, perhaps because in the gay world the term "open relationship" has come to mean something much more open than what they have.

Defying those inside and outside the gay male community who for years have said it was impossible—or delusional—for gay men to attempt monogamy or even near monogamy, it appears that many gay men in couples are striving to be in sexually monogamous, long-term relationships. Only human, they sometimes don't adhere to this—but probably not as often as many might think. Other couples are making agreements to allow for the occurrence of sex on the outside once in a while by one or both partners, understanding that it simply may happen, but deciding not to discuss it when and if it does. Chapter 6 discusses how these relationship styles differ from the classic, 1970s-inspired gay open relationship.

While the philosophy of the urban scene might deem these couples as regressive, retrograde, and perhaps dishonest, Chapter 6 shows how these men are in fact dealing with the realities of jealousy and resentment, and feel that this is actually the best possible way for them to remain closely bonded. They believe that, though it might work for others, the classic open relationship, which they in the past felt pressured to master, for them would be destructive and counterproductive.

In ways beyond relationships, many gay men are continuing to break the gay molds of the past. Perhaps one of the most important areas where this is occurring is in dealing with the various changes and traumas associated with growing older. Both in the urban centers and beyond—but again, perhaps more prominently outside the cities—there is today more non-sexual mixing and socializing between gay men of all ages, outside of the traditional meeting places such as bars and clubs, and many older men are assuming roles as mentors to younger men. The barriers between the generations are breaking down, helping put to rest some of the most enduring myths about older gay men. Chapter 7 focuses on the stereotype of the "lonely old queen," and how this stereotype continues to plague those caught up in the scene, fearful of aging and of losing their looks and their self-worth. Calling for the death of the stereotype of the lonely old queen, Chapter 7 shows those gay men who are shedding the ugly stereotype for themselves and for the generations that follow them. Their lives will inspire us all.

A PERSONAL JOURNEY

As I alluded to in the very beginning of this introduction, I wrote this book in part in response to some of my own personal experiences as a gay man navigating through life in America in the 1990s. Working as a journalist and author, traveling the country, covering the gay world, it might, for example, seem that I should be informed about safer sex, and that keeping up safer sex practices should not be a problem. And yet, I had in the past found myself, on occasion, engaging in unsafe sex, putting my life at risk. After much soul-searching I wrote about one of these experiences, in a lengthy column for *Out* in September 1994, which focused on what appeared to be a breakdown in safer sex among a great many gay men, young and old, and a rise in HIV transmission in the gay population after several years of leveling off.

Last year I spent a couple of grueling weeks on assign-
ment in Hawaii. One night in a Waikiki gay bar I met
your classic gay hunk: tall and masculine, with a
buzzed haircut, razor-sharp cheekbones, a body of
granite, and a Texas drawl. I'll make you see God
tonight, he promised, trying to coax me to go home
with him. It didn't take much for me to realize I
needed a religious experience; we went to his place.
As usual, one thing quickly led to another. But not as
usual, he didn't put on a condom before we had anal
sex, and I didn't demand he use one. . .

. . . I'd had a couple of Absolut Citrons. And I had
made a quick decision—inside of ten seconds—based
on heat-of-the-moment rationalizations that at some
distance seem absurd: 1) Since he did not put on a
condom, he must be negative; 2) He is a Navy petty
officer and therefore is a responsible "good" boy;
3) Since he's in the military he must be tested every six
months and would be discharged if positive; 4) He's
absolutely perfect—the gay male ideal—and I don't
want to do anything to make him blow off the whole
night; 5) I'm sure it'll be okay as long as he doesn't
come; 6)This is Hawaii, and the AIDS problem can't
be like it is in New York; 7) I'll only do it this one time.

That column resonated with a great many men, and it
received national media attention, inspiring a *Newsweek* piece
and many newspaper articles. *60 Minutes* eventually profiled
me for a piece on unsafe sex among gay men. A second column I wrote on the topic in *Out* was reprinted on the op-ed
page of the *New York Times*. In writing about the issues
involved and speaking with many other men who had similar

experiences, I began to realize how many of us allow the scene, its pressures and its values, to enable us, and perhaps even encourage us, to ignore safer sex—no matter how educated we are on the topic. But clearly, as this book shows, that is just one among many ways that we allow the scene to exploit our anxieties and lead us to extremes. Having eventually tested negative, I felt I had a new lease on life, and I was energized to explore the areas that create tension and conflict for many gay men. For me, this book was thus a personal journey through the scene and beyond it. In researching it, I explored areas of the gay world, and ideas and ideologies that have developed within it, that I had not previously explored and studied in great detail. Many of the conclusions I reached are ones that would previously have made me uncomfortable. Indeed, they might have that effect on others.

In particular, some people may be uncomfortable with the use of the term "monogamy," especially since I am sometimes using it in a context in which it means something other than the technical definition of the word. Monogamy is a word that for many is fraught with problems, carrying the weight of heterosexual orthodoxy; even some gay couples who are technically monogamous do not like to use the term. Nonetheless, as I explain in detail in Chapter 5, it is a term whose meaning seems to have shifted among many gay men—as has the term "open relationship"—and I decided that it was important to allow men to use the terms and labels they chose for themselves, as long as those terms and labels were clearly defined.

Some older gay men, and perhaps some younger gay men, also may not be comfortable with this book's study and critique of masculinity. For many years, gay men were negatively stereotyped as "effeminate," and "womanly," characterizations that were as misogynistic as they were homophobic. Many gay

activists over the decades worked hard to dispel those stereotypes, and to show that gay men were often as "masculine" as
straight men. But as is often the case, we can go too far in the
other direction in trying to dispel stereotypes; in many ways we
have inadvertently demonized effeminacy within our own
community. This book deals with our own anxieties about
masculinity and effeminacy in great detail. It is not meant,
however, to be an attack on masculinity or an attack on male
beauty per se. It is rather a critique of how we often allow these
things to exploit one another and to consume one another.

Similarly, this book is not to be construed as an attack on
sex, sexual attraction, working out, or going to the gym. Like a
great many gay men, I belong to a health club, work out regularly, am mindful about my physical appearance, and greatly
enjoy sex. Some feminist writers in recent years have critiqued
the fashion and beauty industries and have studied many
women's slavish devotion to attaining a physical ideal. At the
same time, these writers have often celebrated female sexuality, sexual attraction, and looking "sexy." For them, it's not
about giving up lipstick, high heels, and physical beauty. It is
rather about not allowing such things to dictate their self-worth
and determine their value to men. In the same way, I set out in
this book to show how and why many gay men often become
obsessed with physical appearance rather than have a healthy
relationship to their bodies as well as to their sexual desires.

It is my hope, and it is the ambition of this book, that many
gay men within the culture of narcissism and hedonism that
envelops much of the gay world will follow in the footsteps of
a great many others, gay men who have discovered a more
rewarding, fuller, and richer life, outside.

PART ONE

LIFE

INSIDE

1

THE CULT OF MASCULINITY

"I want a body just like that," Chris tells me, gesturing to a six-foot-two blond man with a lean, chiseled body. We're standing on a staircase overlooking the main floor at Equinox, the downtown Manhattan gym to which we both belong. Like several other chic New York gyms, Equinox is a workout spa for, among others, countless top fashion models and soap opera stars and well-groomed gay men of every occupation. Chris, who works at an exclusive uptown hair and makeup salon, laments the fact that the gym is filled with "beautiful people" in whose presence he says he feels less than attractive—even though no one has put a gun to his head to join this gym.

"My whole life is like—well, I'm surrounded by the top five percent in the world," he observes, referring to society's hierarchy of physical beauty. "It's really intimidating a lot of the time. I mean, I work all day at the salon, doing the hair of models and actors, and then I come here at the end of the day, and it's the same thing."

Chris will never have the body of the blond man he pointed out because that man is over six feet tall and lanky, and Chris is five foot seven with a thicker, sturdier build. But, at thirty years old, Chris is quite handsome in his own right and has a muscular, tight body, attractive enough to get his share of stares in this attitude-driven place. Chris has just come off of a relationship with a personal trainer who is drop-dead gorgeous. Yet Chris feels inadequate when it comes to his looks. He wants more, he says.

Over espresso at a nearby café, Chris spells it out more clearly: "I want to be physical perfection in the eyes of gay men—totally physically appealing, like the ultimate. The perfect tits and butt, bulbous biceps. I want to achieve symmetry, big and in proportion. I would look like the cover of an *HX* [*Homo Xtra*, a New York bar giveaway known for its covers of hot men]—lean, sculpted, muscular, virile, a stallion, a guy that would make your mouth water. I want to know what it's like to walk down the street and have everyone look at you, absolutely *everyone*. I want to know what it's like to really feel like an *object*."

What does he believe all of this will do for him?

"Honestly, and I'm embarrassed to say it, but I'm hoping it will boost my self-esteem," he admits. "I don't know how to boost my self-esteem now. My feeling is, 'Get a great body and people will admire you. Get a great body and everything will be okay.' There's that voice inside me that of course says that all of that is full of shit. But it's not powerful enough to overcome this magnetic pull, the promise of what the perfect body might bring. It's this belief that if I can just get the perfect body, then I wouldn't be insecure. I would feel more confident. I wouldn't be afraid of certain gay environments."

ONE PILL MAKES YOU LARGER

There's a little bit of Chris in every gay man. And there's a lot of Chris in a lot of gay men. Some are not quite as caught up as Chris and aware of it. Others are just as caught up as

Chris is, or even more so, and not the slightest bit aware. Chris's thoughts and feelings have relevance for many gay men, particularly those who live in the urban gay ghettos, where the pressure to look a certain way is most intense and where even lovers often find themselves competing over their looks.

It was during his relationship with his ex-lover, the drop-dead gorgeous personal trainer, that Chris says his desire to be "perfect" became more acute. "I wasn't as consumed with it as much before Ryan," he recalls. "It wasn't until I felt I was in competition with Ryan. The more I fell in love with him, the more I wanted to own him. I feared losing him to another man with a better body than me. I would see people look at him all the time, and I wanted to know what it felt like."

Chris works out with weights "at the very least" three days a week, except when he's "in a routine, on a quest," in which case he does intense workouts with a trainer twice a week in addition to the three times a week on his own.

"I'm using money on a trainer that I should be using on therapy," he flatly tells me. "It's intense. I spend all my money on supplements too. Right now I wake up and I take a Met-Rx ["engineered food," a meal replacement shake with a whopping thirty-seven grams of protein per serving] and a teaspoon of creatine monohydrate [an over-the-counter powdered compound believed to increase endurance and build muscle tissue]. Then with my first actual meal later on I take four tablets of HMB [beta-hydroxy beta-methylbutyrate monohydrate, an over-the-counter supplement billed as a "protein breakdown suppressor"]."

Chris has in the past used illegal steroids. "I took one shot of steroids, but didn't finish the cycle," he says. "I was living with a guy who is HIV-positive, my ex-boyfriend's ex, and I couldn't believe he was doing all of these unhealthy things to his body. These weren't the steroids that some people with AIDS take for health reasons—these were black market, used for bodybuilding. I figured if he did them, I could. He took B$_{12}$ shots and a cycle of steroids—he was doing Deca and Winstrol, two different steroids. There are many different ways that it works. People just take different things. If you want to get big, there's a steroid to make you big. There is one to make you lean and vascular. There's a pyramid technique too, you can stack up different steroids for a variety of effects. I really don't know much about them, just trusted this guy really. The steroids we took, he got them from [a well-known gay gym], where somebody was dealing them. They're from Russia."

Chris had this friend inject the steroids into his butt with a hypodermic needle. He describes looking at the liquid before it was injected: "It was like looking at the rainbow and seeing what it would be like to be on the other side, that this liquid could make me the object of someone's desires. That's what it offered to me I guess, the chance to get to the other side. I was looking at it and thinking, What would it be like to have the control and the power to say *no* to a gorgeous guy who was trying to pick me up? That's more power—I wouldn't even say yes, because half of them are cheeseballs. I want to walk among them to pick and choose and be able to turn them down."

That first week on steroids, Chris says, was a bit "crazy," as the physical and emotional effects of the steroids kicked in. "I found myself a bit more explosive," he recalls, describing what are commonly known as "roid rages." "There were times when I'd be feeling these feelings and turn to a friend and just roar. I felt unstoppable. That first week, nothing could stand in my way. I was walking heavy. I felt strong, like, *Don't fuck with me!*"

Chris soon became afraid of the dangerous aspects of the steroids, not only to his psyche, but also to his body. He was well aware of what the steroids could do to him physically, damaging his liver and kidneys permanently, particularly since he was not using legal steroids under the supervision of his doctor (for medicinal purposes) and didn't really know what he was taking or whether the doses were truly safe. "I'd paid three hundred dollars for the cycle, but I was afraid to go through with it," Chris says. So he stopped taking steroids after that first week. But now he's thinking about the idea all over again.

"At this moment, this afternoon, speaking to you, there is a part of me that is so desperate and feeling so low," he confides, "that I'm thinking about taking the steroids again and running the risk. I inquired about them again last night, and I guess I feel that if I did it in moderation, it would be okay. Like I said, there is another side of me saying that that's just bull. That side of me says I'm attractive, I'm witty, I have a good sense of style, I have a good body. Why not spend the time, the money, the energy on something that's going to actually show achievements? Why not put myself into my career, or travel, take classes, educate myself, work on myself from the inside out, rather than the outside in? I don't know why I don't do those things instead. I don't know."

Chris realizes that many guys who are as caught up in their physical appearance as he is, who are going to similar extremes, don't have nearly the same awareness of it that he does. And he's not sure who is luckier: them or him. "That's why I can't figure out why I'm doing this," he says. "I mean, because I know better, and yet I proceed. I talk to a lot of these guys, and they haven't thought much at all about what they're doing. Who is really better off? At least these guys aren't fretting about it. These people I want to attract, most of them don't have any awareness of anything I think is important. Why do I even want to be involved with them at all? Why would I want to be around people who are so consumed? They're not physically fit, they probably won't live to be fifty, they take drugs that will do damage to their liver, their kidneys, they could have a heart attack early, and they run the risk of losing their hair—and their skin often reacts badly to the drugs and is being ruined too."

Many—perhaps most—gay men today in the urban centers are focused to varying degrees on achieving the masculine ideal Chris describes, putting a lot of time, effort, and money into looking a particular way. No matter what we do, however, most of us will never become the masculine ideal we are striving for. But that doesn't stop us from trying.

"It really is like a cult," Chris observes. "It's like we're trying to get to the *promised land*—that's what we believe the perfect, masculine, muscular body really is—and what we're hoping to find in the promised land is confidence, a sense of self, power, and control. You can't help but get caught up in this, and once you are, you're hooked."

What Chris describes is an example of the intense preoccupation with, and outward appearance of, a particular kind of masculinity that has developed in urban gay culture over the past few decades. Today, however, for a variety of reasons, it is more acute and pervasive than ever before. It has become a phenomenon mostly about artifice and manner—how we *appear*—and is not necessarily indicative of our being wrapped up in masculinity as it has been defined throughout history. Masculinity has, for example, been associated with specific and sometimes brutal *behaviors*, such as invading foreign lands or subjugating women. Gay men as a group do neither. Nor do we necessarily take on some of the deeper psychological qualities and complicated behavioral traits associated with heterosexual men. Many of us, rather, emulate a traditionally masculine *look*, wearing a particular kind of masculinity as a costume and exaggerating it for effect. Ours is more a postmodern masculinity, associated with performance and looking the part—what someone described to me as *virtual* masculinity.

This phenomenon might have in the past seemed harmless; to some, it might even have seemed liberating. But that is no longer the case, at least for a great many of the players themselves. Our preoccupation with appearing masculine has begun to exploit our anxieties and chain us to certain behaviors. For many of us, it has become an addiction, difficult if not impossible to break from.

It is the cult of masculinity.

OBSESSION

In the past, writers have looked at masculinity as a small cult within the larger gay world. "Many of the problems that haunt gay love relationships spring from the difficulties of two men each imbued and trained in the demands of masculinity as defined by our society," Dr. Charles Silverstein, celebrated gay psychotherapist and co-author of the classic *The Joy of Gay Sex*, wrote in 1981, in his book *Man to Man: Gay Couples in America*. "In its most extreme form I call it *cult masculinity*, in which symbols of masculinity exert more influence over behavior than the need for love. Cult masculinity is excitement seeking carried to its most extreme form."

An obsession with masculine appearance is not, of course,

confined to gay men; we live in a culture that is slavishly focused on physical beauty and where men are often highly insecure about masculinity. Certainly, like Chris, many straight men who are not professional bodybuilders also take steroids, work out, and obsess about their bodies, conforming to a masculine ideal. Studies in fact show that this obsession is particularly acute among heterosexual teenagers today, increasingly influenced by advertising that props up the male ideal. But the cult of masculinity plays out in distinct and unique ways among gay men.

As a community, we don't like to discuss the topic. We're loathe to be reminded of some of society's worst (and particularly simplistic) stereotypes about gay men: We are "narcissistic," "hedonistic," and "self-absorbed." However, it is probably safe to assume, for reasons that are not difficult to understand, that a greater percentage of gay men than straight men are highly concerned with their physical appearance. According to an *Advocate* sex survey published in 1994, in which *Advocate* subscribers and readers in general were asked to fill out a lengthy questionnaire and mail it back, 19 percent of those who responded said they pump iron six hours or more per week (which, if the average workout is one hour, breaks down to lifting weights almost every day), and 59 percent said they lift weights regularly but less than six hours per week (an average of three days a week). Thus, a whopping 78 percent of the thirteen thousand gay men surveyed by the *Advocate* regularly pump iron. I conducted informal surveys of more than six hundred gay men that showed 67 percent of them regularly worked out at the gym or lifted weights. Though this is a lower percentage than the *Advocate*'s findings, it still indicates a vast majority.

My surveys and the *Advocate*'s are of course problematic

in that they are not random samples. Those who responded to either or both surveys might be men who for whatever reason are more or less inclined to go to the gym. Still, though the actual percentages of gay men who work out regularly might be lower than these surveys suggest, they are in all probability not as low as the surveys on fitness taken of the male population in general. In a 1990 U.S. government study, for example, only 44.7 percent of American men over the age of eighteen reported that they "exercised or played sports regularly," a statistic that is so open-ended it presumably includes those who weight train as well as those who take a brisk walk daily or play tennis once a week. A 1994 poll of fifteen thousand American households commissioned by the International Health, Racquet and Sports Club Association determined that only 7.7 percent of the male population over the age of six belonged to a health club. Of course, if the survey was solely of men over the age of eighteen, the percentage would be substantially higher, and this figure does not account for men who might lift weights or exercise at home. Still, even taking into account these variables, the figures seem comparatively quite low. And since the results of any such study regarding fitness and exercise would invariably include a number of gay men, the percentages of *heterosexual* men who regularly play sports or exercise, or who belong to a health club, are perhaps slightly to moderately lower than even these figures represent.

Not all gay men agree that the obsession with body image and physical appearance is more acute in the gay male community. Gay men I interviewed and surveyed were just about evenly split. In surveys, they were asked a two-part question: "How do you feel about the focus in the gay male community on youth, beauty, and muscles? Is it any different from the straight world, and if so how?" Forty-eight percent of those surveyed believed there was no difference in this regard between the gay and straight worlds, while 52 percent said there most certainly was a difference. What exactly they believed the differences were broke down in more complicated ways and tended to reflect their own experiences.

"It's no different from the straight world," responded a thirty-year-old from Birmingham, Alabama. "And I find pockets of the gay world—the 'bear' subculture—to be much more affirming and accepting than any part of the straight world."

"It is different—it's too unrealistic," said a twenty-three-year-old Kansas man. "Not everyone can look like a porn star."

"It is NOT any different in the straight world," a Vancouver forty-two-year-old insisted, passionately capitalizing for emphasis. "We get attracted to the same aspects of youthfulness, virility, so on and so on."

"There is far more emphasis on youth, beauty, and muscles in the gay world than in the straight," wrote a seventy-two-year-old from State College, Pennsylvania.

OTHER MASCULINITIES

Many of those men who did not feel there was a difference between gay and straight culture tended to have found subcultures or groups within the gay culture itself that they believed were more accepting than the larger gay culture (and clearly much more than the straight world). "Bears," for example, are gay men who break from the dominant notions of male beauty in the gay world and celebrate a much broader range of body types—particularly big and overweight bodies. They revere body hair wherever it may naturally occur, rather than subscribe to the current rage for trimming, plucking, shaving, and waxing as reflected in the dominant commercial gay culture.

In fact, the cover of *Bear* magazine, a publication for gay bears, has its motto emblazoned across the top: "Masculinity without the trappings."

In this sense then, the cult of masculinity—the obsession with attaining a commercially promoted physical standard—does not necessarily encompass all of the various masculinities within the gay world and its subcultures. Rather, the cult of masculinity is about the overriding, highly commercialized and quite rigid body culture that is most visible in the ghettos of New York, Los Angeles, San Francisco, Chicago, Washington, D.C., and Miami Beach. But even if one submerges oneself into one of the various sexual subcultures, the overriding sexual culture is difficult if not impossible to avoid.

Similar dynamics play out within racial and other minority groups within the gay world that carve out their own space but are always touched in some way by the more physically rigid and very white mainstream gay sexual culture. For example, many African-American men who noted that they socialize not in the larger white gay male community but in the black gay community said they believed the black gay male community was not as rigid with regard to physical appearance as the larger white gay community, which they saw as much more acutely focused on youth and muscles than American culture as a whole. Yet some have noticed changes among some black men, particularly where whites and black intersect in the gay world.

"You always had spectacular muscle queens [in the black gay community], and a lot of them were men who didn't work out much at all, but who were naturally muscular," says Rodney, a forty-two-year-old Los Angeles travel agent, "and they've always been the stars. But there wasn't this urge to segregate among them, to hang out just with each other. They wanted to hang out with other African-American gay men of all kinds. That was more important, and so the clubs and bars always had a variety of African-American men. But now I see a lot of younger [black] muscle men, hanging out with white muscle guys, and not wanting to hang out with men who aren't muscular, whether they're African-American or white. They're on the party circuit, which is mostly white, and so the thing that bonds them is not race, but body type. Then when they do hang out in a black environment, they still have that attitude, staying together in a pack, avoiding people who don't look the part."

VICTIMIZER AND VICTIM

Many gay men who said in surveys that they saw little or no difference between the gay and straight worlds regarding male physical beauty seemed very concerned about the gay community being stigmatized as "narcissistic" or falling prey to negative stereotypes, and they expressed strong feelings about this, like the Vancouver man who capitalized the word NOT. In some cases, the fear of stigmatizing the community seemed to perhaps outweigh answering the question honestly. Still other men, indeed the great majority who said they saw no difference between the gay male world's and the straight world's focuses on youth and beauty, were making their decision based on comparing gay men to straight women (not straight men), noting the equal pressures put on the two groups to look a certain way.

"No, I don't think it's much different from the straight world," opined an eighteen-year-old high school student from Beloit, Wisconsin, who then added: "Men in the straight world always want their women to look beautiful, thin, etc. Gay men do the same in the gay community, but they admire [male] beauty, muscles, thinness, etc."

"When I was younger I was considered attractive in a non-pumped-up, masculine-but-not-macho, hunkish sort of way, but I still had the same opinion then as I do now on this," a forty-one-year-old molecular biologist from Short Hills, New Jersey, responded in one of my surveys. "I believe that men, gay and straight, have tended to objectify their sex objects so as to create an idealized, fragile, ephemeral form of beauty that few can attain and none can retain. This was the impossible standard that feminists saw as causing self-dissatisfaction—self-loathing—in so many women, and against which feminists rightly rebelled. What feminists failed to address—like the heterosexists they were raised to be—was that gay men typically held up analogous, impossible standards for their own objects of desire."

Similar responses ware also prevalent in lengthy personal interviews with a vast cross section of gay men. Those who believed the gay male community to be no different from the larger straight culture generally tended to compare the attention gay men pay to their appearance to the attention that women are pressured to pay to their physical appearance. Most gay men interviewed agreed that the majority of straight men were not generally as focused on attaining the "ideal" male body, though some believe that this is changing, sometimes crediting the influence of gay culture on straight men. They tended to agree that, while our larger American culture is obsessed with physical appearance and body image, the onus seems to be greater on straight women and gay men.

That is not to deny the rich and intricate realities of the various other gender and sexual orientation combinations, and many men were quick to point this out. Many lesbians, for example, say that some lesbians objectify other lesbians similarly to how gay men objectify other men and that such objectification is increasing, particularly among the younger generations of lesbians. Certainly there are straight women who hold straight men to rigid notions of male beauty, and again some might say that this tendency is on the rise. There are also straight men who do not hold women to rigid physical standards. And there are of course many gay men who do not objectify other men and who put other qualities ahead of physical appearance in choosing a mate or sexual partner.

But looking at what *predominates* in the different groups, it appears the dynamic described above dominates in the gay male world in a way it doesn't in other groups, and it is often so powerful that it affects all gay men eventually, even if they break from it on an individual level. In *Culture Clash: The Making of a Gay Sensibility*, cultural critic Michael Bronski, discussing gay pornography, notes that "while it is true that the viewer, sexually aroused, lusts after the object, it is equally true that he may also want to be that object. This element of identification with as well as desire for the sexual object distinguishes gay and straight porn."

Expanding that idea beyond pornography to all visual elements of gay sexual culture, it is not difficult to see that many if not most of us become both the rigidly objectified as well as the rigid objectifier, holding ourselves and *each other* to rigid standards of physical beauty. These standards become a significant, if not the most important, characteristic in choosing a mate or sexual partner. For many of us the preoccupation with physical appearance and the cult of masculinity become the mechanisms that drive most aspects of our lives.

STRAIGHT-ACTING AND -APPEARING

"Sometimes I feel like I'm maybe depressed," Alex tells me. "No, let me clarify that: I *definitely* feel *really* depressed, and it's not just *sometimes* — and then I look at all of this and I say to myself, Hey, quit your complaining." He's standing on the balcony of his spacious two-bedroom twentieth-floor apartment overlooking lower Manhattan, waving his hands over the city as if it were his own empire. He bought the apartment three years ago, two years after his career "took off." Alex is a consultant in a specialized field and works out of his home, earning a comfortable six-figure income. He is an attractive thirty-two-year-old man with sandy blond hair, golden skin (he takes a lot of vacations to warm destinations, he says), and bright green eyes. He's quite proud of his well-developed body, which he works on "almost daily," and which he reluctantly admits is his "best asset." Asked to describe his personality Alex says that he's "a happy-go-lucky kind of guy," popular at parties, traveling within a wide circle of friends. But he consistently brings the conversation back to his body: "I'm the kind of person I am because I feel good about my body. It makes me confident, self-assured, and happy because I wouldn't be confident if I didn't feel good about my body." He cracks a smile. "When I'm not feeling good about my body, I'm, well, pretty miserable."

Alex sounds not unlike Peter, a thirty-one-year-old Miami Beach accountant who spends eight hours a week in the gym: "My work is dull. I don't have a wife and children like some of my colleagues. My social life and my friends and all of the 'hot boy parties,' and the clubs are important to me. It's my outlet to the rest of the world, to having a life outside of the office. There's no way that that kind of social life can be important to you if your looks and your body aren't important to you. When I *got* a body, when I started working out, that's when I really became happy, when I started getting a lot of attention. . . . Sometimes, if I haven't worked out in a while, then I feel kind of blah. I sometimes won't go out at all."

Roger, a Los Angeles student who is twenty-five years old and who has what he says his best friend calls "a flawless body," nonetheless has days and nights when he will not venture to West Hollywood, to the swank parties filled with pumped-up men that a "plugged in" friend takes him to. "I have to feel just 'perfect' for all of that," he explains. "I know it sounds crazy, but I can't enjoy myself if everything's not right and if I don't feel confident about my body."

Alex, the New Yorker, describes the kind of guys he likes: "Big, built, strong. I definitely like *very masculine* guys; I don't want to use the politically incorrect term 'straight-acting' and I don't think it applies anyway, since who is to say that 'masculine' means 'straight'. . . but anyway, you get the idea of the kind of guys I like." Plenty of other men, however, are not so averse to the term Alex is careful about. "Straight-acting and -appearing," states Philip, a Dallas insurance broker. "I just can't go with an effeminate guy." Archie, a Chicago business owner, says he won't date anyone who "seems gay" at first glance. When it is pointed out to him that, in the big cities at least, many heterosexuals can easily pick out some gay men precisely *because* of their hypermasculinity—the big pecs, tight shirts, close-cropped hair—and thus the term "seems gay" could in fact mean someone with those qualities, he rephrases: "What I mean then is any guy who has womanly traits on the outside, you know, of how he acts."

Defining himself as similar—in terms of masculinity—to his ideal mate, Alex says that he'd "be pretty good boyfriend material." He concedes that as much as he entertains the thought of getting into a relationship, it's not a top priority. He's never had what he describes as a "serious" relationship. "I'm not obsessed with the idea," he observes. "It's like, if some-one comes along who is just right for me—and they'd have to be pretty hot and pretty wonderful, I'm very picky—that would be fine. But it's not stopping me from enjoying life. I like my friends and I like my work. I date on and off, have sex now and then. I really, honestly, like my life—at least *a lot* of time."

AT THE SEX CLUB

But a lot of other times, Alex says, "things break down." In those moments not only is he not so happy but he also kind of "freak[s] out" and does things that later, after he thinks about them, make him uncomfortable. This is an experience that a great many gay men described to me to some degree or another, even if the impetus and the scenario itself are different.

Alex recounts a typical night out: "I went out with a friend. We went to a nightclub; I was in the mood to dance, but I was also in the mood to cruise. But when I think back to it now, I wasn't in the mood for *sex*. I really wasn't horny—I was just into *cruising*. I wanted attention. And when I think about it even further, I think I wanted that kind of attention because I'd had a bad day: I lost one job to a competitor, someone I've been going head-to-head with. On another job, the client wasn't pleased with my work and dumped me, told me that was it and they weren't using me. Then, while I was on the phone with someone, I found out that a close friend tested HIV-positive. That was the second friend in six months, and this one is only twenty-five, and it just hit me like a tidal wave. I was even more upset because he didn't tell me himself—I found out through someone else, who was like, *gossiping*, you know, and who didn't know that this was a really good friend of mine. Basically, you could say I felt like shit."

Alex decided to go out to a gay nightclub, the kind that plays nonstop house music and where pumped-up men dance to all hours of the morning, snorting Special K, an animal anesthetic that is popular in the clubs, and downing hits of Ecstasy, the psychopharmacological designer drug popular on the party circuit. Alex wanted simply to have a few drinks and loosen up. He was stressed and needed some old-fashioned fun. But instead of relaxing him, the atmosphere seemed to make him more stressed and a bit anxious.

"No one was looking at me," he says. "I mean, no one that I really thought was *hot*. And I guess that made me think I wasn't looking good that night, and then it's kind of like downhill from there. You're not feeling good already, and then feeling worse because no one is paying attention to you, and sometimes you're not sure if it's all in your mind. Maybe people really *are* looking, but you're just not picking it up. I think my mind plays tricks on me in that way.

"I think I use my body a lot as a way of feeling good about myself," Alex continues. "I'm sure other people go out, just have a drink, and maybe shrug off the problem, but me, I go out, I think, sometimes, to feel desired and wanted and that makes me feel superior, and then it offsets my feeling bad."

Jeremy, a Washington, D.C., lawyer, says the same dynamic operates within himself. "There's nothing that can make me feel better if I'm feeling down than getting laid," he says. "Nothing at all. But I should stress that it is not the actual sex that does it as much as feeling completely and utterly validated by someone. Sometimes I don't even need to actually go home with someone when I'm in this state—just flirting in a bar and knowing they want me can be enough." For Alex and many other men, however, "just flirting" is not enough.

In his quest, Alex decided to go to another bar, hoping his luck would be better. He drank some more. And some more. But even there, he says, no one was cruising him, and he could not get his validation fix. He went to still another bar, but to no avail. Finally, he went to a sex club, a small place near his house where men meet in the near darkness and have sex with each other in cubicles and corners.

"I had no intention at the beginning of the night of having sex or going to a sex club," he recalls. "What I mean is, I wasn't horny and that's not why I ended up in the sex club. I ended up there because I needed attention, validation, and, remember, I had been spiraling downward all night. I needed to be worshipped because I felt I was being ignored. And if someone would worship my body, I'd realize that I'm not unattractive and that all of this—my thinking no one was interested—was in my mind."

He met a man "almost immediately" who took him in a corner and performed oral sex on him. "He wasn't totally hot, didn't have the hardest body, but he was cute enough," Alex says. "And he worshipped my body the whole time, which is what I needed. When it was over, he stood up and put his hand over my chest, and said, 'You remind me of why I go to the gym—because I want to have a body just like yours.' That was really weird and unnerving, because it felt great to hear that, made me definitely feel superior. So I guess I'd finally gotten what I really wanted. But I also realized at that moment that I was making him feel lousy or, rather, contributing to his making himself feel lousy. I got over my own negative feelings, got past my feeling bad about my body—but it was at the expense of someone else, making someone else feel inferior about his body. It's like a contagious disease—you just pass your insecurity on to the next guy."

Maybe. Or maybe the man already has the "disease"—low self-image, that is—and having a man like Alex is actually making him feel better, making him feel that he is worthy enough to get such a hot stud as Alex. Either way, however, that sudden feeling of greater self-worth is fleeting and does not even begin to get at the underlying issues that created the low self-esteem in the first place.

Alex explains that he sometimes goes to sex clubs simply for "fun" and with what he considers a good attitude; he is not "against" sex clubs and seems to have a relatively high regard for them. "Look, I don't want to put down sex clubs, because I've gone to them and met guys and had hot sex and it was all great and made me feel good," he says. "But this wasn't like that, and this does happen often these days with me it seems. It's not something I feel good about because it's motivated by my feeling bad about myself, and later I realize that the fix is really empty. It doesn't really end the problem, my feeling insecure about myself and how I look—it only comes back. I don't know what would really do that, actually. Maybe just drop out of the system, you know, and just do something else. It's this system that we're all in, you know, the gay system: 'Look like this. Look like that. Always look great. Always look better than the next guy. Make them look at you, but don't look at them. Treat everyone like shit.' Sometimes I wonder what the hell I'm doing."

IMPRISONED ON THE DANCE FLOOR

If the "system," as Alex calls it, can have this kind of effect on someone whose physical appearance certainly fits in, it's not difficult to image how it affects those who do not fit in.

Walt is a thirtyish (he's so hung up about aging that he refuses to tell his real age) Boston public relations professional who goes out a lot to gay dance clubs and all-night parties and often travels to New York and other cities to party on weekends.

He's five foot tall, skinny, and average-looking. "This scene," he says, "is fun and dandy but if you don't got what they're looking for, it's just not worth it—and I don't got what they're looking for. I have gone through so many head trips about this. Sometimes I'm standing there on the dance floor and maybe I've got a hit of Ecstasy in me and I'm still saying to myself, What are you doing here? You've got to be the gay white male equivalent of 'sexy,' and I'm not. I'm short and skinny."

Why, then, does he continue to go out to these places and subject himself to the kind of rejection that only feeds his low self-image? "I want to feel I'm completely involved in the scene, in what's happening," he tells me candidly, with only a hint of embarrassment. "If I don't feel I'm at the center of the hippest people, of that 'in' crowd of the sexiest and most A-list men, then I'll just feel worse. At least I'm *there*, you know— even if it does make me feel that compared to these guys I'm inadequate."

Walt says that he has thought a lot about changing his life, but he sees few choices, at least in the gay world he lives in. "I have questioned everything," he says, "and I'm back to square one. It all seems like it's going nowhere. I live in Boston, in a big gay community, and yet I feel disconnected from what's going on in the outside world. I definitely feel like I'm in a prison, like I have to follow a strict set of rules and can't seem to find another way. I guess I'm not willing to do anything about it, or condemn it—out of fear that there's nothing else—but it definitely is a prison." In order to feel better, Walt hits the dance floor, he says, high on drugs. "I'm on Ecstasy, but still, when I'm looking around at all the guys on the dance floor it depresses me, so maybe I take another hit. But it'll be a while before it works, so I take a hit of poppers, and then everything is fine, wonderful, I feel I belong. And then in a bit my second hit of Ecstasy kicks in, and I'm doing good for the night."

But this feeling of inclusion is artificial and fleeting. Later, when the night is over, Walt usually winds up home alone. In his case, that means getting on the phone and having phone sex, sometimes all night and the whole next day, after having snorted some methamphetamine, better known as crystal or crystal meth, an amphetamine stimulant (curiously, much more popular on the West Coast then anywhere else), which Walt says he also now uses at work, to "get through the day."

Larry, a twenty-seven-year-old Miami nurse, has a story similar to Walt's. Unable to fit the physical paradigm (he is, he says, "tubby," at five foot nine and 220 pounds), he goes out to bars and often to sex clubs and baths and often does drugs. In his case, however, Larry finds himself all too often engaging in unsafe sex. "I've allowed men to fuck me without condoms on more occasions than I can count, quite honestly," he says nervously. "It's like this: I'm high. But not always—I've even allowed it to happen when I was on nothing at all. I meet someone who's really, totally attractive, someone I've always wanted—which is not very often, but enough of the time. I let him call the shots, tell him we'll do whatever he wants to do. My goal is to get the guy to go home with me, and I'll do whatever it takes. I can't believe he'd even consider having sex with me. And when he does, it's anything goes. I just don't think about it. I'm too caught up in it. And he is too, because he doesn't think about it either."

It appears that gay men's own perceptions when they compare their bodies to others, even if those perceptions are different from the reality, enable them to put themselves at risk. At a Dallas gym, an old friend I ran into—a thirty-four-year-old who has a great body but nonetheless believes he looks "terrible" compared to some of the beefcake there—pointed to a hunky guy doing crunches on the floor while we were having a discussion about safer sex. "If I were drunk, I'd probably allow him to fuck me without rubbers," he said flatly. "What worries me is that I feel so beneath guys like that I'd allow them to do *anything*."

LIVING THE FANTASY

Even if one eschews the pumped and hairless clone and has access to a wider variety of gay men and gay subcultures, the shaved muscle boy aesthetic and all of the baggage that comes with it is omnipresent. In New York, for example, one can forgo the Chelsea pumped-up crowd for the skinny, tattooed queers of the East Village, but it's nearly impossible to escape the glossy little publications like *Next* or *Homo Xtra*, stacks of which abound everywhere in the ghetto and even beyond, their covers, not to mention pages and pages of ads, promoting huge biceps, cut abs, perfect pecs, and bubble butts. In Fort Lauderdale, it's *Scoop*. In Boston, *The Guide*. In Los Angeles, *Edge*. Every major American city in fact has one—and sometimes three or four—"bar rags" filled with images of "perfect" gay men, the ideals that set the standard. Most of the pictures are being used to sell us something: gym memberships to the trendy gyms of choice; all-night parties at nightclubs filled with near-naked, young-and-buff men; phone sex; and even actual sex in the guise of "escorts." These same images are played back to us again and again in gay porn, on safer sex posters, and in dozens of gay newspapers and several glossy national magazines that often sport pumped-up coverboys and fetching ads selling products and events, from underwear to hot parties. And that is not to mention the nightclub parties themselves, where the go-go boys from the slick party invitations suddenly leap to life, standing on pedestals, gyrating their wares.

As young men enter the gay community, coming from far and wide, crowding the restaurants, bars, and coffeehouses of the ghettos, this ready-made lifestyle is sold to them: a fast-food lifestyle for people with a fast and furious appetite. After a few years, they become quite conditioned to it, like the rest of us, programmed to the McDonald's-like ease of buying a life.

Part of the reason it all sells so well is perhaps that gay men, breaking free after eons of repression, have for almost three decades been told—or rather, have told themselves—that they can and are *living the fantasy*. The average straight man, on the other hand, may have his *Penthouse*, but more often than not he doesn't have the time or the will to play out those fantasies. He is in fact conditioned in another way: to sow his wild oats at a young age, get his act together, and settle down. With a wife, a house, a family, and a career to keep his hands full, he not only often has little time to live out all of his sexual fantasies but he also doesn't have the time to *be* the Calvin Klein model whom women so desire. So even his own potential muscle body often remains in the realm of fantasy too, and he vicariously lives through Schwarzenegger, Stallone, and other action figures. Perhaps this is one reason why, according to *Sex in America*'s 1994 study and contrary to popular mythology, most heterosexual men have, on the average, five sexual partners throughout their lifetimes, which, even if off by a few, is a great deal fewer than that of the average gay man.

For a great many gay men in the urban centers—the majority of which, some studies since the 1970s have shown, have hundreds of sexual partners throughout their lives—living the fantasy has of course all been under the guise of liberation. But perhaps there is no such thing as true liberation.

When we break from one rigid system, we often create another. It's true that most gay men in urban America are not living a life of *enforced heterosexuality*, as gay liberationists might call it, with a driveway, a picket fence, and children to nurture. Many are, however, instead living a life of *enforced cult homosexuality*, with parties, drugs, and gyms ruling their lives.

Some men have in fact found that there is a thin line between liberation and oppression. "I joined the gym I'm going to now about four years ago," says Jonathan, a thirty-five-year-old Washington, D.C., man. He'd moved to Washington from Connecticut, where he was not out, hoping to enter a community he thought would be accepting. "For the longest time it used to just sort of kill me that these guys who looked as if they stepped out of an International Male catalog worked out there," he says of the Washington Sports Club in Dupont Circle, the gay ghetto of D.C. "My initial reaction—well, it made me very, very depressed. I would say that I was very intimidated, and it depressed me to think that here is the ideal of beauty, and I personally fall so far short of that mark. I felt that if that's what it takes to make it, then, *wow*, I'm screwed. Because it's genetically beyond me, and therefore I'm doomed to failure no matter how hard I work out. I mean, I wanted to go to a gym that was *gay-friendly*, which is why I went there, because these guys are gay. But for a long time I felt totally oppressed there—my friends and I called it *body oppression*."

BODY FASCISM

"Body oppression"—or "body fascism," a term several writers including myself have used–is perhaps one of the most detrimental effects of the cult of masculinity in the gay world because it devalues so many men in the eyes of both themselves and their peers. Not surprisingly, in interviews and surveys it is the primary criticism that most gay men have of the gay world.

"If there is one thing that I would have to say is a downside in the gay community it is this obsession with looks and having the perfect body," notes Victor, a twenty-three-year-old Los Angeles waiter, making an observation that men of all ages within many urban centers make. "It's so competitive, and it wasn't what I'd expected. It's like you have no choice but to become a muscle robot."

Body fascism can perhaps be defined as the setting of a rigid set of standards of physical beauty that pressures everyone within a particular group to conform to them. Any person who doesn't meet those very specific standards is deemed physically unattractive and sexually undesirable. In a culture in which the physical body is held in such high esteem and given such power, body fascism then not only deems those who don't or can't conform to be sexually less desirable, but in the extreme—sometimes dubbed "looksism"—also deems an individual completely worthless *as a person*, based solely on his exterior. In this sense it is not unlike racism or sexism or homophobia itself. In this worst-case scenario, the only way one can become valued *as a person* is if one conforms to the set of standards—if one is lucky enough, from a genetic perspective, to be able to do so.

"There are these guys, hot guys with, I mean, the really chiseled bodies, who I used to look at in awe, who wouldn't give me the time of day," recalls David, who is a thirty-two-year-old hotel desk clerk and lives in Minneapolis. "I didn't exist to them. I wasn't a person. I'd try to strike up a conversa-

tion at the bar, and they'd just turn away, in a mean way—
treated me like shit. Now, here it is four years later, and I'm all
built up, got my forty-two-inch chest and my big biceps, and
now these guys are all over me—they can't get enough of me.
And, well, I have to say it does make me feel powerful. I've con-
quered them. That is a feeling of power."

THE NEEDLE BREAKS

Back in the locker room at Equinox, Chris, the uptown hair-
dresser, is telling me all about that supposed power.

"I needed to achieve that confidence I told you about, that
sense of control," he says, explaining why he has now gone
back on steroids. "I just felt, you know, I wanted to look really
perfect and have that kind of power."

It's been eight months since we'd last spoken, when he told
me he'd tried steroids but didn't finish the cycle for fear of what
he might be doing to his body. He's still afraid, but the perceived "payoff," he says, is now greater than his fear. He bought
the steroids from an acquaintance, someone whom he says
"knows all about steroids."

"What kind of steroids did you buy?" I ask, having learned
a great deal about steroids in the time since we last spoke and
having learned that many steroids, particularly on the black
market, are more dangerous than he might think.

"Oh, I don't know," he says.

"What dosage are you taking?" I ask

"I don't know," he says. His acquaintance usually injects
him. "I just know he uses the whole vial."

Chris then pulls down his shorts to show me the spot on
his butt where he'd this morning injected himself—for the first
time—and made a major blunder. He displays a purplish black

lump the size of a golf ball. It appears to me, from what I've learned from interviewing doctors, researchers, and many steroids users, that he has an intramuscular abscess, a product of improperly administered intramuscular injections (steroids must be injected into muscle tissue as opposed to intravenously), which can be quite dangerous. In the worst-case scenario it must be surgically drained and can still create a serious gluteal muscle infection or even gangrene.

"I can't believe this," he says, getting a bit upset. "I tried to do it myself, and I didn't get it deep into the muscle, and then the needle broke too. And now I don't know what I did."

He cracks a nervous smile. "I've got to be crazy, right?" he says. "Why on earth am I doing this?" He pauses, sits down, and asks rhetorically, "How did it all come to this?"

Indeed, that is the question many of us have been asking ourselves for quite some time about our own lives and about the gay world we live in.

To answer it, and to even begin to come to terms with it, we must first squarely face the fact of what the cult of masculinity truly represents. We must look at how it evolved within gay culture, and we must understand how it has come to have such a powerful grip on so many of us.

2

THE ORIGINS OF THE CULT

The cult of masculinity can perhaps best be viewed in the way its name suggests: as a religion. Looking at it in this way in fact allows us to have a broader understanding of its grip on our entire culture, and on gay men specifically.

The cult of masculinity is not organized in the way some traditional cults and religions may be organized—with one or two charismatic leaders or founders, a centralized and hierarchical structure, and a written set of doctrines—but that does not mean it wields any less power over its followers. In postmodern capitalist America, with its hyper-media and ever present advertising bombardment, such obvious characteristics are no longer necessary to define, create, and maintain cults.

What *is* necessary is a vulnerable, easily exploited *audience* ready to buy into the cult, and a broad *promise*—an idea that is captivating enough to sell—that convinces followers to give themselves over to the cult.

The cult of masculinity in the gay male community began developing immediately after Stonewall and the birth of a broad-based commercial gay sexual culture. It reached its zenith during the second wave of AIDS in the gay world of the 1990s. Like most cults, the cult of masculinity revolves around an obsessive devotion to a principle, a belief—in this case, a rigidly defined physical ideal of "masculinity"—that followers see as a source of control over their present lives as well as future happiness. Like followers of other cults, followers of this cult have a tendency to be suspect of, hostile to, or ignorant of criticism of the cult. They may laugh off or ignore warnings by others that the cult or certain aspects of it might be detrimental to them physically or emotionally. They might in fact find it ridiculous even to imply they are part of a cult. But they are.

The cult of masculinity, like other cults, is also fundamentalist and doctrinaire; while not all of those caught up in it follow its most extreme tenets, enough do to keep the cult thriving and bringing in new converts, often when they are young and newly out of the closet. These young men are *not* being converted to homosexuality—they've already realized that they're gay. Rather, upon coming out, they are often confused, seeking direction, and not finding other routes to integrate themselves into the lesbian and gay community, no matter how visible those other routes seem to be. Or perhaps, being afraid to access other avenues and still unsure of themselves and vulnerable, they simply join the alluring and seductive cult of masculinity. It defines them and guides them, offering meaning and purpose, as well as a social life and the promise of love and sex. J. Gordon Melton, in the 1992 revised edition of *Encyclopedic Handbook on Cults in America*, notes that cults tend to attract "single young adults (18–25)," in particular people for whom traditional religion, the family, and other institutions have failed.

In *Cults in America: Programmed for Paradise*, Willa Appel describes those who follow cults as people "whose expectations have undergone sudden change" because they are "frustrated and confused," attempting "to re-create reality, to establish a personal identity in situations where the old world view has lost meaning." Cults "offer community, meaning and spiritual direction," Appel observes, and keep members "in a kind of limbo, permanently suspended from the surrounding environment." People who are marginalized are especially attracted to cults, Appel says, because they "have no political voice, lack effective organization, and do not have at their disposal regular, institutionalized means of address."

THE BIRTH OF A CIRCUIT QUEEN

"When I was twenty-three and just sort of coming out, I was kind of lost," says twenty-eight-year-old Roger, who lives just outside Washington, D.C., and works for the federal government. He grew up in Baltimore in a working-class Irish Catholic family. He's single and is today very active on the international circuit of gay dance parties that take place throughout the year in various cities around the country and around the world. Thousands of men travel to them, particularly to the hottest of the parties—the Black Party in New York, the White Party at Vizcaya in Miami—and the events often turn into several days of partying. Recreational drug use is rampant and almost universal among attendees, and the atmosphere is sexually charged as men dance for hours on end, their shirtless, smooth, sweaty bodies crammed up against one another. The crowd is mostly a very attractive, body-conscious crowd in their twenties and thirties, although there are some men in their forties and beyond. They are mostly professionals, men who can afford to travel to the parties and pay for the drugs.

The term "circuit queen" is used by those on and off the circuit to describe the average repetitive attendee, although few men will label *themselves* a circuit queen. Roger and many other men I've interviewed who are on the circuit even bristle at the term, finding it "derogatory." I met Roger at a circuit event when I saw him gyrating on a speaker; he agreed to sit down with me at another time and talk.

"I knew from when I was young that I was gay, and I tried to suppress it, but I couldn't and I felt an enormous amount of guilt," he tells me. "I was raised Catholic and my faith was important to me. And wow, this, my homosexuality, was really troublesome for me, it was conflicting. I eventually strayed from the church and felt bad. I guess it was guilt, but it was also a sense of losing something important to me, something that was a real part of my life. The church always gave me a direction and hope, and I felt an emptiness. But then, not long after I came out, I just became filled with a new feeling, a great feeling, you know, a really proud feeling, and I came to realize that I hated the Catholic church and didn't need it."

Roger says that at that time he didn't know of the gay-centered Metropolitan Community Church or of the many mainstream churches that are gay-positive. He also was not drawn to gay social and support groups while in college or after he'd graduated. Describing how he came out into the gay community once he'd come to terms with his homosexuality himself, Roger tells a story similar to those of many gay men I have interviewed and surveyed who live in the urban centers: "I knew I needed people my own age around me who were gay and I saw a lot of the guys in the bars who I wanted to be friends with. I didn't know where else to find people my age then. I was just testing the waters, and, you know, you gravitate toward what is most obvious; I didn't know about any groups, or workshops, or anything like that. I don't think I was aware of them, or maybe I was but they didn't make an impression on me. I guess I would have been embarrassed or something to go to a meeting or something like that at that point. No, I only knew the bars and the clubs. That's really when things changed. I found new friends and a new life, where I was accepted for being me."

But just how much was Roger really accepted, as he says, "for being me"?

"I immediately began working on my body. I was in pretty good shape already, but some of the guys I started hanging out with were in a lot better shape and I had to pump up. We were doing a lot of the parties and going to Tracks [a Washington nightclub] on Saturday night and traveling a bit and everybody looked great. It was like a slap, you know, like 'wake up and get in shape!' There were also other guys, in different crowds on the scene, at the clubs, who wouldn't talk to me or look at me, and I admit it, I wanted to hang out with them—and sleep with them.

"I also started dressing more with-it, more hip, wearing clothes that would show off my body. Before that I was flaming a bit, wearing, you know, some flamboyant and wild things— very faggy!" Roger laughs, uneasily. "But, you know, those clothes aren't going to get you dates or get you laid." He laughs. "So yeah, I started dressing right, and walking the walk, and talking the talk, you know. I also had to get a better haircut— no more fluffy do!" He laughs again as he recalls his transformation.

"I noticed an amazing difference within a year after I began working out, not just in my body, but in my whole life, my social life. I soon had so many new friends and men were trying to pick me up everywhere—and I got in that crowd I was desiring to get into. I was having the kind of hot sex that really made me feel special, sex with real meaning; I mean, for me sex became even spiritual in a way, but it had to be with the right guy, the guys I would be fantasizing about. I'd see a guy on the dance floor and for weeks I'd plan it out and fantasize about having him, and then I'd have him.

"I'm happy I got to where I am. It just meant a lot of hard work and discipline. I had to get my biceps to sixteen inches and my pecs to forty-three, my calves to sixteen—that was my goal that I set for myself. And I realized that having goals like that is a good thing. It gave me something to strive for. I was taking in huge amounts of protein. A lot of egg whites. No fat. *Never!* My eating is the most boring you can imagine. I've gotten my body fat down, but there are times when I'm depressed about the body fat thing. You look at these guys with the rippled abs, and that's like *zero* body fat and that's what you've got to get to."

THE RITES OF THE CULT

Roger's replacing his previous life—one that was devoutly religious—with a new one that required a similar amount of "discipline," as he says, in return for giving him a sense of community and "meaning," is all too typical among gay men. While not the case with everyone in the cult of masculinity, the cult for Roger in particular fills a void and offers him a "new life."

In her 1991 book *The Beauty Myth*, the feminist writer Naomi Wolf looks at the similar phenomenon among American women, what she calls the "Rites of Beauty," and she does not mince words about its role as a replacement for traditional, oppressive religions. Her critique could just as easily be applied to gay men:

> What has not yet been recognized is that the comparison should be no metaphor: The rituals do not simply

echo traditional religions and cults but *functionally supplant them.* They are *literally* reconstituting out of old faiths a new one, literally drawing on traditional techniques of mystification and thought control, to alter women's minds as sweepingly as any past evangelical wave. . . . The Rites of Beauty are able to isolate women so well because it is not yet publicly recognized that devotees are trapped in something more serious than a fashion and more socially pervasive than a private distortion of self-image. The Rites are not yet described in terms of what they actually are: a new fundamentalism transforming the secular West, repressive and doctrinaire.

Wolf shows, for example, how the cosmetics industry and the diet industry, with their gurus and preachers, their calls to discipline, their promises of "a new you," have as powerful a grip on many if not most American women as any organized cult. The cult of masculinity has a similar hold on many gay men. Like other cults, it encourages conformity, in looks as well as thought. It homogenizes all gay men today—the circuit clone with his huge muscles, close-cropped hair, and shaved and waxed body being its main cookie cutter image today—in the same way that all Hare Krishna devotees look and dress the same. "Consumer culture," Wolf observes, "is best supported by markets made up of sexual clones." Indeed, not only do commercial cults thrive under a free market economy, but a free market economy also thrives with commercial cults. This dynamic, reciprocal relationship has made gay men in America, in fact in all of the capitalist West, ripe for the cult of masculinity. It came about and grew to the immense proportions it inhabits in gay culture today as the result of two conditions that have worked in tandem:

- The anxiety about masculinity that has played itself out in western and particularly American culture for at least the past century among all men, but particularly among middle-class men.

- The sudden, broad-based commercialization of gay sexual culture that came about shortly after Stonewall and the birth of modern gay liberation.

The commercial gay sexual culture of the 1970s zeroed in on gay men's anxieties about masculinity, anxieties that had over the decades narrowed the idea of what it meant to look, act like, and be a man. The commercial gay sexual culture, which has expanded dramatically since the 1970s, promoted and continued to narrow that masculine ideal.

CRISES OF MASCULINITY

There may not have been circuit queens pumped up on steroids, dropping Ecstasy, and dancing the night away at the turn of the century. But there was a similar anxiety about masculinity. This "crisis of masculinity," as some have called it, had its high and low points throughout the twentieth century. The historical moments when anxiety about masculinity peaked, which resulted in shifts in how men who had sex with men perceived one another, were:

*These historical formulations are based in part on discussions I had with David Gerstner, who is working on his Ph.D. dissertation on queer modernism and American creativity. They are also based in part on my reading of his Spring 1997 *Film Quarterly* article entitled "The Production of the Closet: Making Vincente Minnelli's *Tea and Sympathy*."

- The Oscar Wilde trials of 1895
- The rise of the women's suffrage movement in the beginning of the twentieth century
- The Great Depression of the 1930s
- World War II and its effect on the burgeoning gay ghettos
- The McCarthy Era of the 1950s
- The sexual revolution of the 1960s
- Stonewall and the onslaught of commercial gay sexual culture
- The shock and panic of the initial AIDS crisis of the 1980s
- The second wave of AIDS in the 1990s.

These periods and moments in history highlighted, and greatly effected, a change in the dominant "gender style" that was the sexual object-choice of men who had sex with men.

Within western culture, the criteria that define a "masculine" or "feminine" manner and appearance have changed over the centuries. In the eighteenth century, for example, wearing a frothy wig was considered to be a fashion mandate for any stylish man or woman. And roughly a hundred years ago, if a man was considered "effeminate" by prevailing standards, his manner and appearance did not signify to others that the man was engaging in, or desired to engage in, sex with other men.

Just prior to the turn of the century, just before the infamous trials in 1895 in which Oscar Wilde was convicted of committing "gross indecency" with another man, men who had sex with other men in England and America were, for the most part, sexually attracted to men who were effeminate. Their sexual object-choice tended to be the young, soft, cherubic man and the gentle aesthete, the dandy. This particular manner and appearance, however, was not at that time a signifier of these men's homosexuality, at least not to the culture at large.

Throughout the 1800s homosexuality was viewed as an "act" not as an "orientation." It was considered a nasty act at that, but conceivably it could involve *anyone*, not just individuals who exhibited certain behaviors or had some inherent qualities. As the British historian and scholar Alan Sinfield shows in *The Wilde Century: Effeminacy, Oscar Wilde and the Queer Movement*, all that changed after the widely publicized trials of Oscar Wilde.

The trials, front-page news across Europe and the United States throughout 1895, put the homosexual on the social and cultural map for the first time. Coming at approximately the same time that a homosexual movement in Germany was evolving, and, as philosopher and historian Michel Foucault showed, the western scientific community was forming ideas that began to regard homosexuality as state or a class, the trials had a major impact on how people came to view the newly emerging homosexual.

Like other literary and artistic figures and many leisure-class men of his day, Wilde, as Sinfield writes, "had adopted the manner and appearance of an 'effeminate aesthete,'" which, prior to the time of the trials, mostly was defined as "being emotional and spending too much time with women" but did not necessarily indicate in a man a desire to have sexual relations with another man. That is, not until after Wilde became the queer poster boy of the era. "The image of the queer cohered at the moment when the leisured, effeminate, aesthetic dandy was discovered in same-sex practices," Sinfield notes. "Until the Wilde trials, effeminacy and homosexuality did not correlate in the way they have subsequently. . . . Up to [that time]—far later than is widely supposed—it is unsafe to interpret 'effeminacy' as defining of, or a signal of, same-sex passion." After the trials, many of the characteristics that Oscar Wilde exhibited were assigned to the homosexual: The effeminate man was still a sexual object-choice of other homosexuals but was now labeled as a homosexual and easily marked. All men began to experience anxieties about exhibiting feminine behavior because they were afraid of being marked as homosexuals.

In the first decades of the twentieth century, a homosexual culture formed in cities like New York, but it was decidedly different from gay culture today. Particularly among working-class men who slept with men, there existed "fairies," effeminate men who took the submissive role in sex, and "trade," masculine men who were for the most part straight—or "normal," as they were called—and took the dominant sexual role in their encounters with the fairies. The fairies had sex with one another and with trade, but the trade apparently did not have sex with one another, having homosexual sex for the most part only with fairies. In the homosexual culture of the turn of the century, well into the 1920s, the fairies, who were the effeminate men, were the sexual object-choice of one another as well as of the masculine trade. The trade in turn were the sexual object-choice of the fairies.

There was another category at the time: "queers," a term that then signified a decidedly different group than it does today. "Queer" today connotes a more radical, in-your-face segment of gay activists as well as some academics and others who eschew the label gay because it has come to represent a white middle-class aesthetic. At the turn of the century, however, those who identified themselves as queer were, ironically, mostly white middle-class men who did not consider themselves heterosexual or "normal," like the working-class trade (though many of them were attracted to and had sex with trade), but who disdained the fairies because of their "womanlike" qualities and their flamboyance. Queers could, among themselves, be just as campy and effeminate as the fairies, but they simply didn't want to be identifiable in public as homosexual.

"The cultural stance of the queer embodied the general middle-class preference for privacy, self-restraint, and lack of disclosure," historian George Chauncey notes in *Gay New York*. The middle-class queer, in wanting to distance himself from the fairy, was reacting to the developing crisis of masculinity in American culture, a crisis that was particularly acute for middle-class men in the early years of the twentieth century because of women's demands for equality. "Many men believed that women were threatening the sanctity of other male domains as well and were trying to take control of the nation's culture," Chauncey notes. "The women's suffrage campaign seemed the most direct challenge, for many men interpreted women's demand for the vote as a renunciation of men's prerogative to represent the women in their families in the (male) public sphere. . . . As middle-class men's anxieties about their manliness intensified, a preoccupation with threats to manhood and with proving one's manhood became central to the rhetoric of national purpose."

The effeminate male had been coded as homosexual since the Oscar Wilde trials. In order to prove their "manhood," their heterosexuality, it became increasingly important in the first few decades of the century for homosexual and heterosexual middle-class men — who were less secure about their masculinity than working-class men, whose livelihood, after all, was earned by performing "manly" labor — to exhibit what was considered at the time masculine appearance and behavior.

During the Great Depression of the 1930s these anxieties became even more enflamed. A great many men lost their jobs — the markers of their manhood. Later, with the onset of World War II, women would be more visible in the workforce, taking the jobs that men who went to war would traditionally have taken, and in many cases demanding to stay in those jobs and professions after the war. The tensions and anxieties caused by these changes in the roles of men and women made homosexuals into scapegoats. "As Americans anxiously tried to come to terms with the disruptions in the gender and sexual order caused by the Depression and exacerbated by the Second World War," Chauncey observes, "the 'sex deviant' became a symbol of the dangers posed by family instability, gender confusion and unregulated male sexuality and violence."

As the homosexual was ridiculed more intensely than before, many men began to distance themselves even further from homosexuals and homosexual activity. The category of "trade" would begin to disappear in coming decades. The two predominant male sexual categories shifted from "fairies" and "normal men," which were based on gender persona, to "homosexual" and "heterosexual," categories based on sexual object-choice. The term "gay" soon came into wide usage to refer to all homosexuals regardless of the subtle or not-so-subtle distinctions between them. And the fairies and their effeminate style would become decidedly less desirable to other men who slept with men. "The transformation in gay culture suggested by the ascendancy of *gay* was closely tied to the masculinization of that culture," writes Chauncey. "Jeans, T-shirts, leather jackets, and boots became more common in the 1940s, part of the 'new virile look' of young homosexuals. Increasing numbers of conventionally masculine men identified themselves as gay, in part, because doing so no longer seemed to require the renunciation of their masculine identities. Many gay men still considered themselves 'sissies,' but it was no longer as necessary for them to do so, and growing numbers adopted a self-consciously masculine style."

World War II saw many homosexual men brought from their homes in towns and cities around the country, where they might not have dared ever act on their sexuality, to a militaristic, hypermasculine environment. Stationed on army bases around the world, on ships in diverse ports, or in bases around the United States, they got their first taste of independence, of life away from their hometowns. For many of these men it was their first introduction to other gay men. While the all-male environment provided a cover because men could spend a lot of their time with love and sex interests without anyone getting suspicious, behaving masculine in this environment was often literally a matter of life and death. Though some gay men of the time report that higher-ups and others simply looked the other way, thus accepting their homosexuality, for a great many gay men, being too overt about their homosexuality meant they might get bashed in such close quarters. Anxieties regarding masculinity indeed escalate in these kinds of cramped, all-male environments, particularly since the very mission at hand in this case was also quite a masculine one: war.

In this type of environment, at a time when the homosexual is a known entity, many men, straight and gay, perhaps try to behave in a hypermasculine manner precisely because of the elevated tensions associated with the homosocial surroundings. For many gay men in the military at that time, hyper masculinity perhaps became second nature, not to mention even more sexually arousing. Many of these gay men would leave the war, as historian Allen Berube showed in *Coming Out Under Fire*, and move to the big cities of America and populate the emerging gay ghettos that would grow well into the Stonewall era.

Anxieties over masculinity reached a fevered pitch again in America during the paternalistic, conservative McCarthy Era, as homosexuals were swept up in the anti-Communist purges led by the infamous Senator Joseph McCarthy. He was greatly assisted by his closeted gay aid, Roy Cohn, a man who embodied the fear and revulsion of homosexuals that at the time was prevalent even among homosexuals themselves.

Just as the middle-class "queers" of the turn of the century had distanced themselves from the fairies and lived more discreet lives in order to prove their "manhood," the middle-class homosexuals of the McCarthy Era found it perhaps even more necessary to show their "manhood" because of the ways in which homosexuals were being demonized. A fascination with bodybuilding and physique magazines, not unlike the "cult of muscularity" that George Chauncey describes as having developed at the turn of century, returned in the 1950s among homosexual and heterosexual men alike. Homosexuals had since the beginning of the century been described by American psychiatry as "inverts," literally as women on the inside. Now they were being attacked by politicians as a danger to national security. There were purges throughout the government and the private sector of men known or thought to be queer, and many of them had their lives and careers forever ruined.

Also during this time, as historian John D'Emilio has noted, the famous Kinsey Report was released, which was a comprehensive study that for the first time showed a high prevalence of homosexuality in the United States, higher than previously believed; 8 percent of men were reported to have been exclusively homosexual at some point in their lives. Kinsey also broke the myth that all homosexuals were effeminate, showing that homosexuals exhibited a range of gender styles. As the McCarthy purges and the Kinsey Report underscored to the public that the homosexual could indeed be anyone, anxieties over masculinity heightened even further. Many men felt that even their masculinity itself could not ensure their manhood—their heterosexuality—to others. The homosexual was thus further reviled, resented, and hated.

The fear that swept gay men at the height of the McCarthy Era cannot be underestimated. It exploited a prevailing fear in American culture at large of effeminate men and instilled it further, even among gay men. Not only would men, gay and straight, not want to appear effeminate lest someone think they were homosexual, but the profusely masculine pose that straight men adopted in the 1950s had a profound effect on gay men that lasted for generations. Homosexuals are, after all, attracted to men, and if men in a given culture are assuming an even more masculine appearance than previously, thus redefining once again what it *means* to be a man, homosexuals will perhaps by default become more attracted to that more masculine appearance.

In other words, the sexual object-choice that gay men found themselves increasingly attracted to may have been dictated by the larger heterosexual male population and what it defined as "manly" at a time when both gay and straight men alike were experiencing acute anxiety surrounding their masculinity. The effeminate homosexual continued to become at best someone to avoid, even among a great many gay men themselves.

LIBERATION AND BEYOND

The sexual revolution of the 1960s actually saw a loosening up of the constraints of masculinity, even if it was short-lived. The youth movement rebelled against the dominant order and celebrated free love and androgyny. Women began wearing men's clothing, long hair was the rage for men, and the term "unisex" began popping up all over the place. It was a mood that lasted among some circles well into the 1970s. For some gay men—as well as for many women and even some straight men—this lifestyle provided a way to break loose of the gender constraints society had long imposed. The sexual revolution, coupled with the emerging women's movement, inspired the first gay liberationists. Indeed, many of the leaders and participants of the Stonewall Rebellion in New York, the riots that ushered in the modern gay liberation movement, were hippies and counterculture types, among other gender violators, including drag queens, transsexuals, and butch dykes. Their mission was, among other things, to break free of the rigid constraints of masculinity and femininity as they had been defined and which they believed pulled gay people down.

The advent of Stonewall and its demand for sexual freedom, openness, and outness also saw the beginning of the first commercial gay sexual culture, which grew rapidly in the 1970s. Having their liberation movement suddenly swept up in capitalism and the free-market economy was decidedly not something that the leftist gay liberationists had planned on, but it was perhaps inevitable. For the first time, the sex that gay men had known for decades—which previously had to be anonymous, furtive, and fleeting—could now be celebrated openly, and in America that invariably means being sold in the marketplace.

While there had been some gay commercial establishments in New York and other cities throughout the earlier decades, before Stonewall they were vulnerable to police and constantly under attack. For a great many men, deeply closeted, these social and sex establishments were unsafe places where they might risk arrest. Indeed, for the vast majority of men engaging in sex with other men from the turn of the century until Stonewall, in the cities as well as outside the urban centers, the closet and its furtive sexuality was always the established mode, with tearooms, rest stops, and public parks—themselves dangerous places because of the periodic crackdowns from the police or other government forces—being predominant locales for sex and for meeting sexual partners. But after Stonewall, men could congregate much more confidently in commercial sex establishments and be free of harassment.

"The change that came after Stonewall was not that men *stopped* having public sex, but that they stopped doing it furtively," author Michael Bronski has noted. "They felt better about it, less guilty, and—most importantly—they felt it was their right."

In his 1996 book *Sex Between Men*, journalist Douglas Sadownick expands upon this idea: "For the first time ever, [directly after Stonewall] a community standard developed that transformed anonymous sex into a good thing. . . . Casual sexual encounters no longer took place simply because men needed to conceal their identities but because it was considered hot to separate sex from intimacy."

If many of the early gay liberationists were dismayed that gay men had taken to the new and highly commercialized sexual culture, they were particularly disappointed and sometimes angered that such hedonism seemed to be at the expense of involvement in political activism. Although many men were coming out for the first time as gay, they were remaining closeted by day, in their jobs and to families. More important, they were still *men*. They continued to rest on their privilege and power in society. Before Stonewall the most visible sign of oppression for many of these men had been that they had to sneak around peep shows and back alleys, fearful of arrest. With that fear gone, a great many of the mostly white middle-class gay men of the urban ghettos, unlike gay men of other racial or socioeconomic backgrounds, lesbians, transsexuals, and others, had relatively few pressing issues of concern. With the police off their backs, many simply did what men have empowered themselves to do for centuries: They became as sexually adventurous and indulgent as they wanted to be, denying any responsibility for themselves or others in the process.

Many lesbians after Stonewall, on the other hand, did more freely what women have been conditioned to do for centuries: They formed stable, long-term relationships and denied themselves sexual adventures. Many white middle-class lesbians of the time joined the feminist movement, which then was attacking pornography and other aspects of culture that activists believed exploited women sexually. Many of these women also created lesbian separatist communities, cutting themselves off from gay men, whom they often disdained for their hedonistic, apolitical lifestyle. The perfect balance—and perhaps the most unique and innovative path—would have been something between these two extremes that many gay men and many lesbians pursued. Both lesbians and gay men were following what they thought were radical new paths but which were in reality new twists on centuries-old, constricting gender roles.

Lesbians, however, because they were involved in and inspired by feminism and the women's movement, were more politically aware and active, and they had other issues to drive them when gay liberationist politics began to fizzle. According to Canadian activist and cultural critic Ian Young in *The Stonewall Experiment*, the gay activism that the early liberationists established lost its allure to many people soon after Stonewall because gay politics didn't have a rich tradition and history and seemed directionless. Whereas lesbians experienced the call of feminism, for gay men there wasn't much else beyond gay activism other than sexual culture. Young observes that there existed a "lack of awareness of gay history and ideas" shortly after Stonewall, and the prevailing political ideology of the gay liberationists was what he calls an "armchair Marxism converted into a procrustean bed for the militant gays who squeezed themselves into it. Sloganeering and dogmatism alienated more people than they attracted," he writes. "As a result, many were simply turned off the gay movement and drifted, disappointed, into the faggot lifestyle. . . . With the streets and neighborhoods unsafe for gays and social institutions unwelcoming, the ghetto offered the only refuge, and especially in North America, bathhouses seemed to many like a zone of safety. . . . As the bath is a traditional symbol of healing and regeneration it is not surprising that it became a central institution of post-Stonewall gay life."

It wasn't that the gay activist spirit and energy died, however. It was, rather, transformed in a way that would celebrate the commercial sexual culture, a way that appealed to many men rather than pushing them away. It was true that the gay liberationists Young writes of, who in New York founded the

Gay Liberation Front (GLF), had believed that traditional gay modes of sexual interaction—baths, parks, bookstores, porn movie theaters—had to be discouraged because they exhibited the closeted, furtive mentality of the past and were throwbacks to a preliberationist time.

"When they discussed what it was like to be gay, radical male GLFers rapidly agreed that they found gay life unpleasant and unsatisfying," historian Toby Marotta observed in *The Politics of Homosexuality* in 1981. "This led them to conclude that male homosexuals who wanted to be fulfilled sexually had to abandon traditional styles of promiscuity and to avoid subcultural institutions like bars, bathhouses, and pornographic bookstores." One manifesto of the GLF demanded "the complete negation of the use of gay bars, tearooms, trucks, baths, streets and other traditional cruising institutions." The members of the GLF were in essence revolutionaries as opposed to reformists, demanding radical change in the traditional gay sexual culture rather than accommodating it to the new "out" political order.

When these calls to action were not taken up rapidly by the many men coming into the ghetto to enjoy the new sexual freedoms and the GLF politics rather quickly petered out, the newly formed Gay Activists Alliance, which included some people who'd broken from the GLF, took center stage in New York in the early 1970s. According to Marotta, the GAA brokered a kind of compromise by institutionalizing "the cultural reformist approach to gay liberation [by] promoting the idea that enjoying traditional gay pastimes was not only moral and salutary, but political. As more and more homosexuals, often without appreciating the political outlook most responsible for legitimizing and encouraging their activities, followed the lead of the first cultural reformers," he notes, "there was a surfacing of the gay subculture and a proliferation of identifiably gay bars, discos, restaurants, bathhouses, bookstores, sex shops."

There had been a few gay bathhouses in New York, San Francisco, and other cities in the early part of the twentieth century and up to the Stonewall Era. But compared to the explosion of bathhouses and sex clubs that occurred post-Stonewall, these establishments were small in number and scale and operated below the radar, their owners fearful of police raids, which occurred often in the early part of the century. Their 1970s descendants mushroomed in New York, San Francisco, Los Angeles, Washington, Chicago, Miami, St. Louis, Minneapolis, Seattle, and many other major American cities. They were not only much safer from the authorities and much greater in number, accommodating a much larger community that was coming out politically as well as sexually, but they were also for the first time open to business from an emerging *market*: the market of out-of-the-closet gay men. For the first time gay sex was advertised in a broad-based way in gay publications and manuals, and written about openly in books and magazines.

The bathhouses and sex clubs of the 1970s were among the first shrines of the emerging cult of masculinity in the gay world. These were publicly marked places where the furtive, anonymous sex of the pre-Stonewall days could be acted out in a safe space. They represented the introduction of capitalism and the American marketplace to the sexual activity gay men had known for decades. The cult of masculinity needed this commercialism to take root and grow.

THE BIRTH OF THE CLONE

A key factor in the formulation and promulgation of the cult of masculinity that also dismayed the gay liberationists was that the dominant gender style was now supermasculine. It was as if the 1960s and the counterculture androgyny never occurred. Gay male culture was still reeling from the crisis of masculinity that had affected homosexuals for decades. Gay men, attracted to the masculine ideals they'd cultivated in the furtive days prior to Stonewall, seemed now to institutionalize and exaggerate a heterosexual-inspired, macho look. The 1970s clone was born, and his look exploded on the streets of rapidly growing gay ghettos in dozens of American cities.

"I got back from India in 1974, having been gone a couple of years," remembers Craig, a forty-three-year-old New Yorker. "I was twenty-one, and I had long hair and a full beard, and I couldn't get laid. People told me I was cute but that I'd better shave and get a haircut. Everyone looked like the Marlboro Man. You had to look like a straight, macho guy—with a mustache, work boots, and plaid shirts." The clone was in fact described by many writers at the time. Edmund White, in his classic 1980 book *States of Desire: Travels in Gay America*, described the "Castro Street Clone" as having "a strongly marked mouth and swimming, soulful eyes (the effect of the mustache): a V-shaped torso by metonymy from the open V of the half-buttoned shirt about the sweaty chest . . . the feet simplified, brutalized and magnified by the boots." Indeed, this was the look that hundreds of thousands of men in the rapidly growing gay ghettos of America's urban centers were copying. Whether it was San Francisco, Chicago, Boston, New York, or Los Angeles, many gay men were conforming to the same rigid ideal: the image of the rugged, muscled, working-class straight man.

The dominant gender style for sexual object-choice had thus narrowed dramatically. The more effeminate style sexually desirable among Wilde and his contemporaries had all but disappeared from the forefront of homosexual life. By the time the Stonewall-inspired bathhouse and sex club culture of the 1970s rolled around, the established gender style of the gay male community was masculinity as it had been heterosexually defined, but it now became exaggerated into a hyper masculinity. Charles Silverstein had in fact observed this phenomenon in *Man to Man* in 1981: "Just a hundred years ago the English dandy was all the rage, with Oscar Wilde and a cadre of Cambridge scholars as the role models. . . . [W]hatever the reason, the 'queen' stood as the apex of homosexual openness. Now the image has changed completely—'queens' are a dying breed (unfortunately, so are their art and wit), replaced by the 'macho man' who ironically has become more macho than his heterosexual model."

Perhaps even more significant, however, the "macho man" was the sole gender style openly marketed to the emerging gay male community as the appropriate sexual object-choice. It didn't matter if masculine gender style was, or ever actually had been, the gender style of most gay men, and it didn't matter if it was, or ever had been, the gender style that was the sexual object-choice of most gay men: It was now marketed as such, and as a testament to consumer culture, it would simply become even more so.

It also didn't matter that there were at that time, and always had been, men who sexually desired effeminate men. It didn't matter that there were men who were not necessarily effeminate but who did not fit the rigid masculine ideal of muscles and mustaches. It didn't matter that there were plenty of effeminate men as well as drag queens, cross-dressers, transvestites, and transsexuals who might look to *one another* to find sexual object-choices. While some of those individuals were prominent in the arts at the time and in gay activist politics—many of them in fact were among those who had led the Stonewall Rebellion—they were virtually invisible as sexual object-choices in the gay sexual culture as it was now represented in its media, advertising, pornography, and sexual nightlife culture, its baths and sex clubs. The allure of baths and sex clubs in fact was their hot, "masculine" sex, as evidenced by the name of one popular New York bathhouse, Man's Country.

NO FATS, NO FEMS

"All the looks anyone needs can be bought at the local gym and from the local pusher; the lisped shriek of 'Miss Thing!' has faded into passing," Edmund White wrote in *States of Desire* in 1980, discussing New York's gay sexual culture. Indeed, the bathhouse and sex club, the apex of that culture at the time throughout urban America, was a place for macho men to meet macho men, and the effeminately attired man or the drag queen was not welcome (unless of course they were performers). Many sex clubs in fact did not admit drag queens (similar to several sex clubs today in New York and Los Angeles, which, in addition to drag queens, do not allow overweight or physically underdeveloped men either) and had dress codes that were decidedly masculinist: at New York's Mineshaft, for example, one would not be allowed in if one didn't wear something that connoted masculinity: work boots, leather jacket, ripped jeans. Another sex club of the time had a backdrop that included elaborate stage sets of trucks and prison cells and other exclusively male backgrounds.

This macho atmosphere of the baths and clubs often seemed to bring out in men a callous bravado that resulted in a disregard for one another, as well as a kind of aggressive desperation. "Some gay men behaved in brutally rude ways to each other," Doug Sadownick writes in *Sex Between Men*, about the baths of the 1970s. "Men deemed too fat or too old were treated as pariahs; they in turn could be seen to paw at younger men without permission. Those whose dicks did not measure up perhaps suffered worst of all. . . . Men tweaked on speed, hungry for the touch they didn't get, headachy from amyl, became sexual predators."

The image of the new, out gay man portrayed throughout the gay media and promoted by its commercial establishments was perhaps best epitomized by the Village People song of the time, "Macho Man." There may have been differences in the image—the motorcycle dude, the cop, the leather daddy, the obedient son, the boyish youth, the bodybuilder—but they were all variations on one theme, one gender style. On everything from advertisements for poppers to bathhouses, the hypermasculine male ideal appeared, beckoning gay men to *have* him and to *be* him. Indeed, he was the man gay men were to desire. But the only way to have him, gay men were being told, was to look just like him.

These images, it appeared, appealed to many out-of-the-closet middle-class white gay men of the time—men who had money to spend in the new commercial sexual culture. Those within this group who were genetically lucky found it easy to fit the ideal. But others within this group tried hard, drawing upon their middle-class values and dollars, working out and dressing the part, vowing to *be* the ideal, even if such attempts were in vain. That, after all, is the false promise of the cult of masculinity and indeed of any cult: Hard work and discipline will bring fulfillment, love, and adoration.

All other gay men either joined in, reluctantly or not, or in time found other subcultures within the gay world that were less visible but where they felt more comfortable. Within these subcultures they were made to feel they were in a minority, when in fact they were, in all probability, the majority.

VOICES OF DISSENT

This narrowing and promotion of the masculine physical ideal did not go unnoticed by writers and cultural critics in those early days of the commercial gay sexual culture. Several prominent writers and activists of the time were in fact disappointed and sometimes angered and valiantly shed light on the emerging cult—even if many men would not heed their warnings. Activist and scholar Martin Duberman wrote several articles in the 1970s critical of what, in his 1996 memoir *Midlife Queer*, he described as

> that segment of the gay male community that seemed to have narrowed its existence to achieving perfectly symmetrical bodies and inscrutably haughty veneers, and to displaying both as often as possible at stylish watering holes and disco palaces (or, alternately, at déclassé meat racks and backroom sex bars). . . . If you were a young middle or upper-middle class gay white male living in a big city, doing the latest designer drugs, disco dancing till dawn, taking advantage of the many outlets for casual sex, then you fit the current media image (and subsequent mythology) of the 'gloriously indulgent' 1970s. . . . But the vast majority of gay men and lesbians did not fit that image.

The late author and essayist George Whitmore, in 1982 as the 1970s gay sexual culture reached its peak just prior to the full-blown AIDS epidemic, observed that "almost all our common commercial institutions" were designed to promulgate the masculine "Rebel lifestyle." "The most visible aspects are [the Rebel's]," Whitmore noted, "and the ones glorified by most of our magazines and even our ideologues." Whitmore called this phenomenon "a new kind of victimization, this unexamined life."

Larry Kramer had begun taking on the gay sexual culture with the publication in 1978 of his book *Faggots*. Perhaps the most controversial gay book ever written, it is a stirring, satirical treatment of what he saw as the excesses of gay life. In interviews in the late 1970s and early 1980s Kramer took aim at sex clubs like the Mineshaft, discussing the pressure men felt to participate in the sexual culture it embodied and how men were made to feel "square" if they chose not to participate. He railed against the gay sexual culture, charging that it alienated men from political activism and was nothing but self-indulgence and escapism. To Kramer, the commercial gay sexual culture was unhealthy and could only lead to catastrophe.

Many writers, Duberman and Whitmore included, thought Kramer to be exceedingly moralistic and sex-negative in his critiques. Regardless, while they split hairs about how delicately Kramer had treated the subject, Duberman, Whitmore, and many other writers at the time were, like Kramer, all pointing to the same thing: a new rigidity that had overtaken gay culture, a lockstep mentality that was damaging to both individuals as well as the entire community, one that seemed to exploit an insecurity that dwelled within us all.

They saw that the commercial gay culture and its "cloning" of the masculine ideal was not at all liberating and was in fact for some not any less confining than life in the closet had been. In many ways, the heterosexual power structure was simply allowing gay men their excesses, perhaps even encouraging them, not only to make money off of us—many heterosexuals, after all, owned many of the sex establishments—but to keep us from being politically engaged.

"Gay clones were a homosexual version of what masculinity had become, and was becoming," Ian Young observes in *The Stonewall Experiment*. "When it became clear that gays weren't going away, a commercialized, consumerist version of our sexuality was conceded to us, a sexuality all the more frantic for being emptied of deep emotion. This fueled a machine without oil, which could only burn itself out until it seized up completely."

THE NEW RELIGION OF SEX

The cult of masculinity could not, however, completely solidify in the gay world unless the commercial sexual culture became an all-consuming, frenetic, collective obsession, something to literally believe in. But that was practically a fait accompli. The late 1960s and early 1970s was, after all, a time when traditional religion in general was loosening its grip on America and traditional religious institutions were experiencing a decline. And most gay men felt rejected from the religious institutions they had been brought up in anyway, bashed as demons and banished as sinners, simply for being who they were. But people don't easily give up thousands of years of religious ritual, with its promise of fulfillment, stability, and a connection to something larger than themselves. The breakdown of religion within a culture, or even among one group of people within that culture, occurs only when other institutions rise to take its place.

For many gay men, sex and the sexual culture, with all of its intricate rituals, came to fill the void; indeed, by the 1970s gay sex had gone from being an isolated event—a quickie in the men's room or a longer but quite singular good time in the park—to being a publicly acknowledged and preached-about religion.

"I would say that with the collapse of other social values (those of religion, patriotism, the family, and so on), sex has been forced to become our sole mode of transcendence and our only touchstone of authenticity," Edmund White noted in *States of Desire.* "The cry for scorching, multiple orgasms, the drive toward impeccable and virtuoso performance, the belief that only in complete sexual compatibility lies true intimacy, the insistence that sex is the only mode for experiencing thrills, for achieving love, for assessing and demonstrating personal worth—all these projects are absurd," he wrote, and then prophesied: "I can picture wiser people in the next century regarding our sexual mania as akin to the religious madness of the Middle Ages—a cooperative delusion."

Or, as a cult.

The cult of masculinity grew rapidly in the 1970s, supplanting many other institutions that might offer meaning. Rampant sex and drug use were written about as liberating, as important cultural, social, and political acts. The nightclubs and parties, with men disco dancing until dawn while high on a vast array of drugs, were considered spiritual rites of passage in the gay world, events at which people bonded with themselves and others. Indeed, for a great many gay men, the cult and its shrines—bathhouses, sex clubs, nightclubs, and bars, where many men went every night—were their only salvation in a hostile world, places where they obtained a sense of community.

Having grown exponentially in ten years, by 1980 the cult of masculinity had all the earmarks of some other doctrinaire cults: It offered a sense of community and meaning, filling a void in people where both politics and traditional religion had failed; it promoted drugs and sex as important and even transcendental experiences and as spiritual rites; and it subjected followers and would-be followers to repetitious bombardment of visual images and icons, in this case the gay male ideal seducing men to join the cult in return for a new life suffused with purpose (superficial as it might in reality be).

Quietly during those years, however, unbeknownst to the cult's promoters or followers, the cult was also helping to create the superhighways for a lethal virus that was finding its way into the gay world. During this time there was an explosion of multiple-partner sex and the dropping of the fairy-trade "role-playing" that meant more men were now both getting fucked and fucking. As Gabriel Rotello shows so lucidly in his 1997 book *Sexual Ecology*, this allowed HIV to spread rapidly in the 1970s in the urban gay ghettos. One famous study by researchers Bell and Weinberg at the time showed that almost half of the white gay men surveyed in the San Francisco Bay Area—recruited from bars, baths, community groups, and commercial mailing lists—reported having "at least" five hundred sexual partners throughout their lives. One-third of black gay men reported a similar number of partners throughout their lives. Ironically, the AIDS crisis almost ended the cult.

As the bodies began piling up and the AIDS crisis mushroomed in the early 1980s, the cult of masculinity in fact came to a momentary standstill. Bathhouses and sex clubs eventually closed down in cities like New York and San Francisco. Fearful for their lives many men settled into relationships, lowered their number of partners, or stopped having sex altogether. The gay resort mecca, Fire Island, previously at its peak, awash in hedonism, excess, and hot, masculine bodies, was almost deserted. The gay ghettos of the urban centers, once vibrant and alive with activity at all hours, became somber places. Even nightclub and bar culture in many cities practically died. Gay men were in a panic, rightly so, as friends and lovers sickened and died and the government responded with callous disregard. Many assumed they would be next. The sexual culture was stunned.

THE CULT RESURRECTS

But the cult of masculinity was not dead yet. It was simply lying dormant. By the mid to late 1980s, the community mobilized and pulled itself together, as we learned it was a virus that caused AIDS. Soon, the HIV-antibody test was developed; men could find out if they were infected or not, and the condom code came into play. The gay community formed a myriad of AIDS service organizations. Activists protested and demanded government action. But in our zeal to protect gay sex from being viciously demonized by the likes of religious zealots like Pat Robertson and Jerry Falwell, who attacked gay men from their pulpits and charged gays with spreading a pestilence, we resurrected a stronger-than-ever cult of masculinity.

Gay AIDS-prevention leaders told gay men they could continue in the behaviors and lifestyle they'd been used to in the past but to simply "use a condom every time"—something we learned years later was easier said than done. Many activists, beating back an antigay and right-wing backlash that was intent on seeing gay sex further criminalized, implored gay men to "save our sex" by continuing in their previous lifestyle.

The safer sex message was thus soon incorporated into the cult. "Safer Sex Is Hot Sex," blared HIV-prevention posters that were plastered all over New York, San Francisco, and Los

Angeles, showing two spectacularly well-defined, hairless, and completely naked men engaging in anal sex. Other placards and posters implored gay men to "Do it!," again using the images of sexy ideal men—and reminding them that they should, by the way, also use condoms.

ACT UP and later Queer Nation, two groups I was very much involved with in New York City, were highly successful in shifting the debate on AIDS, eventually forcing the government to respond, and promoting queer visibility. For many of us the groups were instrumental to our survival. Chapters of both groups sprang up in several dozen cities across the country in the late 1980s and in the early 1990s, bringing thousands of gay men and lesbians to direct action, many for the first time. These groups provided many with the very sense of community and sense of purpose that the cult previously had given them. And the consciousness they created sent ripples out into the respective communities in each city, far beyond the actual people who were involved in the groups.

But these groups, perhaps inadvertently, also eventually promoted the cult and its apolitical and self-indulgent attitudes, as well as its robotic lifestyle. We perhaps contributed to bringing the cult back to life—even if that might not have been our intent, and even if the kind of apathy, lack of involvement, and selfishness it cultivated was everything that ACT UP and Queer Nation were against. We were, of course, attempting to make people feel good about sex again, to get them out from under the shame that our enemies had exploited during the crisis. "Sex-positive," was the phrase we'd in fact used. But we rather idealistically expected that the vast majority of gay men viewed gay sex proudly, would treat it responsibly, and understood the importance of promoting the sexual culture for political and liberationist reasons while at the same time staying completely safe (for health reasons).

To be sure, many men, just as they had nearly twenty years earlier when the Gay Activist Alliance made a similar call to celebrate gay commercial sexual culture, took us up on our call to sexual action, but not always for reasons of "pride," and certainly not because they were the slightest bit politically minded (or, for that matter, "sex-positive"). Rather, reeling under a horrendous epidemic in addition to the usual homophobia in society, and knowing nothing else but the cult as a salvation in life, they were more often than not operating out of self-indulgence, fear, low self-esteem, and a nostalgic yearning for the only thing that gave them meaning in the past: the perfect cocktail—especially if you throw in some of the newer mind-altering drugs—for an eventual breakdown in safer sex.

THE CIRCUIT EMERGES

By the early 1990s, bathhouses and sex clubs began to trickle back—those that had never closed down were once again packed, while in other cities they reopened, or opened for the first time. Back rooms became all the rage in many bars. The drug-induced nightclub culture experienced a boom in the urban centers. Fire Island and other sexually charged gay resorts were raging again. And the international gay party circuit, as we know it today, was born.

The circuit—with its jet set "A-list" of well-heeled and muscular gay men—had actually been in existence in the pre-AIDS time, albeit it was small and very exclusive. It consisted in the late 1970s into the early 1980s mostly of about a thousand men who flew back and forth between New York and Los Angeles, going from the famous parties at the Flamingo and the Saint in New York to the ones at Probe in L.A. But in the

1990s the circuit grew to consist of parties all around the country, indeed around the world—from Miami to Montreal, Vancouver to Sydney—with tens of thousands of men who regularly attend events. In the early 1990s there were only a handful of events; by 1996, according to Alan Brown in *Out and About*, a gay travel newsletter, there were over fifty parties a year, roughly one per week. Typically these are weekend-long events, more a series of all-night (and daytime) parties stretching over a few days, often taking place in resort hotels, each punctuated by almost universal drug use among attendees.

Curiously, the circuit—as well as the "minicircuits" within the urban centers around the country, the local nightclub dance parties—grew in the early 1990s along with the decline of ACT UP and Queer Nation. There are still today many active and vibrant chapters of ACT UP, but their membership has declined dramatically. And most Queer Nation chapters, like some ACT Up chapters, have folded. As with the Gay Liberation Front roughly twenty-five years earlier, ACT UP and Queer Nation could not sustain themselves for a great many people, with members battling among themselves over politics and process; many of ACT UP's goals in particular—like streamlining the government's drug-approval process for drugs to treat life-threatening illnesses—were met, and people within the group differed on the direction the group should take. When the Clinton administration replaced the Bush administration, the enemy was also no longer so well defined. For many, focusing on direct-action activism had become frustrating, and they did not quite know how to take on a more gay-friendly administration that nonetheless was negligent. People began to leave the groups, pursuing other activities, and quite a few of the formerly politically engaged ACT UPers and Queer Nationals became fixtures on the circuit in the 1990s, either attending the parties, or even working them, sometimes promoting them, and often becoming as apolitical and party focused as the next circuit queen. The cult indeed seemed to absorb the energy that for many men had previously been poured into activism; not to mention that the cult of masculinity, rather than gay activism and gay politics, would now once again provide a sense of meaning and purpose for many men, particularly younger men coming into the community.

"Cults form out of the same conditions that determined women's recent history," Naomi Wolf observed, discussing how many women became more submerged in the Rites of Beauty in the years after feminism lost its steam; the analogy applies equally to gay men and the decline of activist politics. "Active rebellion," she notes, "is followed by passive withdrawal. When activism is frustrated, the activists turn inward."

As the community itself came to deal with AIDS and survive its devastation, and as gay politics, as before, lost its sparkle, the cult of masculinity flourished and became an important mechanism for many in coping with the tragedy of their lives, whether they'd lost people to AIDS or were infected with HIV themselves.

AIDS had almost destroyed the cult roughly ten years earlier. But, ironically, the newly risen cult now became a psychological antidote to AIDS. It provided a release for gay men reeling under a horrible epidemic. For many it is in fact their only connection to something larger, their only opportunity to bond with other men amid the pain and loss. The connection and the bond themselves, however, produced many more anxieties than they alleviated: The competitive commercial body culture became more rigid than ever before, and the drugs became more potent and more destructive.

THE CURRENT CRISIS OF MASCULINITY

AIDS exacerbated the century-old crisis of masculinity with a hysteria more extreme than even that of the McCarthy Era. Homosexuality once again came into the glare of the public spotlight and was looked at as something dirty and dangerous. Many straight men felt the need to distance themselves further from the homosexual, to prove their heterosexuality, their manhood. Gay men too experienced this and perhaps even more acutely: Now the sexual "bottom" was the focus of negative attention. In much of the public's eyes—and certainly in the eyes of many gay men—it was the submissive "feminine" role in homosexual sex that led to disease. Being healthy was now associated with taking the "manly" role in sex, the top— or at least pretending to. The term "straight-acting," a term to signify masculinity, became more popular than ever in the personals of gay publications and throughout gay cyberspace and was seemingly accepted—or at least reluctantly so—by much of the community.

"They're saying, 'I'm a man's man, and I only want to go out with real men,'" notes Los Angeles psychiatrist Duane E. McWaine, an African-American gay man who treats mostly gay men and people infected with HIV. "When you look at some of these ads, it makes me kind of ill sometimes. I wonder if I was looking through a publication and I saw 'black male wants white-acting female,' what kind of uproar that would raise. [Gay] publications are full of that, however."

Being healthy and disease-free also began to mean having muscles and a strong, sturdy body. As the 1990s raced on, we were out to prove we were supermen despite AIDS.

"People are trying to prove they're healthy, and this includes people already infected," the late Victor D'Longin, a professor of political philosophy at the University of Hartford, told writer William J. Mann in an article widely syndicated throughout the gay press in 1995. "For a long time, outside and inside the community, the face of AIDS was the emaciated body. The image of gay men, both inside and outside the community, has become just the opposite: hunky, healthy bodies. . . . It's a desperate attempt to appear healthy."

The ideal got tougher, bigger, harder. Huge chests, bulging biceps. But the ideal also needed to be clean and free of disease—pubescent, innocent. Our anxieties about disease and our own fears of AIDS were ever present, and they too would be exploited. From the late 1980s and into the 1990s, in advertising within the ghetto, in gay porn, and in gay fashion spreads, youthfulness and healthfulness, with all of its images of innocence, was *in*. Body hair—a sign of experience and maturity, and thus disease and guilt—was *out*. No one wanted to look like they might have "it." More significant, no one wanted to sleep with anyone who might seem to have "it."

"I know men who had wasting syndrome [in which a person with AIDS loses muscle mass] who were afraid of walking through Chelsea because of the pity and revulsion they feel," notes New York psychotherapist Rosemary Caggiano, whose clients have included many gay men with and without AIDS throughout the 1980s and 1990s. "Nurturing might go on at the community center, but on the streets, where you have your cruising, they became a threat and an embarrassment to the community."

Exploiting that fear and anxiety, the gay porn industry, centered on the West Coast, helped define the ideal further: the corn-fed, youthful, hairless, white, muscle man-boy with a healthy California tan. He was every bit a man, and he was disease-free. The irony of this of course—beyond the fact that at the time perhaps as many as half of all gay men in some large cities were infected with HIV, no matter how healthy they looked—was that many men who came close to being the ideal were taking dangerous illegal steroids to get that way, drugs that made them anything but healthy.

Technology in fact, medical and otherwise, had a great impact on the cult of masculinity in the 1990s: As gym equipment became remarkably advanced, as scientific knowledge of how the body builds muscle grew, as the development and use of food supplements and drugs to enhance muscle growth became prevalent, and as cosmetic surgery for men—from liposuction to pectoral implants—became refined and more popular, the masculine ideal became more precise. It also became much less attainable for most men then ever before, unless they were willing to go to ridiculous extremes, investing a great amount of time in building their bodies, taking dangerous drugs, and opting for surgery. Even then, genetics still played a role, since most men would not be able to fit the new ideal unless they were precisely genetically blessed with a specific body type.

Even *that*, however, even with hard work, did not assure fitting the ideal. The ideal, as presented in advertisements and photos was, more and more, computer enhanced (butts made rounder, bigger, the biceps accentuated, the waists slimmed in) to proportions that were physically impossible to emulate, even with drugs and surgery.

Indeed, by the late 1980s and into the 1990s the ideal was no longer something that occurred in nature. It was a completely manufactured man, an artificially created version of masculinity. The masculine body type that was now most revered could perhaps only be attained by surgery, drug use, and computer enhancement of images. No one, in essence, could really be the perfect man. But that would not stop the members of the cult from trying.

The frenetic lifestyle, the highly competitive body culture, the rampant drug use, and other pressures of the cult of masculinity certainly created some of the conditions that kept young men and older men alike from using "a condom every time." The reports issued in the early 1990s, and which continue to come in, which are indicative of the so-called second wave of AIDS, have been devastating: A San Francisco Department of Health study in 1991 found that among men ages seventeen to nineteen, 43 percent said they had engaged in anal sex without a condom. A University of California, San Francisco, study that same year found that for African-American young gay men, that number jumps to 52 percent. A 1995 study funded by the Centers for Disease Control and Prevention reported that more than two-thirds of gay men surveyed in Chicago, San Francisco, and Denver had had at least one unsafe encounter—unprotected receptive or insertive anal intercourse—within an eighteen-month period.

Not so surprisingly, all of this unsafe sex has been taking its toll: A 1992 study of HIV infection rates among gay men in four cities—Baltimore, Chicago, Los Angeles, and Pittsburgh—concluded that one-third of all currently uninfected twenty-year-old gay and bisexual men will seroconvert by the time they are thirty, and the majority will eventually seroconvert.

PROTEASE DIS-INHIBITORS

The greatest news we have received in recent times has been about protease inhibitors, the new class of drugs to treat HIV. Doctors and researchers are astounded by the remarkable advances that have been made with various triple combinations of these powerful new drugs. A great many gay men using these drugs are responding dramatically well, seeing their health restored practically to normal; their viral load often plummets to the point where there is no HIV virus detectable in their blood. We are watching ourselves, our lovers, and our friends suddenly spring back, rebounding with energy. In a happy ending that would have seemed impossible just a few years ago, many people with AIDS may live long and normal lives.

Treatment researchers as well as prevention experts say, however, that safer sex is even more crucial now than ever before. It is still uncertain, for example, as to whether or not HIV is hiding in the lymph nodes or other places in those people with AIDS who now show the virus to be undetectable, ready to multiply, perhaps mutate into a drug-resistant strain once they come off the drugs. And no one knows how long the drugs will work even if people stay on them indefinitely; HIV could still mutate around the drugs in time. Another problem is that some people with AIDS cannot stomach many of the protease inhibitors. Their bodies react violently, though their doctors keep trying various combinations of the various drugs. The drugs are also not working for a substantial number of people; their bodies simply do not respond to the drugs. There is also the danger that many people will not take the drugs properly; the drugs must be taken at various times throughout the day, on an empty stomach (no food for two hours before and two hours after). If a person misses a day or two, or is not digesting the drugs properly, HIV could mutate around the drugs rather than being killed off, and thus resistant strains are likely to develop. And the drugs are cost-prohibitive for a great many people with HIV infection.

The fear among prevention experts of course is that, with enough people around who are developing drug-resistant strains, if safer sex uptake is not improved, a new epidemic of drug-resistant HIV, a sort of super-HIV, will inevitably develop. Yet some researchers believe that because protease inhibitors are showing great promise for many, they have lead to many HIV-negative gay men disregarding safer sex practices: They're perhaps believing that they can now let down their guard precisely because there are now drugs to treat them if they become infected. In effect, the drugs are *disinhibiting* them with regard to unsafe sex. (It's not hard to believe, considering that a substantial number of men were engaging in unsafe sex *before* protease inhibitors.)

In a 1996 study of gay and bisexual men in South Beach, the southern tip of Miami Beach, William Darrow, a professor at Florida International University and one of the most respected AIDS researchers in the country, found that 16.1 percent of gay and bisexual men there aged eighteen to twenty-nine were infected with HIV, while 38.6 percent of those aged thirty and older were infected. South Beach is a haven for many gay men in their twenties and thirties, one of the cult of masculinity's hot spots, now home to several circuit events throughout the year. It is a gay resort destination that caters to a gay fast crowd looking for action.

"It's a very transient population. . . . People come and they get caught up in the holiday mood," Darrow observed to Reuters. In his study, more older men than younger men said they'd recently engaged in unsafe anal sex, albeit only slightly greater. Both figures, however, were astounding: 72.4 percent of men aged eighteen to twenty-nine, and 78.6 percent of men aged thirty and older reported that they had engaged in unprotected anal intercourse in the last year. These figures, the researcher observed, are "the highest levels of unsafe sex that anyone has reported in the last ten years."

"Gay and bisexual men have gotten all the messages that we want them to get, but they still are engaging in high levels of risk," Darrow said, noting that the positive news about the new drugs to treat HIV infection, the protease inhibitors, were perhaps contributing to the impression that AIDS is now curable, and thus the impression that safer sex is not important. "Now maybe they are more optimistic, that some drug is going to come along, a magic bullet," he observed. "That worries us, because we think that it's inadvisable."

There is also an evident fear among some people in HIV prevention that some HIV-positive men who are on protease inhibitors, believing that their undetectable viral load level is an indication that they cannot be infectious, believe they may not need to use condoms to protect others.

"They're calling and asking, 'I can have sex without a condom now because my HIV blood levels have gone to undetectable and that's the same as being cured, right?' And I say, 'Whoa!'" Bruce Patterson, director of the Gay Men's Health Crisis hotline in New York told *Long Island Newsday* in December 1996. In the same report, award-winning AIDS reporter Laurie Garrett noted that, looking at preliminary data, National Institutes of Health researchers "found no correlation between the amount of HIV in an individual's blood and the quantity found in sperm" and that "some individuals whose blood levels were extremely low still had what are assumed to be infectious quantities of HIV in their semen."

Certainly, the cult of masculinity and its various pressures are not the sole force influencing gay men in their decisions about safer sex. But they certainly contribute dramatically. A Band-Aid approach, in which HIV prevention groups and AIDS organizations try to get men to use condoms even as many men continue to construct their lives in ways that enable them—and sometimes even encourage them—to forgo safer sex, does not appear to cut down on unsafe sex enough to stem the epidemic. Fearful of appearing moralistic, many prevention leaders refuse to acknowledge that, in addition to their current efforts, the cult itself, and more specifically, encouraging and urging gay men to loosen its grip over themselves, is what also needs to be discussed.

For even without AIDS as a major concern, it's quite clear that our slavish allegiance to the cult of masculinity has for decades affected many gay men in detrimental ways, from the physical to the emotional, from the psychological to the spiritual.

And unless we weaken its pull, the cult will continue to have a stranglehold on so many of us. That includes a great many gay men of future generations, men who will be seduced into joining the cult's fastest growing institution as we approach the millennium, an institution that ultimately affects us all, even if we know little or nothing about it: the Evangelical Church of the Circuit.

3

THE EVANGELICAL CHURCH OF
THE CIRCUIT

"My first circuit party was in June of 1994, aboard the aircraft carrier the Intrepid *in New York, on the weekend of the Stonewall 25 celebration. On that night, I was baptized by drugs. And after that party, my life changed forever."*

—Juan,
a thirty-one-year-old
Miami Beach art director

The bulging men on the covers of the gay glossy magazines and the hundreds of bar rags in thousands of bars and nightclubs in cities across America are the cult of masculinity's deities, worshipped and adored, looked up to and revered. So are the go-go dancers, the top-notch hustlers, and of course, the gay porn stars. "He is a *god*," we tell one another, describing these men; if we can only get near them, receive their blessing, perhaps some of their holiness will rub off on us.

Gyms are the cult's temples. Nightclubs and sex clubs, its

shrines. And the drugs—whether they are the steroids and other compounds many men use to transform their physical bodies, or the Special K, Ecstasy, cocaine, and crystal meth many use to alter their minds—are the mystical elixirs and potions that will take us to a higher place where all is well and where we will bond with one another's souls.

"There's a lot of ritual to the drug intake," says Jay Corcoran, director of the 1996 film *Life and Death on the A-List*, a documentary about the handsome model, actor, and photographer Tom McBride, a circuit A-lister who died of AIDS in 1994. Corcoran, an actor himself and a friend of McBride's, knows the circuit well. "The drugs are very much like the [Holy] Communion and the wine, treated very sacredly. People are so into the maintenance of their drugs. The way they store their drugs, their stash, it's very holy, like the Chalice. The drugs bring them somewhere. They're very important."

Thus the drug-fueled parties of the circuit, weekend-long events attended by men who make pilgrimages from places far and wide, are spiritual retreats for the most devoted. They are the evangelical or fundamentalist wing of the cult of masculinity. Some of the circuit's devotees even espouse what can only be called a *church theology*, often describing the circuit as a sort of religious institution—one that draws upon ancient traditions of faith, and one that requires its adherents to conform to shared behavior and thought.

"The intensity at the core of the circuit," the quarterly publication *Circuit Noize*, the bible of the circuit, informs us, "is created by the music's heavy bass beat that resonates deep within one's chest, the flow of alcohol with its loosening effects, the rush of adrenaline from smuggled substances, the sexual tension, the smell of the sweaty half-naked bodies that surround, oppress, and ignite the 'group think' that allows us to behave with new levels of abandon, the rampant desire stirred by the presence of so many fantasy esquires."

In *Circuit Noize*'s theology, the circuit has a certain "spiritual power" that creates a "single dance floor organism" that harkens back to a day many thousands of years ago when religions on earth focused on "the mother goddess." In those days, *Circuit Noize* tells us, people stayed in an "ecstatic state for days at a time" with the help of "herbal substances" while celebrating the feasts of the goddess. These events could sometimes also spawn "a drunken orgy" or two, bringing people to "new heights of public depravity." Today's circuit parties then, *Circuit Noize* suggests, are "a genetic memory of the traditions which existed for thousands of years before being suppressed by the patriarchal religions." And the men who attend the circuit's "celestial celebrations" are "transformed by the energy of their gatherings," overcome with "the same spirit that was present at the feasts of the goddess."

It is safe to say that the theology of the circuit, as espoused by *Circuit Noize*, is probably not shared by most gay men; it might not even be shared by most men on the circuit itself. And though the circuit is larger than ever and continues to grow, bringing in new converts every day, it is not directly within the experience of the vast majority of gay men.

Yet, the circuit and its philosophy and lifestyle are not as far removed from the average gay man's life as we might like to think. Like the omnipotent Vatican, or like the fundamentalist Protestant churches, which influence all of American politics and culture, the highly visible and doctrinaire aspects of the circuit affect all of gay culture and, ultimately, each one of us individually.

That is true whether we belong to it or not—even if we've

never taken drugs and danced all night on a dance floor. Many gay men are inextricably linked to the circuit simply because the circuit is one of the driving forces that fuel the cult of masculinity within the gay world.

FEAR OF THE UNFASHIONABLE

The circuit and the culture that both built it and now fosters it—the "minicircuits" of hot boy nightclub parties in each individual city, the national gay media, which it promotes and which support it (including *Out* magazine, for which I write a monthly column), the infinite number of local sex rags in cities across the country—are to the gay male world what Hollywood, the fashion industry, the cosmetics industry, *Vogue*, and *Glamour* are to American women. Just as the average American woman has never been to a Seventh Avenue runway show, the average American gay man has never been to a circuit party. Yet, what happens at both events—what is shown, what is performed, what is telegraphed to the larger community—dictates an accepted and expected mode of behavior and expression. Both events deem "unfashionable" all those who don't buy into them.

For some of those newly on the circuit, avoiding the "unfashionable" label seems to have been their motivation in fact for joining in. "I never did drugs, and I had never been to a circuit party and I was afraid to go," says Andy, a twenty-two-year-old San Diego student who after working out for a while now does drugs, goes to circuit parties in L.A., and has "the circuit boy look," as he calls it. "I was really out-of-it before. I was very moralistic, you know, looking at drugs as bad and stuff. I was kind of dull."

"I think that everyone who is considered, you know,

'plugged in' is on the circuit to one extent or another, and everyone on the circuit works hard on their body and gets high," says David, a twenty-seven-year-old San Jose computer consultant. "If you're going to go out at all, meet hot men and have a good time, drugs are like a prerequisite, and if you don't do them you'll be considered kind of out of it. And I think on the circuit, without doing drugs, like, you're bored out of your mind. I understand people who don't do drugs and don't do the circuit, I mean, that's their choice. But I would say, yeah, maybe I'm biased, but I think that they're not so cool and they're kind of, like, prudish. It's the same with working on your body. It's like, if you don't want to do that, fine. But I like having a tight, muscular body. You know, that's where it's at. If you don't want to do it, then cool, you're not into being where it's at, and if you can live with that, go ahead."

"I moved to Miami four or five years ago," recalls Juan, a thirty-one-year-old art director who grew up in Puerto Rico and attended college in Nashville before moving to South Beach. "Soon after I moved, I kept going to clubs, to the dance floor, and seeing all of these shirtless men dancing and doing these choo-choo trains and they would never go home, and it took me years to figure out why. For some reasons they had the energy of death. It's Ecstasy, I later figured out. At the time, if someone had offered me drugs, I wouldn't have done it. I was on a different track."

But after a couple of years, Juan fell in love with a man, someone on the circuit with whom he eventually broke up, and like a lot of people who fall in love, he did things he'd never done before. "To be honest with you, I discovered all of this by accident," he says of the nightclub scene in South Beach and the circuit, which he now travels. "My ex had done it. So I was introduced to it pretty much for the wrong reasons, not because it was great and I wanted to have a ball with people, but because I allowed myself to be influenced by him. He wanted me to do it, and I would have been on a different wavelength, I felt, if I didn't do [the drugs and go out dancing]. And in his mind, if you were cool, you did it. He was a person who enjoyed escaping reality—looking back he had the brain and maturity level of a fifteen-year-old. I remember doing [Ecstasy for the first time] and holding the pill in my hand and I remember asking, 'Is this going to fry me for the rest of my life?'"

Juan laughs, noting that he later realized that was "an overreaction." In fact, he says, that first party also made him realize what he'd been "missing out on" all that time he was standing on the side of the dance floor and not knowing what was going on. His story illustrates the hypnotic power that the circuit has on many: It offers up the rituals and merrymaking of childhood and adolescence that most gay men, closeted well into early adulthood and beyond, were never previously able to experience *as gay men*, and its ever increasing visibility in the gay world in many ways sets a standard for how all of us are to be gay.

"That first circuit party I did, it was like going to the circus," Juan continues, "and seeing things I had never seen before, seeing people have sex on the dance floor, onstage, in the dark rooms, seeing the drugs, everyone out of control, people doing [Special] K on the dance floor, the intensity of the music, people gyrating, the sexual feeling. Wow, I was feeling that this was a new thing for me, and I was seeing that this is what being gay was, and it was so primitive and powerful. That first night, I was like a kid in the candy store. I was salivating. I thought that that night, it was never going to end, that it would be there permanently."

Juan goes on to describe that first night on drugs as being, literally, a religious experience. "It was phenomenal," he says. "That night I was baptized by drugs." And thus began his induction into the Evangelical Church of the Circuit and the cult of masculinity. From that moment on, though he and his boyfriend broke up (a direct result of the pressure the circuit put on their relationship), Juan would travel around the country from party to party, getting high and partying. He would also begin to work out vigorously, even though he is thin and finds it difficult to bulk up, and take all kinds of compounds that promise to build up his muscles.

"I'M NOT THE IDEAL BUT I WANT THE IDEAL"

The physical paradigm the circuit creates and the pressure to conform to it, however, are present even among many of those who, unlike Juan, never got sucked up in the circuit and haven't ever been anywhere near the circuit, which underscores the circuit's reach far into the gay male community. Vincent, a thirty-two-year-old New York schoolteacher who lives on Long Island, New York, has never used drugs other than marijuana and has never been to a circuit party (he can count on one hand in fact the number of times he's been to a gay nightclub). Yet the circuit and its paradigms are one of the reasons he offers for why he keeps working out; he refers to the circuit men in much the same way the average woman might refer to, say, the new generation of supermodels.

"You gotta keep up with the Chelsea circuit queens," Vincent says, laughing. "They're spreading like wildfire. If you don't keep up, you'll wind up getting passed up." Marty, a thirty-nine-year-old Chicago journalist, puts it into a bit more perspective: "No matter where you are, even if you don't like the circuit or even know about it, you feel a pressure to buy into that look. I don't go to circuit parties. I don't like the music. I think the crowd is boring. And I'm not into drugs these days as much—just sort of once in a long while. But the body, well, yeah, that I do try to keep up and, yes, I would say I do feel a pressure to emulate the circuit muscle boy. It's the aesthetic now, and I'm trying to fit it, and I think most of us are."

Even among many men who claim to disdain the shaved, pumped circuit look, there is sometimes a glaring contradiction in their logic, one that betrays their reverence for the physical ideal the circuit promotes. "I hate all those guys," says Alan, a forty-two-year-old florist who recently moved from Atlanta to Washington. Alan is slightly shorter than average, and quite thin. "They've all got attitude and they're transparent. Plastic. I don't understand it. They don't look at people as people, just as objects. And what about when they look at me? Why can't they just like people for who they are. I'm a talented, knowledgeable person, very successful, and financially secure. I have a lot of interests and I think I'm the kind of man who is a good companion. But those fellas don't want anything to do with me because I don't have a body like theirs."

But then why does *he* want *them*? Why doesn't he go for someone who looks like him?

"I'm just not attracted to that type," he says, at first seeming not to notice the irony in what he has just told me. "I don't like skinny guys. I like them with some meat. When it comes to sexual attraction, I like the muscled guys, I like the circuit guys. I wish I could say I didn't, but I do." He puts his hands up, exasperated, and laughs, finally realizing the contradiction. "Well, I guess that's just how I am. I see all of those guys going to clubs, with their tight shirts and big pecs and beautiful arms, and it does it for me—even if they all look the same." Alan reiterates the dilemma—the catch-22—that many gay men find themselves caught in: *I'm not the ideal, but I want the ideal, and I can't get the ideal unless I am the ideal, but I'll never be the ideal, so I hate those guys—even though I want to have sex with them!*

And though we are individually responsible for buying into it, it is the circuit that increasingly dictates and further promulgates that ideal. The circuit parties today are aggressively promoted to the gay male community in advertisements that prop up the circuit body through the sophisticated and ever present local and national gay media. The man with the circuit body is the man to emulate, the man to meet, the man to hang around with, and the man to have sex with. And the only way we'll meet him, whether or not we have the "right" bodies, is at the circuit party.

WHO ME? I'M NOT A CIRCUIT QUEEN

"I want to find something to do with my life," the twenty-five-year-old blond man tells me. We're sitting on a small plane filled to capacity, a Saab Turboprop thirty-four-seater, flying high over some treacherous-looking mountains, headed for Palm Springs. He, like me and most of the men on the plane, are attending the VII Annual White Party, taking place on Easter weekend, and billed as "the largest party in the world ... with over thirty thousand of the world's hottest men." Almost since we took off from Los Angeles on this Friday morning—Good Friday—the blond man has been talking to me, telling me his life story, even though I haven't asked.

He's been living in Miami for the past couple of years, having moved from up north. His family has money, he says, and he was expected to follow in his father's footsteps, going into the family business. He was even married to a woman for a year or so, but couldn't keep his true self suppressed. He divorced his wife and came out. Soon after, his family disowned him. So he moved to Miami.

These days, his life is a strange mix of anxiety and boredom. "I want to do something creative, I guess," he says, "but I feel kind of lost, without any direction." His family's rejection seems to have hurt him deeply, not to mention that it has thrown him for a loop in terms of finding an occupation. He reluctantly admits that he works in a dull, nine-to-five clerical job, not the kind of job that would give him the status and money he would have had in his family's business. And he hasn't a clue as to what he'll do next.

So, he plods around from party to party in Miami, something that, crazy as it sounds, does offer him the status he's been denied elsewhere—or at least some semblance of that status. He describes his friends, some of whom are on the plane, as on the cutting edge of the gay party crowd of Miami. "You know, we're the people everyone looks to for excitement, and for what's hip," he says with pride.

One of his friends on the plane had actually gotten this young man's plane ticket and hotel room for free, he tells me. The friend is working the party, a go-go dancer performing in one of the stage shows. I'm not sure exactly how that warrants getting a free ticket for a friend, but I'm assuming this young man is probably working the show too, doing makeup or odd jobs or dancing himself, and is simply too proud to tell me. He seems intent on letting me believe that his fabulousness is what has carried him this far. As if this far is really so far.

Much of the plane in fact is filled with people who are performing in the shows; some are drag queens, and some are African-Americans—not staples of the mostly white gay party circuit, and indeed quite unlike most of the men I will meet this weekend. They're laughing and carrying on wildly, as the plane bobs up and down over the mountains. I'm not sure whether the pilot—who, in this small plane, can view the entire passenger cabin through the open cabin door—is more uncomfortable with the queens' flamboyance or with the plane's erratic activity.

"It's a bumpy ride when you're trying to get over the mountains in this heat with this many people," the pilot warns as I nervously open a copy of *Circuit Noize* that someone has passed down to me. "So please keep your seat belts fastened and hold on tight."

Circuit Noize is a glossy little publication clearly created to pump up the scene, its motto emblazoned across its cover: "A rag custom designed for crazed party boys." The publication includes reports about parties in various cities, a sex column (entitled "Safe Slut," and which, to its credit, dispenses sound and quite sophisticated advice on navigating safer sex), humor pieces that make light of drug use ("Wobbly Wally's feet don't quite work any more . . . his movement is toddler-like as he attempts to navigate the stairs or other mountainous objects. Strange how this barely attracts notice in the twisted arcade of the dance tunnel."), a calendar of circuit parties throughout the upcoming season, and of course page after page of party advertisements propping up the waxed and chiseled ideal circuit men.

As the bumps subside and the plane comes in for a landing, I read a passage on *Circuit Noize*'s contents page, a passage that will stick out in my mind all weekend: "The circuit is a series of queer parties that are held in North America. A circuit party gives us the chance to escape the pressures of our day-to-day existence and to enter the altered world where man-to-man sex is not only accepted, but is celebrated. When the circuit comes to town, that town becomes an instant gay ghetto full of hot men who are behaving as queer as they care to be."

THE BOYS' CAMP OF YOUR DREAMS

Soon after I check into my hotel, I venture out to get a feel for Palm Springs and the White Party weekend. It's a small desert town with a spectacular backdrop, nestled at the foot of the towering, dramatic San Jacinto Mountains. Basically, thousands of gay men have taken over three chain hotels (the official hotels of the party), as well as many other hotels and smaller motels and inns, in the middle of the desert to cavort and play. The expansive Wyndham Hotel is where most of the festivities will take place, and it is entirely booked with White Party attendees. By day, the faux southwestern-style lobby is abuzz with activity, overrun with excited and jovial muscle boys wearing juvenile little shorts and tops. The men are mostly white, and the bulk are in their twenties and thirties, though there are some men in their forties and older. The younger ones tend to be local Californians; many of them drove in from L.A. or San Diego and are sleeping five or more in a room.

"A bunch of us went out partying last night in L.A., stayed up all night and just got in the car and drove here," a hunky, hairless little guy tells me as he holds another fellow in a headlock, a man who like him is probably no older than twenty-three. "And I kidnapped Joe, here. We met last night and he didn't know he'd be coming here." Joe gives me a blank smile and is clearly not operating at full capacity at this moment.

The older men tend to be well-off professionals who've flown in from around the country and around the world. Some of them are quite remarkable, on the surface the kind of perfect man who in your wildest fantasy comes and saves the day, men whom you thought existed only in a Danielle Steel or Judith Krantz TV miniseries—except of course that they're gay. Roget, for example, is a six-foot-six Swiss stallion with a perfectly symmetrical, lean but big and firm body, a gorgeous face with razor-sharp cheekbones, and a wicked smile. He likes running around here wearing only Calvin Klein briefs and work boots. But despite his overzealous circuit attire, he is warm, friendly, and modest, quite unlike most of the Californians and other Americans I will meet here. At thirty-five, Roget is already quite wealthy, an interior designer who lives in Zurich in a huge house cut into the side of a mountain, and who designs the homes of Europe's elite. He travels the circuit around the world, rarely missing a party, and he's just fallen in love with a man he met at the now very popular annual White Party at the sixteenth-century Vizcaya estate in Miami several months earlier, a man who, except for the fact that he is Hispanic, looks very much like Roget, standing next to him at this moment in matching Calvins, matching work boots, matching musculature.

Looking around the Wyndham Hotel as men arrive and settle in while others are already off to events and gatherings brings you back to your childhood. Everywhere, men in kiddy outfits are darting about, hauling bags, carrying clothes; the mood is not unlike the first day of check-in of boys' summer camp.

Late at night and into the early morning hours, however, as both official parties in ballrooms and private parties in suites are still going on, the Wyndham has a decidedly different feel as the entire hotel—all four sprawling floors of it—becomes a virtual bathhouse. This now happens regularly at motels, hotels, and resorts around the country and the world that cater to the major circuit events, where sometimes tens of thousands of gay men meet almost every week (as there are now over fifty circuit events per year). In spite of this, circuit parties are often described as somehow being less focused on sexual activity, perhaps because the events are not as raunchy as, say, the events that highlighted fist-fucking performances onstage at the Anvil in New York in its 1970s heyday or at the Saint in the early 1980s.

"What has replaced sex is the idea of sex; what has replaced promiscuity is the idea of promiscuity, masked, in the increasing numbers of circuit parties around the country, by the ecstatic drug-enhanced high of dance music," wrote Andrew Sullivan in the *New York Times Magazine* in November 1996, discussing the circuit party phenomenon. He may be right that the parties themselves do not include the kind of sexual activity onstage or on the dance floor that was much more prevalent in the 1970s, although, as Juan, the thirty-one-year-old Miami man notes, such activity still occurs at many parties and clubs in back rooms and even on the dance floor itself. The four-day takeover of chain hotels by thousands of gay men—which did not happen in the 1970s—seems to be making up for that.

At the Wyndham during the White Party weekend, every night and into the next day, men stagger from room to room, half-naked, often stoned out of their minds; others are looking out of their peepholes, checking out the men aimlessly wandering the hallways. Some men go from room to room, joining orgies, bringing with them groups of men they find along the way. Some doors are slightly to fully ajar. Their occupants flash their wares and beckon strangers whom they might like—and slam the door on those whose musculature does not meet the standard.

"OUR OWN LITTLE WORLD"

The actual White Party takes place at the Wyndham on Saturday night in one of its ballrooms. But on Saturday afternoon, the pool and grounds of the Wyndham Hotel are the site of a massive party. From a vantage point on a balcony high above, overlooking the pool, it's a scene out of a Cecil B. De Mille epic: a huge Grecian-style swimming pool with fountains spraying out of the middle and from off the sides toward the center, and thousands of half-naked men flailing about in the water and on the enormous grounds that surround it. They're gyrating and dancing in the ninety-five-degree dry heat to the primitive beat of a deejay spinning off to the side of the pool, all under a magnificent desert mountain. The only element missing, one imagines, is Larry Kramer coming down from the mountain, clutching a couple of stone tablets and then hurling them at the crowd.

Indeed, looking around, I'm struck by the thought of how, if even half of this party energy could be put toward political action, gay men would be light-years ahead of where they are, both politically and in terms of visibility, having shattered the closet once and for all. But I'm also not sure many of these men, deep down, would really want that. They seem in fact to like the covert, under-the-radar status of the parties, of having a secret gay society.

"This is, like, a little world that we've created—our own little world," a Houston doctor tells me a few minutes after offering me some cocaine as we chat on the edges of the pool party.

"This is the great part about being gay, the best-kept secret about being gay: We actually do have more fun than straights, and that we actually revel in our being pushed off to the side. I wouldn't trade it for anything. "

"For me, it's like, I'm HIV-positive," says a thirty-four-year-old San Francisco man who becomes annoyed with my questioning, and who is much more candid about his HIV status than most men here seem to be. "I lost a lover. I've lost several close friends. I feel like all of this stuff is the thing for me, you know. This is my once-in-a-while escape into a group of people that is going through the same thing but wants to make believe it's not really happening—*just for a moment*. We get high, we dance. We touch each other's bodies. We put the real world on hold for five minutes at a time—that's what we're doing. I've done the support groups and the therapy and the whole nine yards. But this [going to circuit parties] keeps me *not* talking about it all the time, *not* thinking about it, *not* discussing it. I'm sick of it. I like this as an underground life. It's all about parties, and having fun, and sex. I need that. We all need that."

For other men, however, indeed for what seems like a great many men on the circuit, this is not a "once-in-a-while" escape. "I *live* the circuit," Jim, a thirtyish Long Beach, California, waiter-model proudly tells me. "I try to go to every event I can, and I party my ass off with my friends. I have so many friends on the circuit, and they *all* party really hard. You only live once, you know, and you have to make it a ball yourself. If you don't, life is dull and depressing and can be very, very difficult and very painful. Who needs that? The only way you make it something else is by putting a lot of effort into it. I'm into *celebrating* life."

In ways similar to those of these men, many others talk of the circuit as offsetting the tragedies they experience, particularly with regard to AIDS. They literally look to the circuit as part of their mourning process, as a psychological remedy to the epidemic.

"The advent of the party scene is very much linked to the development of AIDS and the community's response to it," says Alan Brown, a sort of spiritual shaman of the circuit who writes for *Circuit Noize*, *Genre*, and *Out and About*, the gay travel newsletter. Tall and slender, Brown is not at all a muscle man and does not see the circuit, for himself, as a sexual playground. He in fact seems to eschew those who are on the circuit because they're into "body worship and for sexual reasons"—yet he also seems not to realize that by doing so he is probably writing off the vast majority of men on the circuit. For Brown, the circuit is a way for gay men to "connect with a larger energy" and is "virtually a religious experience, a spiritual experience." At the White Party, he runs around with gold glitter dust spread across his bare chest and wears flamboyant beads and outrageous animal print pants. He is one of the very few men who do break the monotony by doing something creative and fabulous. His reasons for being here, however, are strikingly similar to others.

"Many of the largest parties we have were born in the AIDS crisis and are benefits," he says, expanding on his beliefs about the connection between AIDS and the circuit. "It's ironic that the organizations that promote safer sex and responsible behavior would often be the beneficiaries of these parties, but every community is self-destructive to one extent or another, and ultimately it's okay to be sick and to be celebrating your life. I think one response of this community [to AIDS] has been an increased intensity in celebration, which is proportionate to [increased] desperation. I mean, personally, having stood at the bedside of several close friends, beautiful men dying of AIDS, has taught me that what really matters is the quality *of the moment*—and the party scene for me is the way of achieving that sort of intensity of affirmation. It's an antidote for AIDS. It's definitely an escape. Many people with AIDS are partying, as are many people who are HIV-positive. They're having the best times of their lives, hell-bent on having a good time."

A SENSE OF COMFORT

Walter, a thirty-two-year-old Los Angeles sales executive I meet at the Wyndham pool party, who agrees to talk to me in depth a few weeks later, tells a story not unlike that of many gay men on the circuit. The names and locations may change, but the scenario is uncannily the same. "When Albert died, it was like, we were all thrown—just beat down," he says, discussing a circuit pal who'd recently died of AIDS at the age of thirty-four. "We went out and partied like mad that night. We really needed to. It felt great. It was a release of tension and fear. We all really bonded and got past so much of the pain. Albert was always with us, but for the last two months of his life, he couldn't party, he couldn't travel. And so he'd make us call him up from different events. We called him from Vizcaya [the big circuit event in December in Miami], and he was just crying like a baby. And so were we, all of us. Then we went to the party and we did some Ex, and just a tiny bit of crystal each, and we really were connected. I felt we'd really become almost like one that night. And I thought of Albert the whole time. That was a very, very special party for me, for all of us. Then, on that night he died, we went to Probe [the Los Angeles dance club] and we just worked it all out, got high, hugged each other, just worked it out."

In his *New York Times Magazine* piece, Andrew Sullivan, discussing his own HIV-positive status and his presence at a circuit party, eloquently made an observation that perhaps sums up what Walter and his friends, as well as a great many other men, are experiencing: "On the surface the parties could be taken for a mass of men in superb shape merely enjoying an opportunity to let off steam. But underneath, masked by the drugs, there is an air of strain, of sexual danger translated into sexual objectification, the unspoken withering of the human body transformed into a reassuring inflation of muscular body mass."

For many of the men I speak with in Palm Springs over the weekend, like many men I've spoken to at circuit parties I've attended in the past, the circuit does provide a reassurance, a sense of comfort, even if their attempts to find that comfort are often desperate and futile, and even if it is sometimes detrimental to their health and well-being. In a rather scary way, they describe the circuit similarly to how people in cults describe the various rituals and institutions of the cults to which they belong: as offering them salvation from a horrible world outside. And like members of other cults, they eschew attention from the outside, often even becoming defensive of criticism of the circuit, deeming the world outside simply incapable of understanding them.

"It's only a matter of time before our rituals of celebration become a hot topic of debate in broader circles," Alan Brown wrote in his "Tales of the Circuit" column in *Circuit Noize*, discussing the fact that right-wing conservatives in Congress had attacked a circuit event in Washington called Cherry Jubilee specifically because the "Recovery Brunch" was held in a federal building where drug use was observed. Brown may as well have been directing his statements to any and all critics of the circuit, including the many gay men and lesbians who are by far not right-wing conservatives but have been more vocal in recent years about the detrimental effects they see the circuit having on the gay community.

"The problem is, no one will understand why we do what we do," Brown continued, "and our parties will be taken out of context. Few will comprehend that only a community so acquainted with grief could sustain such a phenomenon of celebration. Face it—there may even be an element of jealousy going on here. I mean how many hardworking straight adults would like to stay up all night partying and bathe in the glorious energy of self-affirmation in glamorous locations surrounded by beautiful people?"

THE STEPFORD HOMOS

To Brown's credit, and to the credit of some others on the circuit, there is a willingness and desire on their part to at least discuss the circuit in a political, social, and intellectual capacity. These men, however, seem to be few and far between on the circuit. For far too many men I speak with in Palm Springs and elsewhere on the circuit, it appears that a basic discussion about the scene, its physical paradigms, and its negative or positive effects—including drug abuse and unsafe sex—is a discussion they've simply never had; to most, the idea hasn't even crossed their minds. When engaged about these issues, these men offer only blank stares or frighteningly conditioned, robotic responses. They are, for all practical purposes, the Stepford Homos.

"Oh, I don't know, I mean, I, um, I can't really say," a thirty-three-year-old smallish muscle man says with a pained and perplexed look on his face when I ask him some basic questions, as he lies out by the pool, about the social implications of drug use on the scene. "I don't really get into talking about all this stuff. I mean, I guess it's a problem for some people—the crystal [meth], you know—but I don't know."

A thirty-fiveish man, a lawyer from Phoenix, tells me that he hasn't been "aware" that there's been a problem with regard to safer sex in the gay community, a shocking sentiment that I have heard from West Hollywood to Fire Island among well-educated, professional men. "The gay community did a great job in implementing safer sex and bringing the problem [of transmission] down. I don't see how you could say that [there is a breakdown in safer sex]," he says, looking completely awestruck. "And anyway, what does that have to do with what's going on here [at the circuit events in Palm Springs]? These are all intelligent and educated and informed people."

"This conversation is, like, a little too deep for me," a pumped and highly cut and defined twenty-six-year-old young man tells me as I chat him up in a Palm Springs restaurant across the street from one of the official hotels, asking him some simple questions about the pressure on many gay men to mold themselves in the image of the circuit ideal. "I'm not used to these kinds of discussions, especially when I come to parties like this," he continues, giggling a little. "You're lucky you caught me when I'm not high. . . . Hmmm. . . . No, I can't say I've really thought that most of the guys here look alike . . . I mean, yes, they work out and all, so their bodies are built similarly, but they're different heights and they have different hair, so they *are* different. But I guess you do have a point." He describes his own motivations to work on his body, a project that he began two years ago, just as he came out. And he seems not to notice his own contradictions in logic: "I started working out for myself, not because I wanted to look like everyone else.

No, just because I wanted to be attractive, and have a nice body and, you know, fit in."

Beyond the physical energy that goes into the circuit, as I look out at the masses who've shelled out big money to be in Palm Springs for the White Party, it's hard not to think of the financial power that is apparent here too, perhaps several million dollars poured into the parties by gay men from around the world. It's not necessarily, as some gay activists might declare, that a great deal of money is being squandered here that could and should go into political action. Any smart political organizer knows that celebration, if not taken to the extreme, is important in any oppressed community. It releases tension, boosts morale, and keeps people motivated; money spent on parties and celebratory events isn't necessarily wasted.

Far more significant, however, beyond the fact that the White Party often represents partying to a detrimental extreme, is that a lot of the money shelled out here is being blatantly put into the service of homophobia: For example, one of the companies reaping in some of the millions of dollars spent here this weekend is the Marriott Courtyard Hotel, one of the three official hotels of the White Party, added on at the last minute in fact because of the sheer demand. Marriott is an international hotel chain owned by devout Mormons and often touted as such by the Mormon church. Fifteen percent of the billions of dollars the Marriott Hotel chain makes each year in net profits, including 15 percent of every circuit queen's room this weekend, goes back to the viciously homophobic Mormon church in the form of tithing, as all Mormons are required to give the church 15 percent of their income. The church oppresses gays in Utah; over 90 percent of Utah legislators are Mormons intent on keeping sodomy laws in place there and keeping antigay discrimination legal in their state.

The powerful and growing Mormon church exerts its muscle nationally, teaming up with the religious right and the Catholic church to roll back gay rights across America.

It seems at utterly cross-purposes to be pouring money into a corporation that so overtly supports homophobia. Yet circuit party promoters scoff at such criticism, labeling it "political correctness." They often even view the fact that gay men can now openly occupy and promote parties at chain hotels as a measure of the gay movement's success, something that may very well be true but is ultimately a rather shallow victory.

"I think that the circuit parties have a tremendous economic impact on the community," says Steve Troy, a forty-seven-year-old Los Angeles–based circuit party promoter best known for his fabled Dance on Manhattan event aboard the USS *Intrepid* during the Stonewall 25 Celebration in 1994 in New York. That party raised $250,000 for the American Foundation for AIDS Research. Troy doesn't skimp, putting on elaborately produced events, and 100 percent of net proceeds from his events goes to AIDS charities, he says, though he does charge a flat fee for his services. It's a far different approach, several critics say, than that of Jeffrey Sanker, the promoter of the White Party here, which is considered to have "low production values" when it comes to setting the ambiance of the events. There is a downside to Troy's approach: He has sometimes thrown parties, such as Dance on Los Angeles, billed as AIDS benefits, which cost hundreds of thousands of dollars to put on but raised little funds at all.

Troy is a sincere, soft-spoken man who left his executive position in the high-powered ad agency of Ketchum Communications in the early 1990s after having lost a lover to AIDS and is HIV-positive himself; he was in fact out about his status in the late 1980s while at Ketchum and was a tireless advocate for people with AIDS within the company. Troy travels the circuit, often with his current longtime lover, and has a vast network of friends and business associates. They have a Los Angeles home and a Palm Springs place, which is where I met Troy after I was brought to a party at his home by some acquaintances.

"I mean, look at Miami and what happened there—if you go back a few years ago to the beginning of the Vizcaya event, that was the beginning of the scene in Miami," he notes, discussing what he feel is the "power" that the circuit gives the community. "As time went on, the event really became a minor part of the whole experience of the White Party weekend in Miami. Now, all of a sudden, you've got all these dollars being spent. I read the Miami paper on the Monday morning after Vizcaya this past year, and they estimated that fifteen thousand people attended and over twenty million dollars were spent [in December 1996, Miami Beach officials put the figure more at ten million dollars]. That's a lot of economic clout. It gets us recognition in terms of our economic power. I mean, people who go to circuit parties spend a lot of money, on hotels, on airlines, on food—when they're eating." He pauses momentarily, then laughs, referring to the use of drugs, most of which suppress people's appetite.

"I think it's very interesting that companies like American Airlines and Wyndham Hotels and Hyatt Hotels are all of a sudden getting very interested in circuit parties," Troy continues. "They look at how much money they're going to make on a three- or four-day weekend. I think that's positive. And in some ways, I think it gets us more clout than political rallies. We're using our financial muscle to gain acceptance rather than our political persuasions."

Troy certainly makes a point: Circuit parties are often supported and welcomed by municipal governments and local economies. They are major moneymakers for cities, particularly when they involve the influx of tens of thousands of men with money to spend. Often the local mayor or some other local official will even send a letter of support to the promoters or partygoers, letting them know that they are welcome. For the city of Palm Springs in fact, the White Party is the largest moneymaking event on the calendar, and local officials are only too eager to work with promoters and make sure attendees are well treated.

This economic power can be deduced from looking at the average circuit party advertisement in the gay glossies. In 1996, ads were running almost everywhere for the several-day-long Steel Party in Pittsburgh. The ads revealed that the city of Pittsburgh was pulling out all the stops for this event. The Steel Party, a benefit for Pittsburgh's Persad Center, a mental health organization that services gays and lesbians and people with AIDS, is the kind of new circuit event whose arrival on the scene is a testament to the circuit's rapid growth and its reach beyond the coasts into gay Middle America. It also reveals an attempt on some circuit promoters' part to be inclusive: In addition to the standard white muscle boy, the ad's photo also depicted a black muscle man and even a couple of attractive lesbians. Because of its unglamorous location, the Steel Party will perhaps never be part of what is known as the core circuit, which includes the White Party in Palm Springs, Miami's White Party, New York's Black Party, Montreal's Black and Blue Party, Fire Island's Morning Party, and a few others. It is perhaps for that reason that the Steel Party has the luxury to reach out to women and minorities, particularly in its ads: Promoters of core circuit events know that most of the white, upper-middle-class men who attend their A-list parties would probably not attend them if the parties were overrun with lesbians and nonwhite men, and if the ads showcased them.

The actual Steel Party, the ads tell us, scheduled for Saturday night, was to take place at the David L. Lawrence Convention Center. Atlanta deejay Buc, who has a huge following that travels around the country to hear him, was being brought in for the party. The promoters expected a tourism boost for the city—and probably promised that to city officials in return for the facilities. As per the ad, there was to be a Welcoming Party on Friday night at the Andy Warhol Museum, then an After Andy party at a local nightspot. On Saturday night at another nightclub there was to be a Pre-Heat party, just before the actual Steel Party. Then there would be the Steel Party itself, which was to go until 6 A.M. at the convention center. The next day, Sunday, a Recovery Brunch was planned at the Westin William Penn Hotel.

To the extent then that the parties gain the gay community recognition and economic clout from local governments and large and small corporations, particularly in cities like Pittsburgh that are not known for their progressiveness on gay issues, Steve Troy is right: Any power we can use to gain respect from the larger culture is welcome. But I wonder what we really gain from all of this in the larger picture as, day after day and night after night, hordes of shirtless, pumped-up men, each virtually indistinguishable from the next, Stepford Homos, all spaced out on drugs, pluck down their dollars at event after event in Palm Springs. As Troy notes, circuit parties of the 1990s, unlike their more primitive counterparts of the 1970s and 1980s, often have a multitude of corporate sponsors. The advertisements for the Steel Party, for example, list the sponsors: Captain Morgan Rum, Rolling Rock, the Westin William Penn

Hotel, Starbucks Coffee, American Express Financial Advisors, *Out* magazine, and USAir. As circuit promoters note, in these days of the advertising logo as a stamp of approval, the sponsorship can mean a lot, particularly to a minority that is used to being ill treated. Many gay people see it as a sign of success and acceptance when a company like American Express appears willing to go out on a limb to associate itself with gay people, even if that simply means marketing their services to them. But giving American Express the power to make us feel better about ourselves also gives American Express an even greater power: American Express not only legitimizes and promotes homosexuality, it also legitimizes and promotes the circuit parties and the physical ideals, the drug use, and the often unsafe sex that define circuit events.

Back in the 1970s only small businesses such as local bathhouses and bars and local gay media and the relatively small gay porn industry helped to promulgate the cult of masculinity. Now, in the 1990s, it is American Express, USAir, and the Westin Hotel chain that fuel the cult of masculinity in the gay world. Could it be that all we have gained is the dubious honor of having corporate America sell back to us the same oppressive lifestyle we've been selling ourselves for the past thirty years?

As I look around Palm Springs, it seems that this is what much of the gay movement has come to: We've been temporarily allowed to take over three chain hotels in the desert—in exchange for our hard-earned dollars—to act out our anxieties over masculinity, assuage our fears about being perceived as "fags," and help deaden the pain and loss we're experiencing from the effects of a relentless plague. We do that by getting high, flexing our muscles, and having a lot of sex.

There might have been a time when this kind of behavior bucked the system, but now the system has absorbed it. The system has learned that it can achieve its larger agenda of suppressing gay people by actually letting us do what we are doing here this weekend—openly, in their lobbies, at their pools, in their ballrooms.

From the Mormons' perspective and that of most of the larger heterosexual power structure, which is still indifferent to us at best or antigay at worst—and which owns and operates all of these companies that are making money off of us this weekend—why not indeed let the fags blow off some steam, let the fags take their drugs, let the fags have their unsafe sex? Why not let the fags go on infecting themselves with this deadly disease? Why not let them believe protease inhibitors are the cure? Let them perpetuate their rigid physical ideals and bolster their oppressive rules of masculinity. And let them believe that in doing all of this they are achieving true liberation. All of that, after all, will keep them contained in their ghettos and their temporarily rented spaces in the outside world, anesthetized on drugs, under control. It will also keep them busy, away from organizing political action and demanding equal rights. Meanwhile, we can make a lot of money off their expendable cash. The passage from *Circuit Noize* I read on the plane again comes back to me: "When the circuit comes to town, that town becomes an instant gay ghetto full of hot men who are behaving as queer as they care to be." Yet, in the end, it is the Mormon-owned Marriott and other companies that support homophobia who have the last laugh in Palm Springs, who with one hand hold their noses while the other hand dips into our wallets.

PUSHING FORTY AND BEYOND

There are of course many traditionally gay-friendly companies involved in the Palm Springs White Party, as there are at most circuit events. At the Wyndham Hotel pool party, a huge Absolut Vodka bottle, an inflated balloon, stands two stories high on the grass next to the pool, surrounded by throngs of dancing, near-naked men who seem almost as if they're worshipping the phallic, corporate icon that has been so supportive of them. Absolut and other liquor companies of course have known for years that it pays to be gay-friendly and to support the gay community, as brand-conscious gay men buy a lot of booze at events such as the White Party.

As the Absolut balloon bobs and weaves, dozens of men hang over the hotel's balconies overlooking the scene, bopping up and down to the music. Every square inch of the pool area is taken up by flesh and muscles. Those who aren't dancing are swimming, sunning, and drinking. A large crowd of men are lounging, sitting knee-deep over in the children's pool in the corner, a sign above them declaring this the KIDDY POOL.

The circuit parties provide many men with a way to go back in time, to relive the adolescence they were denied as gay men because they were locked in the closet. Jokingly, or even sometimes seriously, many talk of being "naughty" at these events, of doing things covertly, in the way teenagers do. Publications like *Circuit Noize* reiterate over and over again that these are all "crazed party boys"—even if they're pushing forty and beyond.

"For me, this is a chance to get away, get out of the city," a Los Angeles man who claims to be thirty-six explains as we sit in the kiddy pool. "You know, it's also a chance to be *bad*. You're just never bad at home, too much pressure with work and everything. You let loose at these events. I never get high back in L.A., even going out dancing. I'm just not comfortable." He flashes me a wicked smile and then adds, "But here, I do *all* of the things I've always wanted to do."

And for many men I speak with—far more than I would have imagined—part of reliving adolescence is remaining in the closet in their adult lives. The circuit, for these men, provides a secret life away from home, away from family, friends, and co-workers.

"I have the time of my life when I come to these parties," Art, a thirty-two-year-old muscle-bound real estate agent who lives in a large city over 150 miles away tells me. "I'm a very private, reserved guy back at home. My parents don't know about me, and that's the way I like to keep it. Same with the people I work with. And I'm too busy to go out [back home] and I don't have many friends there—it's too close to home anyway, and people know your business. I've been coming to these parties now for several years, and I have a lot of really wonderful, intimate friends. I see them on the circuit, know they'll be here. I love it."

The same seems to be true of some men from smaller cities and towns and even rural areas whom I speak to—some closeted in their hometowns, others not—for whom the circuit either is their only gay social life or augments it. Yet it seems circuit friendships more often than not rarely truly develop, even though men talk profusely about the "bonding" and the "sharing" they experience on the circuit with the new men they meet. Perhaps the reason the friendships *seem* so special is because they always remain in that magical stage when a friendship is first blossoming, rarely able to progress because of the distance many of these men often live from one another. They see one another every few weeks or months at the circuit events and thus rarely go through the stages most friends go through: That first tense argument or the moment of vulnerability when you both find out what you are like underneath the surface armor.

This is similar to the progression of many circuit "boyfriend" relationships, in which two men who live in different cities meet at a circuit event and claim their undying love for each other. The distance that keeps them from being truly intimate keeps the relationship in an adolescent stage, like high school sweethearts. There's an unbearable yearning to be together, yet it's impossible to let the relationship go too far, and so the relationship remains in a kind of puppy love. And these kinds of relationships are prevalent beyond the circuit, filtering down throughout much of the gay world.

Lesbian and gay psychotherapists have long noted that gay men often struggle with intimacy—not quite knowing *how* to be intimate—both in friendships as well as in love relationships. In heterosexual culture, men in general are not taught how to be intimate as they are raised. Women are charged with keeping relationships together on an emotional level, and it is women who are taught the skills of intimacy and nurturing as they are raised. People are often afraid of what they don't know. Rather than build the tools of intimacy, many gay men look for an easy way out. For many, the circuit as well as the minicircuits in gay ghettos around the country provide the perfect landscape in which to fulfill a desire for friendship, love, and closeness without getting involved. In the argot of the cyber age, they become *virtual* friends and lovers. Eventually, these superficial relationships peter out and are replaced by new infatuations that similarly lack staying power.

"I believed my circuit friends were like my best friends in the world, but that was a total illusion," says Skip, a thirty-eight-year-old Washington lawyer who began going to circuit parties in 1994. After two years, he says he is just about "over" the whole scene. The White Party, Skip says, is his last party. He wasn't even going to come to this event but he'd made the reservations long ago. Skip's experience is representative of many men for whom the circuit is merely a short, transitional phase, a temporary stop—a "rite of passage" even. Rather than spend five years or more on the circuit, doing the scene until they're too ill or too old, they do the circuit for a year or two, and then come to see the circuit's limits, often developing a healthy relationship to it.

"I started seeing that these friends didn't really care about me, I mean when it came right down to it," Skip says, "and even some of the guys I've met, who I actually thought I was in love with, it was all pretty surface and fleeting. With the friends you meet on the circuit, you start to realize they're not really people in your life. When they're gone from the scene—maybe they even died—you're not really plugged into it, you lose touch with them, you sometimes don't even notice they're gone until one day you think, Hey where did that guy go? How can you say these were really your friends then, even though you may have had a really close connection with them? That's really what the circuit does, it creates these illusions. If you truly understand that, it can be something you can enjoy once in a while and not take too seriously. But I don't think that's the case with most of the men here."

DOING DRUGS

The pink, sprawling Marquis Hotel up the road a bit from the Wyndham, where many White Party events also take place, is also completely overrun with gay men, with pool parties in the day, and private room orgies by night. At the Marquis on Friday night there is the Hardcore Party in one of the ballrooms, where top porn stars dance on speakers while men worship them. This party is intended to have a more leather feel, but it's leather done in that perfectly chiseled circuit way, all glossed up and shiny. The Marquis is host to a tea dance on its tennis courts on Sunday also, an all-day dance party at which people dance until late in the evening and then head over to a local nightclub for the Closing Party, which goes on well into Monday morning. The entire weekend consists of five huge dance parties, including the Wyndham pool party.

While that would seem to be more than enough to keep the average speed freak up for four days, there are dozens of other parties all over town, private parties in hotel rooms, private homes, and condominiums. There are also after-hours parties that begin at 7 A.M. in small nightclubs and go until noon—when the pool parties start. All of these parties have an intense competitiveness connected to them because people gain status depending on which parties they attended. Some people even miss many of the official events—some don't even go to the actual White Party—seeing them as too "common."

"I skipped the pool party at the Wyndham," a man haughtily tells me. "I was at a private party in a condominium, a friend's." He says it in a way that is supposed to tempt me to ask him *whose* condominium it was. The status-consciousness here is unbelievable. Men are constantly worried and sometimes racked with anxiety, it seems, about which parties they have been invited to and which parties they haven't been invited to. The young blond man I'd met on the plane frantically calls me on the telephone one afternoon, wanting to get invited to an *Out* magazine party, knowing that I write for the magazine. "I'm supposed to be at *every* hot party," he says, laughing, but clearly not kidding. "You've *got* to get me invited to that party."

Circuit Noize has its party in a suite at the Wyndham, promising on the invitation that its party will have "the hottest circuit boys" and "the best music." Every party is in fact obsessed with having the "best" and the "hottest." There are some very wealthy and powerful older men here too, Hollywood big shots mostly, having their own parties in private homes and condos; but the parties aren't anything unless they attract the "hottest" men. Ultimately, having the hottest party means giving out free drugs and paying the porn stars in particular.

In a weekend-long event of this magnitude, a whole set of drugs is required. Drugs to space you out. Drugs to keep you up. Drugs to put you to sleep. Drugs to get you up again. Drugs to get you through the day. Drug dealers abound, at least one to a floor, it seems. They are called upon in their rooms at all hours of the day and night. Ecstasy is a staple, as is cocaine, and Special K—ketamine, a horse tranquilizer, which is snorted. But it wouldn't be California and a weekend-long circuit event if there wasn't crystal meth, a stimulant that keeps people up for hours on end, sometimes for forty-eight-hour stints, dancing, posing—and having sex. Some people snort their crystal in powder form, but more and more men are injecting intravenously after liquefying it.

"I got hooked on crystal, and had to go into rehab," a Palm Springs taxi driver tells me and a few companions as he drives us to a party. "It was great to work to, I mean I could work for two days straight through. And of course for sex. Man, I could just fuck and fuck and fuck."

It seems that circuit events and the sex and partying that surrounds them, for most of the men here, would be completely uninteresting without drugs. That's what almost every man tells me as I casually ask around. There are some men, I'm told, who attend the parties and do not do drugs, but they seem to be few and far between. At the Hardcore Party at the Marquis, I find myself yawning to the point where I have to leave and go to bed. Even researching the scene, chatting with men and attempting to soak in the experience, I'm fatigued by it all within an hour. I'm also completely sober, and in that state the party is boring and monotonous, the same music blaring on, the same muscle men whizzing by.

Yet the grueling party schedule and the sheer pace of the circuit demand more than just being even a little bit high. The next night, at the actual White Party at the Wyndham, wanting to get the full experience of the event and stay up all night with the crowd, I take a hit of Ecstasy, a clean white tablet I buy when some acquaintances showing me around the scene take me with them to one of the drug dealers' rooms to buy their weekend's worth of drugs. Ex is a drug I've used in the past, so I know what to expect. Soon enough, the night whirls into a frenzied and fuzzy collage of colored lights and bodies as a feeling of well-being takes over. Even on the drugs, the scene isn't exciting enough for some. They find it all tedious and dull, even while high. They complain: The music isn't any good, the lights are dull, the Ecstasy is bad, the crowd is too static, "too into themselves, in that L.A. way," one Atlanta man says. Everyone, it seems, just wants more, more, more. Increasingly jaded, nothing will satisfy them.

Off in the distance, outside the ballroom on the grounds of the pool, several men vomit on the lawn, others pass out; at some point, paramedics arrive, and in the blur from the lights and the drugs, I see someone taken out on a stretcher. He overdosed on something. "Another circuit casualty," someone says to me with a smile. Indeed, another man tells me that there's an OD at just about every big party. "That's how you know it's a good party," he jokes, "if you can attract an ambulance or two."

Others have told me about still other circuit casualties, men who don't necessarily pass out at the events but whose lives eventually collapsed under the weight of the circuit: doctors, lawyers, investment bankers, and the like who were forced to often take off numerous days from work to recuperate, or showed up for their jobs too many times completely drained and unable to be productive. Burnt out and sometimes hooked on coke or crystal too, some of these men see their careers and their relationships—not to mention their health, particularly if they are HIV-infected—completely unravel.

The paramedics come and go in a foggy haze, as if it really didn't happen at all. It's easier to dismiss the paramedics and go back into my own world. Like everyone else here, I dance much of the night like a madman. I take my shirt off and make some "friends," those people with whom you bond on Ecstasy and with whom you convince yourself you have a profound connection—until later you realize it was "just the drugs."

Coming down off the drugs, however, particularly if you come to the party alone, as is the case with many more men than I would have thought, there's an intense feeling of isolation and loneliness that is only heightened by the superficiality of the events. The only way to feel connected once again is to take *more* drugs. Indeed, for many men who can't possibly connect without them, the drugs provide yet another way to experience virtual intimacy and virtual love, in the form of either friendships or sexual liaisons.

I find that a little bit of Ecstasy is not enough for an event of this magnitude, one that keeps going. If I want to go on, I'll need more, and more. There are only too many people willing to help me out. Later, however, when the partying momentarily stops and I go back to my room, I'm unable to sleep. I know that if I'm going to experience other events I'll need to sleep—or I'll need more drugs. So I'm already caught up in the drug cycle of the circuit, which makes an "all-or-nothing" demand on you: even if you've only just arrived, even if you're not so taken with the scene. The opposite choice, staying sober (not being "medicated," as one of my new party chums puts it) throughout the events, seems not to offer the authentic circuit experience, and the possibility of finding someone else in the same state is rather nil. Staying sober seems a dismal prospect, as if someone has told a funny joke and you're the only one not "getting it."

THE PRICE OF ECSTASY

Approximately eight months after the White Party weekend, I'm sitting in a room packed with over three hundred circuit men and various others nightclubbers at New York's Lesbian and Gay Community Services Center learning some things about Ecstasy that make me think about my past use of the drug, things that certainly make me think twice about ever using it again. Like many gay men, on and off the circuit, I always thought Ecstasy was much less harmful than other drugs; it certainly couldn't be as habit-forming as cocaine, didn't induce the mad desperation of crystal, and wasn't as headachy and out-of-control as Special K. In the long term, Ecstasy is possibly more damaging than any of the others—which are all pretty nasty drugs to begin with.

"Ecstasy is different from most other recreational drugs," Dr. Ron M. Winchel, an openly gay psychiatrist in private practice and assistant professor of clinical psychiatry at Columbia University, who has spent several years studying the effects of Ecstasy, tells the crowd, most of whom came to this talk after seeing it advertised in *Homo Xtra*. "If you smoke pot, drink some alcohol, do a little bit of coke, those all have their own problems associated with them, but in most moderate quantities, once those chemicals are out of your body and once the cells recuperate from the effects of the chemical, in a day to two weeks, the chemicals' effects on the brain are gone. . . . [Ecstasy, however,] seems to kill off a significant part of the serotonin cells [in your brain] in large quantities, maybe for a long time, maybe forever. Crystal meth is the only other drug that in relatively small doses can also cause long-term changes in the brain."

The cells that Ecstasy appears to damage control the amount of serotonin that stays awash in the brain. The serotonin system aids dramatically in regulating mood, anxiety, sleep, memory, body temperature, sexual function, appetite control, and other functions. "The amount of serotonin in the brain drops rather rapidly," after doing a few hits of Ecstasy, Winchel tells us. "There is a destruction of fibers [on the cells] where the action takes place [in terms of serotonin secretion]. Do they grow back? Well, we're not sure exactly what happens yet, but so far the best evidence is, if they grow back, they grow back very slowly, meaning a year to three years—again, if they grow back at all. And if they grow back, they appear to grow back in distorted patterns, in overabundance and in wild disorganization . . . in a disoriented way."

Winchel stresses that almost all of this evidence about MDMA, as Ecstasy is known in the scientific community, has been from studies in animals and thus should not be taken as definitive. There have been only a few studies in humans to assess long-term effects, though there have been a fair number of clinical case reports of detrimental effects. However, Winchel also explains that with MDMA specifically, "it's a little bit disturbing, but the higher you go on the [evolutionary] tree—the higher the mammal, from mice to rats, from rats to monkeys, and from monkeys to higher primates—the more vulnerable the animal is." Thus, it is reasonable to hypothesize that there are considerable long-term changes in the brains of humans, and they are perhaps greater than those found in any other animals.

Studies also show that, unlike other drugs, the higher you go on the evolutionary scale, the more vulnerable the subjects are to *smaller* doses of MDMA. Thus, it's possible that a few hits of Ecstasy in a night could create a significant serotonin deficit that may last indefinitely. Even if one does Ecstasy relatively infrequently, more than a couple of hits over a several-day period is suspect.

The possible long-term negative effects of MDMA on the brain include mood and anxiety disorders, and severe depression. "Particular symptoms I've seen," Winchel says, "include eating disorders, and jaw-clenching problems. If people have an existing depression it's very hard to effect a treatment if they've used Ex." That is because, in treating depression with antidepressants (such as Prozac) the drugs are greatly dependent upon the serotonin function in the brain; decreased serotonin levels may therefore prevent antidepressants from being beneficial.

"Some of the case reports associated with Ex use," Winchel further explains, "have reported panic disorder, unusual bingeing disorder, flashbacks, cognitive deficits, derealization, sleep disorders, and chronic fears of being ridiculed by other people."

These symptoms might not show up for many years. If there are any significant long-term effects, then gay men and others of the very first generation of Ecstasy users will in fact probably not know them for quite some time. That is because, as we grow older, there is a normal decrease in serotonin. If we've already decreased our serotonin levels significantly with

Ecstasy, that natural decrease may in years to come bring us below "the margin of safety," as Winchel calls it. "Who knows how much reserve we have?" he ponders. People who have preexisting mood or anxiety disorders may be at greater risk, since it is possible that their serotonin system is already vulnerable. Similarly, HIV infection decreases serotonin, so HIV-positive people and people with AIDS who use Ecstasy may also be at even greater risk.

While there are many drugs that gay men on the circuit and off use regularly, Ecstasy has been among the most constant and the most universal. In some cases that has been because people believed it was less harmful than the other drugs, like cocaine and crystal meth. For others it was simply that they preferred a drug that lowered their inhibitions and allowed them to bond emotionally—which is what psychopharmacological designer drugs like Ecstasy do—as opposed to the hard-edged stimulants like speed (crystal and other stimulants), or the tranquilizers like Special K, which are quite disorienting. And for a great many other men, Ecstasy has actually been viewed as the perfect "base": They take other drugs, like K or crystal, on top of Ecstasy, to enhance and alter the Ecstasy's effects as well as the effects of the other drugs.

It doesn't take a rocket scientist to figure out that a drug that may adversely and permanently affect the system that regulates mood and anxiety in ways not yet known is perhaps not the greatest drug for a group of people already racked with anxiety and fear, many being greatly depressed and demoralized. Also, many of those taking Ecstasy on the circuit are HIV-positive and thus may be at increased risk of long-term effects such as severe depression and anxiety disorders.

The effects of Ecstasy on the circuit and on gay men in general, who take the drug to loosen their inhibitions and find intimacy, however fleeting, could actually be creating an even more panic-driven, fear-laden group of individuals, more vulnerable to life's crises than even before. Though it seems as if it couldn't be possible, through Ecstasy perhaps many of us are becoming (or will become) even more racked with low self-esteem, more anxiety-ridden about issues such as our masculinity, and more depressed about our bodies. And when we feel lousy about ourselves, we may also be more prone to unsafe sex.

THE CRYSTAL CATHEDRAL

"I don't think the party scene creates an environment conducive to unsafe sex," the circuit shaman Alan Brown says firmly. Though Brown does peer below the surface while discussing other issues regarding the circuit, he denies the occurrence of unsafe sex on the circuit, defying both commonsense logic about how drugs impair people's decisions and studies that link drug use with increased incidences of unsafe sex. His sentiments are shared by a great many men on the circuit. "I think the circuit actually creates an *awareness* of safe sex," he says in all sincerity. "There are condoms all around, and the parties are AIDS benefits. What other reminder do you need? I would never consider having unsafe sex, and I would like to think that most of my friends feel the same way. But we don't discuss it. No, we don't discuss it."

And that of course is part of the problem: Men on the circuit, caught up in the escapist frenzy, don't want to discuss something as reality-based as safer sex; the AIDS crisis, after all, as many of them reiterate to me over and over again, is something they're trying to get away from. And despite the best efforts of people like the publishers of *Circuit Noize*, who offer thoughtful and sound advice on safer sex in each issue, when many men are high on drugs all of that seems to go out the window.

Circuit promoter Steve Troy, who is HIV-positive himself, is one of the very few men connected to the circuit who will frankly and realistically discuss the issue. Self-reflective and candid, he doesn't pull any punches. "It's the age of AIDS, and I think people's attitude is, 'I don't know how long I'm going to live,'" he tells me. "The majority of people who go to the circuit parties are HIV-positive, I really think so. Their attitude is, 'I'm going to live for the moment.' The circuit parties are the one outlet we have for total escapism. The unfortunate part of it is that when we do the drugs, we become much less inhibited. Things that we might normally not do when we have our wits about us, we actually do." He pauses for a moment, and then says, "And, to be honest, I can't say I'm . . . I can't say that I haven't done that myself. When people are on drugs, the chances of unsafe sex are greater—like ten times higher."

Among substance-abuse counselors, lesbian and gay psychotherapists, and HIV-prevention workers, crystal, sometimes also called crystal meth, a highly refined amphetamine known in the medical and scientific community as methamphetamine, is perceived as contributing greatly to unsafe sex, perhaps more than any other drug on the circuit. It "blurs safer sex boundaries, big-time," says Sam Minsky, administrative director of Matrix, an outpatient drug treatment center in Los Angeles, describing the drug in a stellar article, "Kneeling at the Crystal Cathedral," by journalist Doug Sadownick in the January 1995 *Genre* magazine:

The drug seems tailor-made for the very class of gay men benefiting from the political strides of the gay

movement. "Look at the demographics," exclaims
Matrix's Minsky. He says that he treats several hundred clients a year and the majority of the crystal users
he sees are white, gay professional men. "It's such a
nasty drug," he adds, "the way it destroys the body and
the mind. Crystal is a gay person's drug and a gay community problem."

Indeed, on the West Coast, in San Francisco as well as
L.A., many substance-abuse professionals believe crystal meth
abuse is a full-blown epidemic in the gay community. There is
now a Crystal Meth Anonymous meeting somewhere in L.A.
every night of the week, and twice a week in West Hollywood.

"You get to be a superman when you do crystal," says
Duane E. McWaine, an openly gay Los Angeles psychiatrist
whose clients include referrals from other therapists, gay men
and HIV-infected people who have chemical-dependency
problems, including gay men who have crystal meth abuse
problems. "You can fuck all night. You can dance all night.
People are up for days sometimes. You can be up and be at the
White Party from Friday till Sunday and it doesn't cost an arm
and a leg. . . . Crystal and other stimulants not only apparently
improve those kind of performances but they artificially
improve self-esteem also. That's what's attractive about crystal,
and why cocaine is so big too. . . . But in terms of [safer sex],
people who are on crystal do not have good judgment; they
make decisions that are not conducive to their health. At the
moment you're high, it speeds things up, it speeds up cognition, speeds up heart rate, speeds up blood pressure, makes you
talk faster. It can make sexual functioning appear better. But
beyond a certain dose it decreases sexual functions, it also then

decreases cognition—so many neurotransmitters are being released you can't make sense of thought. After heavy or long-term use, people get paranoid or psychotic. For people with AIDS, well, many of my colleagues are used to saying that all you need to do to eat up T cells quickly is do lots of crystal."

Comparing studies of young gay men in the Bay Area in 1984 and in 1992, Ron Stall, an epidemiologist at the Center for AIDS Prevention Studies in San Francisco, notes that while the use of some other drugs has on the whole declined, the rates of the use of speed, such as crystal, "doubled since 1984. This is a major drag because it is the strongest indicator of HIV seroconversion in the San Francisco Men's Health Study," he explains. "It is far and away the most important predictor of getting infected with HIV of any of the drugs. There's a major speed epidemic happening on the West Coast. We don't know if the speed epidemic will hit on the East Coast. If it hits, it will fuel a lot of seroconversions. Maybe the East Coast will luck out, but it will be the first drug-abuse epidemic I've ever heard about where the East Coast wasn't affected."

IF YOU CAN'T BEAT 'EM, JOIN 'EM

In the middle of all of this are many of our AIDS organizations around the country, entrusted with preventing the spread of HIV, yet, incredulously, throwing their own circuit events in order to raise money.

In 1996, Gay Men's Health Crisis's Morning Party, a circuit event held on Fire Island that benefits the New York AIDS group, was the focus of a controversy that had been building for several years within New York's lesbian and gay community—one that spilled into the *New York Times* and other New York dailies—regarding the rampant drug use at the party and the link to unsafe sex, and GMHC's role and responsibility. Many, myself included, felt that the group should not be putting its name behind such an event, thereby promoting the behaviors the event is known for. "A party whose point is really drug use has no place benefiting an organization that is fighting for intelligent decisions that lead to safer sex," one critic told the *New York Times*. Others felt that GMHC should at least make a greater effort to educate men at the event about the dangers of the various drugs they would be taking. The group, which has been in the forefront of battling drug use associated with safer sex through its Substance Use, Counseling and Education program—a program to which, ironically, the group allocates much of its Morning Party proceeds—produced only a meager flier for the event entitled, "Enjoy Yourself. Don't Destroy Yourself." Perhaps because GMHC was afraid to insult and offend the well-heeled Morning Party attendees, the flier did not go into any of the real dangers of the drugs. Instead it urged users to drink water if they got dehydrated, "go to the First Aid tent" if they felt "dizzy," and "make sure to use a condom" if they had sex. One GMHC board member actually told me these were an example of the group's "innovative techniques" to deal with drug abuse and unsafe sex associated with it.

The Morning Party is one of several major circuit events across the country in which 100 percent of the net proceeds goes to an AIDS charity. The Morning Party raised $450,000 for GMHC in 1996, although, like most other groups that throw their own parties, GMHC pays a flat fee to a producer; even parties where 100 percent of the profits go to charity thus often still represent an income for party producers and promoters.

In other cases, only a portion of the net proceeds of a party goes to an AIDS charity, while an often large percentage of the money is made by promoters, even when the charity group is billed prominently in the party's advertising; the promoters are often only too willing to give some of the money to an AIDS charity so that their event might be legitimized. (All told, according to *Out and About*, circuit parties in 1995 brought in an estimated $4 million to $6 million in ticket sales.) The promoters also know that giving a small portion of the net proceeds to an AIDS group—a tax-deductible donation—can actually help them cut costs: They are more likely to attract corporate sponsors if they can bill the event as a "benefit," which can mean free liquor for the parties, deals on hotel facilities, free airline tickets for the entertainers, and other savings that are ultimately greater than the amount given to charity. They may also cut costs on hiring staff for the events because some AIDS groups will also provide volunteers.

"They can say it's a benefit and get $25,000 worth of liquor," says New York party promoter Marc Berkeley. "Some corporations will only give them something if it's a benefit." And the AIDS groups, always strapped for cash, are often only too willing to let their names be used. "It all depends on how cheaply they'll sell their name," says Berkeley. "Sometimes it's only for ten percent."

The White Party Weekend in Palm Springs advertised for its 1996 Easter weekend event that "a portion of the White Party proceeds" would benefit a Los Angeles group, AID for AIDS, and the Palm Springs AIDS service organization, Desert AIDS Project. Craig Vincent-Jones, director of development at AID for AIDS, says the group was given a flat donation of $5000 from the White Party promoter, Jeffrey Sanker.

Charlie Fraisier, director of resource development at Desert AIDS Project, at first tells me that his group raised

THE EVANGELICAL CHURCH OF THE CIRCUIT

"roughly twenty-five thousand dollars" from the event in 1996, but later notes that it was actually "a little bit less" than that. "All said and done, it was more between fifteen and twenty thousand dollars," he says, further explaining that part of that money came from the group's merchandising of official White Party T-shirts and other items at the event, as promoter Sanker basically had the group sell the White Party merchandise and keep all profits. "There was a flat donation [from the White Party proceeds] of upwards of ten thousand dollars," Fraisier says. "That's the base. We then raised the rest in merchandising money, with [Desert AIDS Project] volunteers selling the White Party T-shirts." The T-shirts and other items, Fraisier says, did not include the AIDS group's name on them.

"We don't give them an actual percentage, just in case it's a bad year," Sanker replies when I ask him what percentage of the net profits the base donations to the groups represented. He hosts the Hardcore Party, the White Party, and the Outdoor T-Dance on the Marquis Hotel's tennis courts, and a weekend pass for all three events costs $75. "If it's a bad year, then it's not as profitable for them, so we just give them that flat rate," he continues. Yet he agrees that the White Party weekend, rather than piddling out, is only growing bigger and bigger each year, accommodating thousands and thousands of men. "You have to look at the larger picture," he tells me. "I give $150,000 to AIDS groups each year from all of the parties I throw, including [a circuit event in] Pensacola [, Florida]."

Labor Day L.A. is billed as "four days of stellar parties," a fund-raising vehicle of which 100 percent of the net proceeds go to the Foundation for Educational Research, which distributes the money out to AIDS service and research groups. The foundation, whose sole purpose is in fact to organize the parties, is a tax-exempt nonprofit organization completely staffed by volunteers. In 1996, the foundation awarded just under $200,000 to AIDS groups, a figure which compared to, say, the $450,000 that GMHC's one event brings in, seems to some critics quite low for four days of parties. "To be honest, we've caught some flack from people in the community in the past," says Don Zuidima, a foundation board member, regarding the net proceeds. "But one of our roles is to provide quality events and parties to the community and there are a lot of costs involved."

There are other similar foundations around the country whose sole purpose is also to organize circuit parties and distribute money raised to local AIDS groups. But unlike L.A.'s Foundation for Educational Research—and perhaps unbeknownst to party attendees—while 100 percent of the net proceeds goes to the foundation, some of these foundations have administrators and staffs whose salaries are paid before any proceeds are distributed to the AIDS groups, a cut that is not insignificant.

Kirk Baxter is the founder of Phoenix Body Positive, an AIDS service organization serving the Phoenix, Arizona, metropolitan area. He was the group's executive director until 1996, when he stepped down, battling AIDS and needing to lighten his workload. He still serves as a consultant to the group, however, and is chair of the Fire and Ice Ball, a circuit event that benefits Phoenix Body Positive. One hundred percent of the net proceeds of the event go to the group, and, unlike other similar AIDS benefits, no flat fee is paid out to a promoter. The event is planned by a committee of volunteers.

Baxter's candid opinions about his group's circuit event, and about the circuit in general, perhaps offer a window on the minds of other AIDS agency administrators and board members who support and sponsor circuit events. Baxter underscores how, though they might try to keep it low-key, many AIDS leaders have a personal relationship to the circuit, actively promote the circuit and its theologies to local gay communities, battle with others in their groups and in their local communities who are critical of the circuit, and rationalize that the circuit is important for financial reasons—as if all other avenues have dried up, and as if *any* means to raise funds is justifiable, even if ultimately counterproductive.

"We're not entirely happy with the outcome of the event, but we're counting on it getting better," Baxter tells me, speaking of Fire and Ice Ball II, in 1996. "We didn't lose any money. The first year [in 1995] we made fifteen thousand dollars. This year we made twenty thousand dollars. The first year we had fifteen hundred people. This time we had twenty-four hundred people. But sixty percent of the people came from outside of the area. We booked people from all over the United States—from New York, L.A., Atlanta, everywhere—and even from as far away as Australia. There should have been another thousand people, and there should have been many more from the local area, and that was the disappointment. Gay Pride here generally turns out five to seven thousand people. So in year three [of the Fire and Ice Ball] we're hoping for three thousand to three thousand five hundred people. We're the seventh largest city in the country and it's time for this community to grow up. We're hoping that the concept of bringing circuit events to Phoenix will push the community along, get people to come to the event, and get more involved in the community and in the circuit.

"One of the reasons I started this party was that for New Year's and other holidays I had to travel to other cities to experience this kind of celebration, to experience getting away from HIV—even if just for a night. So we decided to create this kind of event here. But a lot of the people who are the hard-core dance enthusiasts have died or moved away. And the younger crowd is, well, a different phenomenon. So we had to market the event nationally.

"There have been a couple of antagonists. There's the usual people in the community who tend to be negative about everything, arguing that it's hypocritical for an AIDS group to be holding this kind of event. But we give out packets with condoms to everybody leaving the event. The truth is, people are adults and they make decisions on their own. You've got conservative people who condemn the whole [circuit] phenomenon, people who serve on [our] board—physicians and others, people who we need to serve on the board for the sake of corporate donors, etc. So we do put signs up saying that we do not support or condone the use of recreational drugs. We have worked with the city of Phoenix and the police to make sure there is no selling of drugs at the event.

"The unfortunate reality is that for an AIDS service organization you can only do so many chicken dinners. This is a whole new market to tap. These are people who traditionally don't give. And their consciousness has been raised by giving a check and going to the event. I just challenge the people who are critical to try for one month to be the executive director of an agency like this. People should try to be more tolerant of how we raise money."

While having the names of AIDS agencies on the ads and invitations offers the circuit parties more legitimacy, the AIDS groups, as perhaps the most visible and most respected institutions in the gay world today, become promoters of the parties and everything that they valorize, sending a clear message to young men coming into the gay community. But the AIDS groups are not in this context only giving prospective attendees further permission to indulge in the party and the culture it promotes. As Phoenix Body Positive's Kirk Baxter underscores in his comments, they are also actually asking men to attend the party *for the cause*. Just in case some or many men might have been questioning their own behavior, they can thus be assured that their exhaustive training to attain the physical ideal and their drug-fueled evenings of excess—their spiritual pilgrimages to the Evangelical Church of the Circuit—are all in the line of duty and goodwill: They're fighting AIDS.

Tom Cunningham, the openly gay, HIV-positive mayor of South Miami who works every year on the Vizcaya party, an AIDS benefit, told the *New York Times* in 1996, "I think that anybody who would pay $125 [the price of admission] to support this cause is doing something worthwhile." The irony of all this, of course, is that a great many of these men, having snorted or ingested or shot up drugs that compromise their decision-making processes, will engage in unsafe sex and behaviors that exacerbate rather than fight AIDS.

Still, circuit party planners and promoters don't miss any opportunity to get gay men to "support" the "cause." They know that wherever there might be a large gathering of gay men—such as at the 1992 March on Washington and the Stonewall 25 celebration in New York in 1994, each of which highlighted half a dozen circuit parties at least—that place becomes an economically fertile locale for them to plan a party.

The desire to rake in big money, either for personal gain or for the AIDS agencies, as usual, often has no limits of taste either: In September 1996, in perhaps the most morose party idea yet, there was a circuit party called Reflections planned around the displaying of the Names Project Memorial AIDS Quilt on the Ellipse in Washington. (Reflecting on your dead friends? Reflecting on yourself in a mirror while flying high on the dance floor?) It was billed as "Two Nights/Two Dances/One Cause." The event was sponsored by the National Minority AIDS Council and the Whitman Walker Clinic (Washington's AIDS service organization), and a portion of the proceeds was to go to the Names Project. One ad for this party that ran in the gay glossies featured an illustration of hot, muscled dancers literally dancing on a multicolored patchwork quilt. As if that metaphor weren't eerie enough, several of the dancers were weaved into the quilt, as if the quilt were sucking them in. In some cases only their arms and heads were still visible: They were actually becoming a part of the quilt. (To his credit, the event's promoter, Marc Berkeley, took only 10 percent of the net proceeds, giving the AIDS groups 90 percent.)

The AIDS groups, when they have even responded to criticism of their involvement with circuit events, have argued that they don't want to be moralistic and condemn drug use, thereby scolding gay men, an approach they say doesn't work. Most critics have not, however, asked the groups to scold gay men, but to simply refrain from sponsoring the parties. Some critics, myself included, have even agreed with the groups that they should have a presence at circuit events, educating men about safer sex and drug use in a nonjudgmental way, but that they should not be hosting or benefiting from such events.

Instead, since the late 1980s, many AIDS groups, by putting their names on such events, have accommodated themselves to gay men's sometimes self-destructive behaviors, thereby accepting those behaviors and even encouraging them. As GMHC's deputy director Mike Isbell told columnist Gabriel Rotello in the *Advocate* in 1996, regarding the group's hosting the Morning Party event, "Drugs are an important part of gay men's lives." That may be true as it stands, but if we're not prepared to change that, and if our AIDS agencies are unwilling to at least distance themselves from that drug use, then we must accept that rampant unsafe sex and HIV transmission—not to mention the other short-term and long-term physical and emotional damage that circuit drug abuse causes—will continue to be an "important part of gay men's lives."

Clearly, we must emerge from our collective denial.

HORSEMEN OF THE APOCALYPSE

Even without the drug use, the condom code continually breaks down because of the demands—and more important—the *theologies* of the circuit and the cult of masculinity. The latest craze among many in the circuit set and beyond within the cult is "riding bareback." Another word for "bareback" is "raw," meaning consciously having anal sex without condoms. There are now bareback parties, and bareback clubs. It is no wonder that in the circuit mecca of the 1990s, Miami's South Beach, a 1996 study showed that more than 75 percent of gay men surveyed had had unprotected anal sex within the previous year.

"Business is booming in the gay mecca of South Beach," the Associated Press reported in November 1996. "But the community of glitzy shops, hip nightlife and worship of the body beautiful has been stunned by a study that shows its AIDS infection rate among gay men is one of the highest in the country—and the number practicing unprotected sex is startling. As hundreds prepared for Sunday's 'White Party' at an estate on Biscayne Bay, gay activists handed out pamphlets and put stickers in bathrooms urging a change in sexual behavior—a step toward waking up a community in denial."

But if some of these men having unsafe sex are bareback riders, daredevils who like the risk and see it as a bit less risky now anyway with the new drugs to treat HIV, then all of the pamphlets in the world aren't going to change their sexual behavior.

Among men on the circuit who are HIV-positive and who have sex with other HIV-positive men, riding bareback has gone on for quite some time. Though some doctors advise positive men to protect themselves from other sexually transmitted disease or other strains of HIV, many have decided that the risks are worth it: In their minds they are, after all, already infected with the worst thing one could get. But now, HIV-*negative* men are riding bareback and going to the bareback parties. Frank, an HIV-negative West Hollywood circuit man who has always been what he sometimes describes as "highly sexually compulsive," travels the circuit and the sex club scene often. He says that he is now "fascinated" with riding bareback. He has gone to bareback parties, orgies where everyone has anal sex without condoms, and he has been exhilarated by them. And he says that one impetus has been the new protease inhibitors: They have given him that extra boost to move ahead with his fascination. After all, he says, if he becomes infected, he can take the new drugs. He seems to have no concern for the fact that the drug regimen is excruciating—you must sometimes take twenty pills a day; the cost of the drugs is exhorbitant; no one knows how long the drugs will continue to be able to help HIV-infected people; there are plenty of people for whom the drugs don't work; the virus can mutate around the drug and create a drug-resistant strain; and it is likely that drug-resistant strains of HIV are already spreading throughout the gay community. In short, he doesn't seem to understand that safer sex is more important than ever before if we are to contain and end the epidemic.

"Significant numbers of gay men may believe that there is a cure," Dr. William Darrow, the noted epidemiologist who conducted the South Beach study, observed. "One hypothesis is that gay men are reacting to this bit of news [about protease inhibitors] by throwing caution to the wind."

The circuit crowd, well educated and cyber literate, is very prominent on the Internet, as circuit men leave postings for one another, have their MuscleM4M (male for male) chat rooms, and go to their own popular web sites. *Circuit Noize*, for example, has its own web site with links to various other circuit venues. And it is online where one can meet other bareback riders.

On America Online, for example, one can meet many men who travel in the bareback crowd, though they don't dare admit it outright. Sometimes it's in their screen names in one form or another, i.e., BarebckNY. But often it is somewhere in their online profiles, a euphemism that is rarely explained except by references to not riding horses. They don't want to be stigmatized, and they like having their secret club. You either know what barebacking is and you're into it, or you don't. A sampling of actual notes in various online profiles indicates the degree of seriousness:

"I like doing my pounding bareback—Don't IM [Instant Mail] if not interested in bareback!"

"Bareback has nothing to do with horses. Ride me till I'm raw."

"The only way to do it is bareback. If you're not into it don't bother me!"

"Like taking it up the ass bareback! Also like giving it RAW too. HIV– and you be too!"

"I like riding Bareback, and I am not talking about horses, with HIV–, hung studs. I'm a bottom. blonde, blu, 30. Gif? [photo?] Hell yes, but not available. Don't want the whole city to know that I'm having unprotected sex. Only the chosen few."

Bareback riders are clearly not men who are "slipping up." It's doubtful that they can be reached by AIDS groups and their pithy slogans and campaigns aimed at influencing men's unconscious decisions around safer sex. These men have already made the very conscious decision to have unsafe sex. While there may be a variety of impulses motivating these men, it seems clear that one thing fueling them and enabling them is the cult of masculinity and the self-indulgent, throw-caution-to-the-wind lifestyle it promotes and demands of followers. Bareback riders are indeed making the ultimate religious sacrifice to the cult.

FILTERING DOWN

The circuit mentality and theology creep their way into gay ghettos in cities big and small, influencing national and local gay culture and establishments. In cities such as San Francisco, New York, and L.A., for example, there are now several private clubs for muscled circuit men only, men who travel the local minicircuit of nightclubs and bars. The rules are strictly enforced: No one without the right body is allowed entrance. In South Beach, the club is called Hardbodies, and its recorded message tells prospective members who want to brave it that the club is "looking for a few hard men. That means muscle studs in incredible shape. Expect to take your shirt off to prove it. If you don't measure up, you'll be turned away."

But the circuit mentality, look, and lifestyle is even evident in the most "mainstream" of gay bars and clubs. In New York, for example, the place men flock to from out of town, the place they hear about perhaps more than any other is Splash, a bar that showcases perfectly chiseled and rippled bartenders and dancers. Like similar bars across the country, Splash hosts competitions—butt contests, biceps contests, and other events that focus on specific body parts, holding them up as the ideal and setting the standard for gay men throughout the ghettos. Through the party invitations and other commercial venues, the images of the "perfect" butt, arms, abs, and pecs are sent out to all.

The Evangelical Church of the Circuit is expanding and fueling the cult of masculinity, as its values and ideologies continue to filter down to all of the gay world. Through its ever present advertising bombardment, through its dramatic impact on the bar and nightclub culture, through its explosive visibility in gay culture while so much else of gay life often remains less visible or completely invisible, the circuit will continue to promote its apolitical, uninformed Stepford Homo mentality. And as that mentality continues to grip the ghettos, the ghettos and their minicircuits will in turn continue to refuel the larger circuit—a never-ending cycle, which keeps the cult of masculinity firmly ensconced.

Unless we individually, along with our leaders and our organizations, begin squarely to address the values of the circuit, it will also continue to seduce many gay men into escaping into a bottomless underground as a way of dealing with the ravages of AIDS and homophobia. It will continue to beckon us to return to a lost adolescence, with all of the fun and reckless disregard that goes with it. It will continue to promote its *virtual* friends and lovers, keeping many gay men from developing any real intimacy in their lives. It will continue to keep so many gay men awash in dangerous drugs that might have long-term implications — if the short-term problems associated with these drugs don't overcome them first. It will continue to have many gay men look the other way as they pour money into companies that endorse or at least acquiesce in our very destruction. It will continue to compromise many gay men's abilities to have safer sex and tempt them with the exhilaration of going "bareback."

And it will continue to play upon all our anxieties over masculinity, forcing many gay men to do *whatever* it takes to achieve the demanded musculature. For a rapidly growing number of us, that means becoming immersed in the dangerous steroid craze now overtaking a segment of the gay male world, looking for happiness in a vial.

4

HAPPINESS IN A VIAL

"I wanted to look exactly like these guys I was told were genetically superior to me," states Ralphie, a twenty-nine-year-old Los Angeles talent agent. We're sitting at the pool of the World Gym on Santa Monica Boulevard in West Hollywood. This, as Ralphie says, is the "belly of the beast" when it comes to the gay male body aesthetic. "Steroids do it," he continues. "They let you have that cut, defined, lean, but big, *big* look." Ralphie is HIV-negative and gets his steroids illegally, from a friend who has a "connection" at a local pharmacy that dispenses steroids to many HIV-positive men who use them therapeutically under the supervision of a doctor. "Of course you never tell anyone you're on them, because you're supposed to be part of that *genetically* superior crowd," he continues. "That makes you *naturally* a hot god. But come on, let's face it, don't you see that there is suddenly an explosion of *natural, genetically superior* gay men all over the place, popping up like pod people? Particularly in L.A.? And when you look at the circuit queens, come on? I'm not a circuit queen, but I could be. Anybody could be if they really wanted to. It's all steroids—they're all doing them, almost everyone who has that particular, perfect and cut body is doing them, just like I'm doing them. But nobody's telling."

Ralphie's observations about our desires to promulgate a

notion of total genetic superiority among many gay men (and idolize those whom we believe to have certain genetic attributes) and downplay or hide any kind of chemical enhancement are underscored by publications like *Circuit Noise*, which makes light of party drug use but rarely if ever mentions steroid use on the circuit and throughout the urban gay world. In describing the party scene in Miami's South Beach, for example, *Circuit Noize* makes a reference to South Beach as containing "the largest concentration of genetically gifted/exercised [sic] enhanced gay men in [sic] the planet." The idea promulgated is that all of the gay men in South Beach (or anywhere) who have beautiful bodies are gifted by good genes that they've simply enhanced through some moderate exercise. Talking about steroid use, or perhaps referring to the men as "chemically altered" in addition to "genetically gifted," would be unglamorous and would detract from the air of exclusivity. Not to mention that the bodies would cease to be *naturally* masculine and therefore not really masculine at all.

GENETIC SUPERIORITY

If all this talk among gay men about "genetic superiority" has a fascist tinge to it, it's perhaps not surprising to learn that the Nazis, who elevated the body beautiful in ways not different from today's circuit queens, allegedly shot up the army troops with testosterone back in the 1930s to increase aggressiveness. Becoming aggressive, many gay steroid users will tell you, is something steroids will certainly do for you.

"I turned into a total top on steroids, though I wasn't previously," says Mark, a forty-year-old New Yorker who works for an AIDS agency. More surprising to him, however—actually quite shocking, he says—was when he began "coming out" about his steroid use and found that "almost everyone" whom he had suspected of using steroids confided that they too had used steroids at some point in the past. "Before I was on steroids, I'd obsess about these guys," he tells me, "and I even asked a couple of them, the guys who have that Splash [the noted New York gay bar] bartender look—all cut up, with the perfect abs—and they would deny it, let me think it was just genetic, which made me feel it was daunting and impossible for me to get that way. But then a couple of years later, after I was on steroids and would get some of these guys in bed, many of these same guys admitted to me that they had used steroids. Nobody's out about it, at least not as out about it as me. They'll tell their closest buddies, the guys they do the steroids with or get them from, but it's not something they tell somebody who desires them. And I find if I came out about it, they'd eventually tell me. All of the guys I thought were just that way by genetics, in turned out, were on steroids. It makes sense if you think about it because, in the 1970s, you had only a very small percentage of guys who were true muscle gods like that, the Colt models and that type. I mean, a lot of guys who have big frames can get really big naturally, bulk up and have big bodies, but it's almost impossible for them to get really cut and defined. And a lot of guys who are lean can get really cut and defined, but can't bulk up and get big muscles. Only an extremely small percentage can, without steroids, get that perfect mix of both. But now, with steroids, the number of people with that look has exploded."

JUICING FOR LIFE

Mark, who is HIV-positive, stopped taking steroids because he claims there was a direct correlation between his steroid use and his plummeting T-cell count and rising viral load, a rise in the actual amount of HIV in his body. This is not something that doctors I've spoken to have particularly noticed in their patients with HIV who are on steroids for therapeutic reasons. But Mark believes that because he was not on any antiviral drugs, including protease inhibitors—like many other men with HIV who use steroids therapeutically—the steroids had this negative effect on him. Nonetheless, Mark believes a lot of the warnings about the dangers of steroids are exaggerated, and that steroids can be safe if they are used in proper doses. Ralphie, the West Hollywood man at the World Gym, has a similar attitude. "Yeah, you hear about all the things steroids can do to you—I had a friend whose liver just swelled up beyond belief, fucked him up for good," Ralphie says. "And that kind of got me down on steroids—for a little while. Then I put it out of my mind, because, well, the upside is too great. And besides if you use them right, don't take them orally, but inject them, they're okay—that's what a lot of friends, doctors, told me. You know how the nickname for steroids is 'the juice'? Well, I know you're going to laugh, because I'm about to compare something that is totally healthy for you to something that is totally unhealthy, but, okay, I always see around the gym or in the nutrition shops that book, a huge best-seller, about juicing vegetables, called *Juicing for Life*. And I always say to myself, laughing to myself, yeah, that's what I'm doing—*juicing for life*. Healthwise, yeah, maybe I'm really juicing for death, you know, underneath all of the muscle. *Maybe*—if you really believe all of this negative stuff about steroids. But in terms of what this has done for my ego and self-esteem *right now*, no, it's the opposite. Because this juice, the steroids, has given me a new life. I have the life I want, having the men I want, having people look at me the way I want. Yeah, I'm telling you, I'm juicing for life."

Ralphie sounds not unlike Chris, the New York hair-dresser who was ambivalent about doing steroids but finally gave in: "I looked at the liquid in the needle, and I thought, There it is—happiness, happiness in a vial."

WORKING OUT INTERNALIZED HOMOPHOBIA

The cult of masculinity would not be a full-fledged cult if it did not provide a variety of rituals. Some rituals are about expanding and freeing the mind, losing control, escaping—such as the rituals of the circuit events. Other rituals offer the opposite, a sense of control over one's own physical destiny, a feeling of self-empowerment. These rituals often develop because they have some other function. The pressure to attain the physical paradigm, for men throughout the gay community of the urban ghettos on and off the circuit, has created the rituals of the gym.

Working out, the drugs that enhance the workouts, the obsession with looking the part, are all parts of the ritualistic, religious elements of the cult. These rituals are mandatory for membership in the cult: As the ads for New York's David Barton Gym in the heart of Chelsea commanded in 1994, "No Pecs, No Sex." But the rituals of the gym also offer gay men the opportunity to attain authority over their own bodies and, eventually, over others. In an erratic world where nothing is certain, where gay men historically have not been accepted and have had their lives thrown into chaos, the rituals of the gym give them something they can strive for in the short term and actually attain. That has become even more acute since the AIDS crisis, with disease and death lurking around every corner.

But the rituals would not overwhelm many of us to the

point of obsession if they did not tap into some basic emotional needs present in many if not most of us: The obsession with fitting the hyper-masculine paradigm, predictably, has much to do with internalized homophobia. On a simple level there's the fear of not living up to expected ideas about masculinity and the fear of being marked as the effeminate homosexual, someone who is less than a "real man," something that perhaps has as much to do with misogyny as it does homophobia. Also, in childhood many gay men realized that they do not quite fit in with the other boys and men. That difference, whether they were effeminate or not, often keeps them excluded from the typical kind of macho, heterosexual teenage camaraderie and bonding—as a result, they were not allowed in the "in" crowd of boys. Many of us never quite heal from such exclusion, which is often bitter and painful. Once out in the gay world, we often become obsessed with never being excluded again by the popular crowd. Many of us carry this obsession to extremes. For many young gay men today, that obsession leads them to ingest or inject themselves with powerful and dangerous steroids, a trend that appears to have begun slowly in the 1980s and taken off within the past few years.

THE RISE OF STEROIDS IN THE GAY WORLD

While perhaps almost every gay man living in the urban centers of New York, Washington, Boston, Los Angeles, Atlanta, Miami, San Francisco, and other cities who is the slightest bit aware would make an educated guess that there is a high and increasing percentage of steroid use among young, urban gay men—something my interviews and surveys bear out—there are no reliable figures of any kind regarding steroid use among the men in the twenty-to-forty age group in the heart of the gay ghettos, where most of the steroid use seems to be taking place.

In the *Advocate*'s sex survey, for example, what seems like a low number—2 percent—of the gay men surveyed responded that they have used steroids. But the median age of respondents was thirty-eight, so almost half of the respondents were over forty, not the age group we want to look at in terms of steroid use today. And 22 percent of those surveyed were from small towns and rural America. Of the remaining 78 percent it is not known what percentage are from outlying suburbs and the larger metropolitan areas of the cities and what percentages are from within the actual gay ghettos and their surrounding neighborhoods. If we were to narrow the sample down to a general core of the modern urban ghettos—Chelsea, South Beach, Dupont Circle, West Hollywood—and their outlying neighborhoods, that 2 percent would no doubt rise dramatically.

Another factor that affects the 2 percent figure is that the *Advocate* sex survey was taken in early 1994, just before doctors treating people with AIDS began prescribing steroids to many of their patients on an unprecedented scale. These doctors used testosterone and other steroids to treat men who had low testosterone levels and were suffering from AIDS wasting, or they used steroids as a prophylaxis to prevent wasting.

"We saw a surge in steroid triplicates [the particular prescription form for prescribing controlled substances] in the past couple of years, but mostly in 1996 itself, a huge surge," says one New York pharmacist. "I probably filled one once in a blue moon. Now, I fill a steroid prescription a few times a week, sometimes every day." Some observers believe that therapeutic steroid use by men who are HIV-positive—men who then often build and sculpt their bodies as a fringe benefit of the steroids—has perhaps normalized black market steroid use by HIV-negative men. The resulting overall explosion of steroid-pumped bodies on the streets and in the clubs has perhaps intensified the pressure many young gay men feel to use steroids.

"When all of the HIV-positive guys are looking bigger, hotter, sexier, healthier, than the HIV-negative guys, something weird is certainly going on," an openly gay and HIV-positive Chicago fitness trainer says. "I know of several negative guys who never thought about using steroids before, but who are now saying they want to use them—one is already on them—and each has mentioned positive friends who are on steroids, pointing to how healthy and safe they think the steroids are because their friends are doing so well."

The use of black market steroids by both HIV-negative and HIV-positive gay men has probably been on a slow but steady increase for years, however. Doctors who treat gay men in the urban centers, for example, have noted steroid abuse among their patients throughout the 1980s and into the 1990s. "I certainly have seen it," says Dr. Bernard Bihari, who treats many gay men with AIDS in New York. "I have had certain patients who go through three-month cycles on steroids, who've used steroids, and continue to use steroids, cosmetically, even when they don't tell me. I can tell because the liver function is abnormal. . . . The liver is being assaulted enough to impair its function."

Steroid use today appears to be particularly prevalent among heterosexual male teenagers, a group that itself is also insecure about masculinity and is experimenting, taking risks, and increasingly feeling the pressure to have the ideal body. Many gay men note the influence of gay culture and a gay aesthetic on the straight world, what one survey respondent called "the Calvin Klein dictatorship of America." But studies have been few and far between, in part because since the late 1950s, when synthetic steroids use was first becoming popular, the U.S. government and much of the U.S. medical establishment, in their zeal to discourage steroid use for fear of possible dangers, took an "out of sight, out of mind" approach to steroids. For example, though professional bodybuilders and athletes have sworn by steroids for years, and though there have been some less-than-reliable studies showing that testosterone and other steroids actually do build muscle and increase strength, a definitive study of the efficacy of steroids for building muscle was not published until July 1996, in the *New England Journal of Medicine*. The UCLA researchers who conducted the study determined that, indeed, "doses of testosterone, especially when combined with strength training, increase fat-free mass and muscle size strength in normal men."

The belief for the past twenty-five years and until recently has been that steroids were used primarily by serious weight lifters, Olympic athletes, football players, and other professional sportsmen; these beliefs were in fact backed up by a few older studies that looked at who actually used steroids. But that thinking has changed. The September-October 1992 issue of the journal of the U.S. Public Health Service, *Public Health Reports*, detailing a World Health Organization initiative to study steroid abuse worldwide, notes "that anabolic steriods have moved beyond athletic training and are now being used by nonathletes for cosmetic purposes." In a study done of male high school seniors in the United States in 1988, for example, *Public Health Reports* notes that 35 percent of those who said they were using steriods "did not intend to participate in school-sponsored athletic programs, and 26 percent cited personal appearance as the primary motive for using the drugs."

It is perhaps fair to hypothesize that, with the explosion of the circuit and its physical paradigms in the gay male world in recent years and the anecdotal reports of many gay men that steroid use has increased in the gay community, a similar or higher percentage of gay steroid users (who are not using steroids for HIV therapy) are not using steroids for reasons related to sports and instead are using them cosmetically. In addition to heterosexual teenagers and others, many gay men are in all probability among the estimated one million Americans who, according to a study published in the *Journal of the American Medical Association* (JAMA) in 1993, said they were current or former steroid users. In fact, in that study, which consisted of a questionnaire that was filled out by over thirty-two thousand Americans and which looked at a broad age range similar to the *Advocate's* sex survey (from teens to senior citizens), only nine-tenths of one percent of American men said they were or ever had been steroid users. Gay steroid users would account for some of these men also. The *Advocate's* reported 2 percent figure, therefore, which for various reasons seems quite low, is still more than *double* that of steroid use among the general male population.

"CREATING MONSTERS"

Studies aside, our anecdotal information is powerful. Many of us in the urban centers today have either used or are using steroids, or know of others who use or have used steroids, and we certainly see it all around us in the seemingly sudden prevalence of perfect bodies. A great majority of men who are over forty reported, in interviews and surveys I conducted, their belief that steroid use in the gay world has increased dramatically in recent years. Doctors, nurses, pharmacists, psychotherapists, and other professionals I interviewed who treat and service gay men in Los Angeles, Miami, Chicago, San Francisco, New York, and Dallas also reported their belief that a large number of gay men today are using steroids either therapeutically or for cosmetic purposes, greater than they've ever before witnessed.

"We were much more circumspect and cautious in the beginning, but now we're giving out steroids quite liberally," says Charles, a nurse who treats gay men with AIDS in a community-based clinic in one urban center. He tells me about one HIV-positive guy in his twenties who was formerly a very quiet, meek type, always thin. He then became very ill, began wasting, became skinnier than ever before and quite gaunt. He had several other opportunistic infections, including Kaposi's sarcoma in his stomach. "I really thought that was it," Charles says. But with the help of protease inhibitors and steroids, this man is now quite healthy. More than that, Charles tells me, "He's now a muscle freak, totally built up. He looks healthier than he ever did, even before he was sick," he says. "And he's got a whole new personality, holding himself differently, walking differently. It's a whole new person. And this is just one of so many guys, where the same thing has happened. They just become these huge muscle men, more healthy-looking than before they had HIV, and they just get bigger and bigger, and become 'no neck' monsters. I turned around to the doctor one day and said, 'Okay, what is the end point here? Do we just keep creating monsters?' There's no question too that steroid use in the HIV community has normalized steroid use in the gay community [among HIV-negative men."]

Charles, after looking around at the highly concentrated

gay ghetto in which he works and combining the HIV-positive men on therapeutic steroids with the HIV-negative men on black market drugs, firmly stated that "almost 50 percent" of the gay men in the ghetto are using steroids. Although that seems like a wild exaggeration, Charles's front-line impressions are instructive.

Similarly, fitness trainers interviewed in gyms that cater to gay men in New York, Los Angeles, Atlanta, Denver, Philadelphia, and Boston report a rise in cosmetic steroid use in recent years. Bert, a trainer who works at a gay gym in New York, like several other trainers, tells me that if his clients ask, he now instructs them on how to take steroids—how to inject them—and on which ones to take. He has, sometimes, even helped them obtain the illegal drugs.

"My feeling is, they're going to use them anyway, so they should know what they're taking and know how to take it," Bert says, claiming that he's never used steroids himself but has a lot of friends who have. "I'd rather help them out than see them do damage to themselves. The problem is, they send their friends around too, and I don't want to come off as someone who is promoting steroids, so that's my dilemma. I would say yes, definitely, there are many more gay men doing steroids and wanting to do steroids than I've ever seen, and I've been doing this [work] for ten years now."

In fact no fitness trainer, health care professional, or psychotherapist I spoke with reported a trend in the opposite direction. No one would confirm that there has been a decrease in cosmetic steroid use among gay men or even a stabilization over the past several years.

"The kinds of things that people increasingly will do to try to match that physical ideal just become more and more extreme," observes noted Los Angeles psychotherapist Dr.

Betty Berzon, a lesbian who counsels gay men in Southern California. "The use of steroids is growing, and it is over time going to be extremely destructive for a lot of these gay men."

ROIDBOTS

Southern California and Los Angeles in particular seem to be Steroid Central. The West Hollywood roidbot is a mythical—but all too real—figure in gay culture these days. The current shaved, steroid-pumped body that has come to be the circuit standard and the cult of masculinity's present ideal emanated from the West Coast, promoted in large part by the booming gay porn industry centered in California. Many of the stars of gay porn who emerged in the 1980s—Jeff Stryker, Ryan Idol, Ty Fox—were the epitome of the hairless, healthy, tanned, pumped ideal that was cultivated in California, and these porn stars spread that ideal to bedrooms and VCRs across America.

Unlike in the straight world, where porn stars are at the bottom of the celebrity food chain, in the gay world porn stars occupy mythic status. Porn stars are treated like royalty at A-list gay parties, given even higher status than Hollywood power brokers, and revered by men far and wide. They are perhaps the homosexual equivalent of the Hollywood female movie starlets in the heterosexual world and are deified and held up as the physical ideal. The hairless and healthy California look of the porn stars, big and beefy, was seen by gay men in the 1980s and 1990s as the antidote to ever heightening fears and anxieties about emaciation and death. The goal became to get that Superman look, and using steroids, for many gay men, was the only way to get the Superman look.

In sunny California, where one spends more time wearing

less clothing and where Hollywood has always nurtured artifice and physical ideals, the pressure to conform to a particular
body aesthetic has always been more intense for straights and
gays alike. Cosmetic changes to the body—from plastic
surgery, to liposuction, to tanning beds—have almost been de
rigueur in recent years and rarely raise eyebrows. People don't
of course talk publicly about the work they've had done, but
it's no surprise to most people in L.A. to learn that someone
has had work done. One particular hobby among some
Angelenos I know is trying to figure out which women in a
given restaurant had what particular kind of work done and
which doctor they went to and how much it cost. So for gay
men in Los Angeles in the 1980s and 1990s to use steroids was
not such a major step in the evolution of ways to mold and
shape the body.

THE WEST HOLLYWOOD-IZATION OF GAY AMERICA

Through the porn industry and the circuit, the California gay
body aesthetic influenced gay men nationally in gay ghettos
around the country. In interviews, many gay men in New York
in fact observe a phenomenon that we might call the "West
Hollywood-ization" of New York.

"The Chelsea look, the sculpted, hairless body, very cut
and very pumped, the whole 'roid look,' it's very L.A.," says
Andy, a forty-five-year-old New York architect, talking about
the newly emerging gay ghetto of Chelsea. "The West Village
wasn't really like that—there were a variety of looks. But it's all
become so homogenized now, wherever you go. It's all that
California look, with the tan and all of the attitude too, that
kind of disengaging thing, where it's all about you and not

about anybody else." Billy, a thirty-five-year-old New Yorker refers to the connection between the "attitude" and the body aesthetic: "It's that building up of armor that goes on in L.A., a presentation on the outside, a shell, to mask the inside. I've seen this in Chelsea lately, it's where you build up that armor, the body, as a protection. It keeps you withdrawn and free from really interacting." Interestingly, men in San Francisco, Chicago, Atlanta, Miami, and other cities share similar sentiments, often in fact using the word "homogenization" to describe how much of the gay community in their respective locales is conforming, in their opinion, to a Southern California steroid-enhanced aesthetic.

TESTOSTERONE TO THE RESCUE

But while West Hollywood-ization may have been slowly occurring during the 1980s throughout very specific crowds in the gay community nationally—the circuit, in particular—it was perhaps the advent of steroid use for treatment of people with AIDS that jolted the look to the far reaches of the community in the mid-1990s quite rapidly: As Charles, the nurse in the community-based clinic pointed out, suddenly men who'd never dreamt of looking like circuit queens had became steroid-enhanced. Even those who had disdained the look for years suddenly found their bodies bulging with muscles. They got used to it quickly. Others finally got the muscle body they'd been trying to get for years—long before they were HIV-positive. HIV, in a roundabout way, gave them the body they had always desired.

"My body has never looked so good in my life," Paul, a twenty-nine-year-old Washington waiter, tells me, laughing at his current situation. His doctor put him on testosterone after finding his levels of that hormone were quite low. Paul had been experiencing an overall malaise and had practically no sex drive, but that all changed not long after he began testosterone therapy. And his body changed quite a bit as well. "I ate right all the time," he says, referring to five years ago, before he was HIV-positive. "I ate a lot of protein. I took all kinds of vitamins. I drank all of those carbo drinks and the loading drinks and all that crap. And I worked out like a nut. But I could never get my body to bulk up. Who would have thought it would take AIDS to do it? With testosterone, I don't even have to work out all that much, and I've gotten great results. So I work out less than I used to, and I'm bigger than I was. It's, like, way too easy, but I'm not complaining."

It is not generally known that testosterone has been used in the past to treat illnesses unrelated to AIDS and has been used particularly for men who might have low testosterone levels for various reasons. Because of the abuse of testosterone and other steroids by athletes and others in the past, the health benefits of testosterone therapy have in fact been greatly overshadowed until relatively recently, with their use by people who are HIV infected.

Low testosterone levels in people with HIV usually cause sluggishness, depression, and lowered sex drive. But there are often greater problems associated with low testosterone levels.

"Growing evidence shows that testosterone deficiency can lead to impaired appetite, weight loss, and decline of crucial lean body mass—all the ingredients for dangerous wasting," Bob Lederer reported in POZ magazine in 1996. The groundbreaking studies of testosterone therapy on people with AIDS were begun in the early 1990s by Dr. Judith Rabkin, Ph.D., M.P.H., a professor of clinical psychology in psychiatry at Columbia University, who showed that the problems resulting from low testosterone could be dramatically improved with regularly administered testosterone. Pushing to get research funding for a study of a drug that might help gay men with AIDS improve their sex drives wasn't easy, she tells me. "When I first applied for approval there was one [committee member] who said, 'This reminds me of helping Typhoid Mary get more jobs,'" she recalls. But she got her funding and began her research, paving the way for doctors across the country to take advantage of the therapy for their patients with AIDS.

"We use fairly vigorous doses," she says regarding the amount of testosterone given to subjects, but the doses she used are substantially less than what most bodybuilders and others looking to build up their bodies normally use—though many doctors are giving their patients higher doses than those Rabkin used in her studies. Nonetheless, Rabkin says, most of the men in her completed studies did gain a fair amount of muscle (fifteen pounds, on average), particularly if they worked out. And many doctors, as well as many gay men with AIDS who've undergone the therapy, report the same.

To assess whether or not a patient needs testosterone therapy, doctors perform a bioelectric impedence analysis (BIA) test, which is an early indicator of wasting in a patient before there are any outward signs. If the test results are below normal, the doctor will then do a test to measure the patient's testosterone levels. And if they are low the doctor may implement treatment with testosterone in the form of either a skin patch, intramuscular injections, or a pill taken orally.

Testosterone is a male hormone that occurs naturally in the body and has effects that are androgenic—growth of body hair, growth of facial hair, male pattern baldness, teenage acne, increased sex drive, development of sperm—as well as anabolic—promoting the building of muscle tissue. Anabolic steroids, used by athletes and bodybuilders, are synthetic derivatives of testosterone and are used mostly for purposes of muscle growth and enhancement. They are designed to cut down on undesirable androgenic effects and produce mostly anabolic effects, though all anabolic steroids have, to varying degrees, depending on the particular steroid, androgenic effects. There are no steroids in fact that are 100 percent anabolic and non-androgenic, though that would be the ideal steroid for those who use them for cosmetic reasons. Men using steroids to build up their bodies, for example, don't want to experience male pattern baldness, and many might not need or desire an increased sex drive.

Some doctors, in addition to testosterone therapy or as a replacement for it, prescribe anabolic steroids in order to rebuild muscle tissue in those patients infected with HIV who are experiencing wasting. "We're confident that this is a valid, beneficial treatment for many people [living with AIDS]," Dr. Gary Cohan of the Pacific Oaks Medical Group in Los Angeles told *POZ* in September 1994. In the December 1996 issue of *Out* magazine, journalist Bruce Mirken, who has written extensively on AIDS, noted in an article about the use of anabolic steroids to treat wasting that it is "increasingly clear . . . that doctors and patients need to think about forestalling wasting from the moment a person knows he or she is infected with HIV," as studies have shown a correlation between loss of lean muscle tissue and risk of death. "That means," Mirken noted, "watching lab markers such as blood levels of vitamin B–12, testosterone, magnesium, and albumin, and tracking lean body mass with [a BIA test]."

More controversial, however, is the practice by some doctors with large AIDS practices in the urban centers of prescribing testosterone and anabolic steroids for patients who are not wasting or have no other symptoms associated with low testos-terone; these doctors believe that the steroids can be used as a preventive or prophylaxis for people with AIDS, including those who may be quite healthy and whose BIA tests and other indicators of wasting are normal; they believe that building up the body acts in this case as a sort of insurance against wasting, should it ever occur. Several groups have in fact formed that specifically advocate this kind of liberal use of steroids for treating people infected with HIV.

"The idea is that you put thirty to forty pounds of muscle on a guy, just in case he might start wasting someday," says one critic, an AIDS activist. "It's completely bogus and unnecessary."

Nelson Vergel is the executive director of one such group advocating early use of steroids by people infected with HIV, Program for Wellness Restoration (PoWeR) in Houston. Vergel himself has AIDS and says he was wasting until he began using steroids. "Our main goal is a standard of care guidelines for wasting," he says. "Wasting starts happening in the early stages. We advocate to have a little bit of a buffer just in case you get an opportunistic infection. We have been criticized that we are trying to beautify AIDS, that we're doing this for cosmetic purposes. Some doctors are criticizing us, but the fact is [the use of steroids for people with HIV is] becoming more and more a standard of care. We know of 148 doctors [around the country] who prescribe steroids and we have over three thousand people on our program [of steroid use]."

Vergel is well aware that many gay men are using steroids for cosmetic purposes, and seems to realize the implications of his own work. "There's pressure in the gay culture," he says. "There's social and cultural pressure for gay males to be built up. A lot of it is in the gay media. You look at a gay magazine and most are doing it, building their bodies. There is pressure to be buff. And you see it more in certain cities. We have done seminars [for men with HIV who might be interested in using steroids according to PoWeR's guidelines] in over forty cities, and usually we get like eighty people. But in South Beach, which is a place where there is a lot of pressure to have a hot body, we had rooms full of three hundred to four hundred people."

Vergel is also candid about what steroids have done for him. "It has changed my health," he observes. "But it has changed my life. I look great, I look buff, and my self-esteem — you become a lot more assertive and confident." And he acknowledges the effect that steroid use by HIV-positive men for therapeutic purposes might have on some HIV-negative men. "I really don't know what the answer is to that problem," he says. "I know that a lot of HIV-negative men are getting their steroids from their HIV-positive friends. It's a problem and it might get worse. But all I know is, I'm not wasting anymore and I look great. I look at myself and I think: One day someone is going to come up to me and say, 'Damn, you look so good! You must be HIV-positive!' It's getting to that."

Michael Mooney is PoWeR's media director. He also writes a column for *Muscle Media* 2000 magazine, a body-builder's publication that has come under some criticism for appearing to advocate steroid use for bodybuilding purposes. Mooney's column, titled Medibolics, is strictly about using steroids for health purposes. However, as Vergel notes, "even HIV-negative bodybuilders are reading the column because he has information in there for them, because we're able to portray it as for medical purposes. Legally, Michael can say what he wants."

Mooney, who is an HIV-negative gay man who lives in

West Hollywood, uses steroids himself, legally. He says that his testosterone levels are "just slightly" lower than normal, so his doctor prescribes him steroids. Mooney believes anyone, positive or negative, should be able to use steroids legally. "When you say abuse, there's two sides to abuse, he tells me. "As far as I'm concerned, as a freedom of choice issue, if you want to do them you should be able to. I'm not sure that I agree that people should be prevented from doing dangerous things to themselves. I have a libertarian bent to me. Regardless of that, after all I have studied, [I've concluded] that the side effects are highly exaggerated. Doctors have been taught to read liver function tests wrong. The whole liver toxicity test thing is exaggerated."

PHYSICIAN-ASSISTED BEAUTY

According to several people with AIDS and other observers, a great many doctors also apparently give their HIV-infected patients higher doses of testosterone or anabolic steroids than may be recommended or necessary for the treatments, wanting to fulfill the patient's desires to have a hotter body.

"Here's how it works," says Rosemary Caggiano, a New York psychotherapist whose clients include many gay men infected with HIV. "Let's say that a physician suggests that they get on steroids so that they don't lose muscle tone. And then they decide, since they have more energy, that they're going to go to the gym. And then they notice their bodies are pumping up more and more—better even than when they were well. And so they begin deciding how much of the medication they should be taking. And they tell the doctors they want more, and the doctors give them more, because a lot of doctors say, 'When someone has AIDS, what's the big deal? Why not?'"

Some prominent doctors who treat people with HIV, how-ever, are much more cautious about steroids. "In somebody with HIV who is on several other drugs that are managed by the liver, I'd prefer that the liver stay intact," says Bernard Bahari, a well-known doctor who has treated gay men with AIDS in New York since the beginning of the AIDS epidemic. "I'm using testosterone for people with low blood testosterone levels, for restoring levels of muscle mass, and also to restore sexual function. I would certainly use anabolic steroids in somebody with wasting. But there is nobody now that I would have occasion to use it in. With the triple combination [pro-tease inhibitors], people's T cells are going up and they're putting weight on. The most dramatic increases in weight I've seen are not from steroids, but from the proper antiviral com-binations. I've seen patients gaining sixty pounds. I've certainly had a few patients who've asked [for steroids]. I generally say no. Part of that comes from my background. I've spent most of my career in drug addiction. It makes me a little more uneasy about prescribing controlled substances."

Other doctors in the urban centers, however, seem to be prescribing steroids freely, often not for physically therapeutic reasons at all.

"I know for a fact that many of the gay men coming in here for steroids do not need them," says a San Francisco pharma-cist who works in a chain drugstore. "Sometimes I just know because they're friends of friends, and I inquire and know they're not positive. Sometimes I can also tell from the other medications they're getting—or not getting. It's not usual that someone is at the point where he requires steroids for his HIV infection but he doesn't require any other drug. It's possible, but I take it to mean this person is probably either HIV-nega-tive, or he's positive but not having any problems with his health that warrant any sort of medication — including steroids. But at this point, even if he were positive and newly infected and healthy, he might be on the newer drugs, the protease inhibitors. So it's more likely he's negative. Either way, I would say that giving these patients steroids is a form of abuse."

"Last year, I looked at this guy's information and he was not HIV-positive," a New York pharmacist tells me. "His prescription came from a well-known doctor with a big AIDS practice. But he wasn't on AZT, or any of the antiretrovirals. He has a friend who works in the store, and he later told this friend the truth. He confessed that he was a friend of the doctor and that he wasn't positive. Another guy, an HIV-positive man I know, got a prescription for the steroid and gave the drug to someone else as soon as he left the store."

Another New York pharmacist notes that, since the advent of steroids for treatment of people with HIV, it's easier for abuse to occur. "When steroid prescriptions were rare around here, it would seem odd if one came," he says. "It would be suspicious. In cases where we are suspicious and it's obvious that the patient or even the doctor could perhaps be abusing it, we have to by law call him on it. If you're in the middle of Minnesota or something you might do that. But the population here at this store is mostly HIV-positive men, many on anabolic steroids. So you get a bodybuilder in the mix, someone who's just using steroids to build up and get cut, and you don't call. They slip in, and even if you're suspicious, you just kind of let it go rather than cause a problem. I once said, 'We have to call on this one,' after a young man came in who was a perfectly sculpted, in-the-gym-ten-hours-a-week muscle queen and who was not HIV-positive, and my boss was like, 'No, come on, I know the doctor. It's money. Go ahead.'"

Sometimes doctors who abuse steroids are themselves gay

and often on the circuit: One New York doctor with a built-up body who never misses a circuit party prescribes steroids to almost any HIV-positive person who asks (and some HIV-negative patients as well), some of whom have abused steroids. "When [John] died and they cut him open, they found all of his organs enlarged—they were gargantuan," says Paul, a thirty-six-year-old New Yorker who describes a friend who died of complications from AIDS and who was a patient of this particular doctor. "Even before he died, you could see his organs coming through his torso, under his rib cage, all swollen. He didn't need steroids. He wasn't wasting. And I wonder how much the steroid use might have contributed to his death."

Similarly, asking around casually, I was able to identify gay doctors in Los Angeles, San Francisco, Chicago, and Washington who are on the circuit and who themselves take steroids and/or who prescribe them for patients who more often than not do not need them for reasons related to health, some of these patients being HIV-negative.

"BUY A GOOD BLOOD PRESSURE MONITOR"

The vast majority of HIV-negative gay men using steroids, however, like the vast majority of all steroid users, are obtaining steroids illegally off the black market (according to *Business Week*, illegal steroid sales are estimated to be a $500-million-per-year market in the United States), often getting counterfeit drugs that are sometimes useless and at other times dangerous. These steroids, which Harvard researchers estimate cost the average steroid user roughly $1,700 per year, can be obtained at any major gym in the gay ghettos, where dealers—sometimes fitness trainers, selling steroids on the side— often can be found in the locker rooms.

"We had one guy who used to sell them, and then, for no charge, he'd inject them in you, late at night in the locker room," one Chelsea steroid user, a twenty-five-year-old student, tells me. "This gym is just packed with people on 'roids,' and a lot of them buy them right here. In fact this is where they learn about them, overhearing people gossiping in the corner, wanting to get a piece of the action—that's what happened with me. Sometimes I would stand here and think, What the hell am I doing? What kind of community is this? But there I was, eventually, getting my steroids shot in my butt."

These black market steroids are sometimes cut with other dangerous compound drugs; often the steroids are smuggled in from foreign countries, such as Russia, where they might not be strictly monitored and regulated. Once smuggled out, the steroids are often cut with still other drugs and compounds by dealers in North America. In a raid several years ago on a steroid dealer's home in Vancouver, Canadian authorities seized anabolic steroids that were cut with Armor All, a chemical cleaner used for shining car dashboards.

There are now, in addition to steroids, over a hundred other substances being sold in the United States to build muscle or burn fat, some legal, some not. Not only are the illegal substances not regulated in this country—one argument perhaps for making them legal—they are also not tested in clinical trials for use at specific doses. Clenbuterol, for example, is a bronchodilator meant to be inhaled for the treatment of bronchial asthma. In countries other than the United States, where it is not currently approved for any use, it is also fed in large doses to livestock animals, and it is believed to increase lean muscle mass and inhibit fat from depositing. The drug is sold on the black market to many gay men and others who are taking high doses, although there have been no clinical trials to show the drug's safety or efficacy at these doses. Some people have had harsh reactions to the drug. In 1992, for example, 135 people in Spain experienced headaches, chills, muscle tremors, and nausea after ingesting the drug.

Elite Fitness is a New York–based for-profit institution devoted to helping people "pack on muscle mass and leave you with a hard, muscular, massive physique." Elite Fitness's "Cutting Document" nonchalantly reports that "Clen can have some serious side effects (like sudden death) at very high dosages." The document goes on to advise users: "Clen works but it's hard on your system. Buy a good blood pressure monitor and use it several times a day. Base your dosage on your BP and resting pulse and your lack of side effects."

BARBECUED ORGANS

While steroids and other drugs used by bodybuilders go untested and unregulated, technology continues to create newer versions of these drugs that are more powerful and thus potentially more effective as well as potentially more dangerous.

"Traditional low-dose regimens using anabolic steroids," says three-time Mr. Olympia Frank Zane, "popular in the days when I was competing [the late 1970s], have given way to human growth hormone, insulinlike growth factor, insulin itself, powerful anticatabolic drugs [to prevent muscle breakdown], diuretics [to cut down on water weight], and other dangerous compounds."

Human growth hormone (HGH) in fact is another substance that, after much pressure from activist groups, most notably ACT UP/Golden Gate, was approved by the Food and Drug Administration in 1996 for treatment of wasting in people infected with HIV. It has shown some remarkable results, and it has also been used effectively for years to treat dwarfism. But HGH too is being obtained on the black market and used by gay men, positive and negative, to stimulate muscle growth for the purpose of bodybuilding. HGH has also been touted on the steroid underground as a miraculous new "steroid alternative," leading people to believe human growth hormone is completely safe. Yet the doses of human growth hormone used for bodybuilding purposes—doses often considerably larger than those used to treat wasting—have, according to *U.S. News and World Report*, been known to lead to acromegaly, or "Frankenstein syndrome," a condition that causes a wicked enlarged distortion of the face, hands, and feet and can kill those afflicted. The late football star Lyle Alzado, who died of a rare brain cancer, attributed his illness to years of using illegal drugs to enhance muscle growth and performance, including human growth hormone.

Sometimes, the drugs aren't even so new. The July 1996 issue of *Flex* magazine reported that a black market substance called Hexalon, which promised to "melt off your body fat," was being sold on the Internet. What wasn't told to potential buyers, however, was that the compound had been around for nearly a hundred years, having been shelved because of its deadly side effects. Autopsy reports dating back to the turn of the century (when, as George Chauncey notes in *Gay New York*, the country was overcome with a similar "cult of muscularity") showed that some users had literally "cooked from the inside out," as *Flex* described it. "In every autopsy report on individuals who died subsequent to taking components that make up what we now call Hexalon, there was no pink left. All of the organs of the thorax and abdomen were well done. Cooked. Barbecued."

WHAT'S THE DAMAGE?

The federal Anabolic Steroids Control Act of 1990, which amended the Food, Drug and Cosmetic Act, classifies most anabolic steroids and several other drugs thought to enhance muscular performance as controlled substances. Prior to 1990, doctors could prescribe steroids to bodybuilders more easily; the amendment was passed by Congress and signed by President Bush after many reports in the late 1980s of steroid abuse by teenage boys. The illegal possession and distribution of these substances today is punishable by a maximum sentence of five years imprisonment and hefty fines. But the mere fact that steroids are *illegal* for cosmetic purposes, promoters of steroid use charge, does not necessarily mean that they are dangerous nor that steroids cannot be used safely. More accurately, they say, the U.S. government is being paternalistic and overprotective and does not view bodybuilding as a significant reason to allow people to take calculated risks with steroids and other drugs. Anabolic steroid use for bodybuilding purposes is, for example, legal in some western European countries.

The damage to overall health and well-being and the long-term effects of the various kinds of anabolic steroids have been a subject of debate for several decades. Studies have been inconclusive and few and far between. There still is not enough data available to say that most kinds of anabolic steroids are 100 percent safe when used according to specified dosages and for the short spans of time that some promoters of steroid use advise, but there is certainly enough data to show that anabolic steroids can and are dangerous when used in larger doses and for longer lengths of time. Even the minimal doses of steroids used to be reasonably beneficial, and if used for relatively short periods of time, can lead to some severe short-term side effects. And long-term effects of steroid use, even at small doses, are simply not known.

Ingesting steroids orally is by far the most dangerous way to use steroids, though Dyanabol, an oral steroid, is one of the most popular anabolic steroids today and is used by many gay men.

"I know orals are definitely not good for you," says Rick, a twenty-three-year-old New Orleans student, "but I can't take a shot, it scares the shit out of me. I don't want to be using needles, and I haven't really talked about [my steroid use] with any of my good friends, so I can't ask them to do it, and I think they would think I was crazy. Orals are a lot easier."

Ingested steroids are processed by the liver, and even at low doses, taken for short periods of time, these steroids can wreak havoc on the liver and other organs, acting as toxins, damaging the organs permanently. Injecting steroids in liquid form prevents them from having to be initially broken down in the liver, although they eventually pass through the liver in a somewhat less caustic but still potentially damaging state. Injections cannot be intravenous. They must be intramuscular. A hypodermic needle must penetrate the skin and the tissue under the skin and enter deep into the muscle itself, one to one and a half inches from the skin's surface, preferably at the top of the buttocks, thigh, or deltoid.

BITCH TITS AND SHRINKING BALLS

There are many different kinds of injectable steroids, each of which creates various results in terms of muscle growth, and each of which creates different percentages of anabolic and adrogenic effects. The brand name Deca-Durabolin, known popularly as Deca (pharmaceutical name, Nadrolone Decanoate), is among the most widely used steroids and is among the anabolic steroids used therapeutically by some men with AIDS. It is used both for attaining a very cut look as well as for bulking up. Deca is a highly anabolic, moderately androgenic compound and is said to have minimal liver toxicity. Winstrol (pharmaceutical name, Stanozolol) is another popular steroid, and is used mainly for getting very cut and defined. It's a low-andgrogenic compound.

Steroids are often "stacked," that is, taken simultaneously with other steroids, to both maximize results and reap the different benefits of specific steroids at once. Many men stack their steroids with testosterone, for example, to accelerate the process by which they build muscle. Deca is often stacked with Dianabol. Winstrol is often stacked with Parabolan, a powerful, fairly toxic androgenic steroid. Steroids are also "staggered," that is, several steroids are used in an overlapping pattern over time.

Most steroids are administered in eight- to twelve-week cycles, with an injection once a week, or ingested daily. There is then an off-cycle period, for six to eight weeks, and then a cycle often begins again. Few gay men I interviewed have done just one cycle, simply because they often shrink up if they do not go back on a cycle, undoing all of the effects of the steroids. For results of steroid use to be lasting, promoters of steroids say that a person should go on and off cycles for a period of at least two years, but for others it may take longer usage for muscle mass to stay on. Some men, in order to stay at a particular muscle mass, must stay on steroids indefinitely, an exceedingly dangerous option.

Common side effects even during short-term use of moderate doses of steroids include shrinking testicles and skin acne. More serious problems arising from steroid use often occur because of excessive dosages, prolonged use, prolonged cycles, not enough off-cycle time, using the wrong steroids—such as an emphasis on androgenic rather than anabolic steroids—stacking them improperly, and using counterfeits that are either useless or dangerous.

Steroids put a great deal of stress on the cardiovascular system and often affect neurologic function, testosterone production, and liver function. When taken either orally or through injection, prolonged use of moderate doses of steroids may cause severe liver damage and lead to progressive cholestasis and jaundice, peliosis hepatitis, hemorrhaging, liver cancer, and other forms of cancer. Kidney failure can also occur with prolonged use, and the damage often exhibits no symptoms until the kidney is substantially impaired. Prolonged steroid use also may adversely affect the blood's clotting mechanism.

Short-term use of excessive doses of steroids appear to be damaging to the liver and kidney, and even small doses for a short time may cause what is known as "aromatizing" effect, whereby the steroids convert to the female hormone estrogen and cause a condition known as gynecomastia, an enlargement of the mammary glands in men, commonly known among heterosexual male bodybuilders as "bitch tits." New York's Dr. Bernard Bihari even worries about the possibility of the development of breast cancer in men who use steroids.

"They could be at risk for breast cancer and prostate cancer both," he says. "Breast cancer from the estrogen breakdown—since we see a connection between breast cancer and estrogen in women—and prostate cancer from the androgenic effects. Most prostate cancer is testosterone-sensitive, in that in tests it makes cancer grow. And so prostate cancer seems to be related to testosterone."

THIS IS YOUR BRAIN ON STEROIDS

The greatest effect of steroid use could perhaps be on the brain. Steroid use creates high amounts of cortisol, the body's major stress hormone, which can lead to hypertension and other ailments. Bouts of aggression—the mythic "roid rages"—also occur among steroid users.

"I would go out and have really violent sex," says Eric, the thirty-two-year-old New York financial consultant. "I never got into that before, but I'd go to sex clubs and I'd be all pumped up and raging, and guys would be like, 'Beat me up. Treat me like shit.' And I'd get into it big time, and sometimes go too far, just really raging. It was like I didn't know what came over me."

"I used to punch walls—scream even—then it would sub-side, so I didn't think anything of it," says Arne, a thirty-two-year-old Dallas store manager who used steroids for three years. "I'd go up and down, tremendous mood swings, but when I was angry, forget it. I punched out a customer in the store once over a minor argument—I'd never done anything like that before. And I was beating up my lover—we'd been together for three years and I'd never, ever hit him before, nor had I ever been violent toward him. It started out with just a swing, now and then, and it became a pattern. I'd go into a rage. The last time, I hurt him badly; he had to get stitches near his eye, and he left me for good. That kind of made me wise up a bit and see that the steroids were really doing a major number on me."

A 1994 study published in the *Journal of the American Medical Association* by researchers at McLean Hospital in Massachusetts found that "steroid users displayed more fre-quent gynecomastia, decreased mean testicular length, and higher cholesterol–high density lipoprotein ratios than nonusers. Most strikingly," the researchers noted, "23 percent of steroid users reported major mood syndromes — mania, hypomania, or major depression — in association with steroid use. Steroid users displayed mood disorders during steroid exposure significantly more frequently than in the absence of steroid exposure." Their conclusions: "Major mood disturbances associated with anabolic-androgenic steroids may represent an important public health problem [for bodybuilders] using steroids and sometimes for the victims of their irritability and aggression."

(In her studies using testosterone on men with HIV who had a deficiency of the hormone, Dr. Judith Rabkin says that because the doses she used were comparatively low, such side effects were not a major problem. "The most common side effect we've come across is irritability," she notes. "They're more likely to be aggravated if someone bumps into them in the subway. This is a lot lower down on the continuum of a 'roid rage,' common among athletes who take higher doses.")

A 1993 study led by Dr. Charles Yesalis, professor of health policy at Pennsylvania State University, who is considered the country's top expert on steroids (he has also written a great deal on the beneficial effects of steroids in treating various ailments as well, and is not necessarily "antisteroid"), concluded definitively that "anabolic-androgenic steroids use is highly correlated with self-reported aggressive behavior and crimes against property." Curiously, the researchers also found that "among twelve- to thirty-four-year-olds, [steroid use] was significantly and positively associated with the use of other illicit drugs . . . and alcohol," perhaps indicating that those who might take risks and use recreational drugs might also use steroids, such as the gay circuit crowd. And a study done by Harvard researchers concluded that one-eighth of steroid users suffered from "bodybuilder's psychosis," with symptoms often including delusions and paranoia.

IT'S JUST LIKE A NOSE JOB

Among those gay and straight health care professionals and fitness trainers who contend that steroid use for cosmetic purposes can be physically safe when used according to specified regimens, there is a tendency to downplay both the psychological effects of steroid use on people and, more important, what sociological and psychological factors lead people—in this case, gay men—to use steroids for cosmetic rather than therapeutic purposes in the first place.

Though the sociological and psychological factors that influence gay men to turn to steroids might, for example, seem similar to the reasons people undergo most types of cosmetic surgery, there are some marked differences to bear in mind. A teenage girl with a large nose, for example, might have been taunted all through childhood and ridiculed. She might decide as a young adult to have her nose "fixed" (among the most common types of cosmetic surgery). Her being pressured to conform to society's standards of beauty by having a nose job might indeed seem similar to a gay man's conforming to a physical ideal by using steroids, and perhaps it is just as morally problematic. Why, after all, should a young woman be pressured to fix her nose? Conversely, why should she not feel free to alter her nose? And if we accept that this young woman should not have to be a martyr to the cause of changing standardized notions of beauty (by refusing to get a nose job), why must we expect any more of gay men who are thinking about using steroids to bulk up their muscles?

Yet, even if the impetus to conform is similar in both cases, the urgent necessity to do so in each case differs greatly, as does the risk involved. A one-time, relatively risk-free surgical procedure to "fix" a nose that has been for years the object of scorn and ridicule seems reasonable. In the case of gay men who do steroids, however, most already have bodies that are socially acceptable; in many cases they already have bodies that are considered to be "hot," "sexy," or even "beautiful." They are not then simply "correcting" something that is socially unacceptable by the larger society's standards; they are conforming to a very precise and rigid standard that some within their own community—itself a despised minority within the larger culture—have put in place as a way of exhibiting to themselves and to the culture at large that, contrary to popular belief, they truly are exceptionally valuable, "genetically gifted," and highly masculine.

Again, the physical risks in doing steroids, unlike having the average nose job, are extremely high. Steroids users inject themselves with powerful chemicals weekly, or ingest these chemicals daily, experiencing mild to heavy physical and psychological side effects regularly, and often misuse the drugs and experience permanent, severe damage to their internal organs and other parts of their bodies. They take these drugs over a period of weeks, coming off the drugs for a while and then going back on them again, all over perhaps a period of two years or longer—or maybe indefinitely—not knowing what the long-term effects will be. Comparing this to cosmetic surgery would be equivalent perhaps to a man or woman who is physically attractive or even considered "beautiful" but who undergoes the most intrusive and potentially painful and harmful kind of cosmetic surgery over and over again, not in an attempt to look socially acceptable but to be *perfect*. What's operating here is an obsession with being physically superior, one that has a lot to do with a phobia of being looked down upon—and a determination never to be looked down upon again.

BIGGER AND BIGGER

"It was my dream to get a body," says Mark, the forty-year-old New Yorker who works for an AIDS agency and who says he had an attractive, lean body before using steroids. "I would see all of those guys with their muscles and I wanted to be one of them. It's kind of like when you're a kid in the school yard and the popular kids and the jocks exclude you because you're not cool enough. Especially if you're a gay boy, you were probably excluded from that crowd as a kid, and so when you grow older there is this nagging to be in the popular crowd, to not be excluded. It's not even like I want to really even hang out with the muscle gods, I mean, after I do get into bed with one, it usually is a letdown. Beyond the sex, which sometimes is really dull, I'm usually saying to myself, Why did you obsess over getting this guy? We never have anything in common. They're usually so involved in their bodies—and it really is an all-consuming project to be a muscle god, and work out, like, all the time—that they don't have any other interests beyond talking about the gym and the scene. But that's the thing about it: It's the private club, the world of the muscle gods, and you don't want to be excluded from it, no matter how much you really wouldn't like it if you were included. You'd rather that they invite you and you say, 'Hey, thanks for including me but I'm not interested.' It's not like you really want to hang in with them—you just don't like them excluding you. It pushes all those buttons from when you're a kid. At least for me it does. And that was one of the biggest reason why I started doing steroids."

"I was always the type who was, you know, the cliché, the shy and awkward type," recalls Carl, a thirty-three-year-old Boston hotel maintenance man who tells a story similar to Mark's. "But a few years ago, a friend of mine, an older man, told me that my body was the type that would really become something awesome on steroids, and steroids aren't that dangerous if you use them properly and don't abuse them. And I was glad I took his advice. To suddenly have everyone wanting you in bed and including you in everything, in parties and social gatherings, after years of being the shy awkward type who wasn't looked at—that is a major ego boost."

And yet despite what steroids might do in terms of an "ego boost," many men feel that they can never be big enough, no matter how much muscle mass they put on, or cut enough, no matter how lean and defined they become. When I tell Ralphie, sitting next to me at the pool at the World Gym in West Hollywood, that his body is quite flawless, he frowns and says he's "not there yet—but almost, or at least sometimes I think I'm almost there, while other times I think I'm way off." He then is quick to add, "I would never admit that, of course, to anyone, and I'm only telling you for the purpose of your book, because it's off-the-record. I wouldn't want anyone to think I have doubts, but man, a lot of the time, I have doubts."

Mark, though he's off steroids now, tells me that even when on them, "I was never really a muscle god, well, not like the guys I looked up to. I tried hard, but I never really got there."

"I'm striving for something, and I'm not sure what," says Richard, a twenty-three-year-old Miami Beach hustler and go-go dancer who flies from New York to Miami to L.A. for "gigs," as he calls his different work assignments, and who has a perfectly sculpted, young and hairless body. "I look in the mirror and I'm not happy. Sometimes, I'm really depressed. I look at this or that part of my body and it's just not right, looks weird, doesn't seem like it should look the way it does. I look in the magazines and I see better, and I want to be that. But even when I think I get to that, I see something else that's better, and I just start obsessing all over again."

Kevin, a thirty-seven-year-old unemployed Chicagoan who has used steroids on and off for four years, says he sometimes catches a glimpse of his body in the mirror while quickly passing by and "it looks pretty hot," but that when he studies his body in the mirror for a while, "it just throws me off, gets me depressed." He becomes exasperated and admits, "I think that it's probably impossible to meet your goal because you set a standard you can't possibly reach. Still, you keep trying, getting bigger and bigger."

While many men I interviewed who use steroids were perfectly satisfied with their bodies or even thought their bodies were exceptional, far too many men with bodies that match the physical ideal and who use steroids seemed to have a distorted idea of what their bodies looked like. When they looked in the mirror, it seemed, they saw a different body from the one everyone else did. Indeed, the major problem with steroids might simply be that for a great many men abuse is a fait accompli once they begin to use steroids: They never seem to get big enough to satisfy themselves, wanting to go that extra yard, taking more steroids at once, bigger doses, going on prolonged cycles, not giving their bodies enough time between cycles, and sometimes staying on steroids indefinitely. Bodybuilding advocates for steroids may say that short-term use of steroids can be safe if kept to specific dosages and cycled properly, and perhaps they are right. The study published in the *New England Journal of Medicine* in July 1996 even backs this up—though it notes that with "extended use" steroids have "potentially serious adverse effects on the cardiovascular system, prostate, lipid metabolism and insulin sensitivity." Some advocates however seem not to recognize that the problem for too many men, perhaps already predisposed to obsessive behavior, is that they find it difficult to stick to safer doses and cycling regimens. Even PoWeR's Nelson Vergel sees this problem with his HIV-infected clients who are susposed to be using steroids therapeutically. "I've seen it a lot," he says. " A lot of HIV-positive guys, they gain thirty pounds and they're terrified to get off of the steroids or they'll shrink. We tell them, 'No way. You have to give your body a rest.' But they're terrified to get off."

Some researchers studying steroid users have identified this condition as "reverse anorexia" — or, more accurately, "body dysmorphic disorder" — in which an individual looks in the mirror and sees an image of himself that is smaller, less muscular than is the reality. "I have seen [steroids users] gain a hundred pounds in fourteen months and still not be satisfied," observes Neil Carolan, formerly a director of chemical dependency programs at BryLin Hospital in Buffalo. Carolan has counseled over two hundred individuals who use steroids. Some users, he notes, may fall into a deep depression upon attempting to stop using steroids, which can lead them to turn to recreational drugs to feel better about themselves.

"These guys are out there with really distorted views of what they should look like," notes Dr. Arthur Blouin, a psychologist, director of the Ottawa Eating Disorder Clinic at Carleton University in Ottawa, Canada, and a lecturer at Columbia University in New York. Blouin specifically studies the similarities and connections between steroid abuse and eating disorders. "They are willing to risk the side effects of steroids," he says, "to avoid the negative perception that they are too small and weak."

Not only does it appear that many gay men who use steroids suffer from reverse anorexia, but gay men may also be more prone than straight men to suffer from eating disorders such as anorexia nervosa, an extreme obsession with being thin, and bulimia nervosa, a disorder associated with binge eating and purging. We've all read the accounts, seen the made-for-television movies, and heard the stories of women suffering from these disorders, women who became deathly ill or even died, losing all of their body fat and becoming stick figures. Psychologists have attributed the condition, which overwhelmingly affects women, in part to the intense pressure put on women in this culture to conform to a particular body ideal—exerted by the fashion industry and Hollywood—one that becomes slimmer and slimmer and is almost impossible for most women to achieve.

While there have been no studies specifically regarding eating disorders in the gay male community, some research indicates that gay men are adversely affected by anorexia and bulimia. Looking at a study of people with eating disorders done at New York Hospital–Cornell Medical Center in 1996, Dr. James B. Wirth, director of the Johns Hopkins Eating and Weight Disorders Program in Baltimore, notes that "the general impression is that more men are being treated for eating disorders," adding that other studies indicate that gay men, competitive wrestlers, and other groups may be among the men at comparatively high risk for these disorders.

"In a culture where 'no fats, no fems' is a personal prejudice condoned by the masses even in the most politically correct of times, to be an overweight male homosexual is, in many people's minds, to be the worst thing you can possibly be," wrote Frank DeCaro, who himself has battled a weight problem for most of his life, in the October 1995 issue of *Out*. "The fat gay guy, sadly, has become invisible as more idealized versions of gay men have become more visible."

THE ULTIMATE HIGH

And the fat guy will perhaps become even more invisible, for newer drugs for newer generations of gay men promise to further solidify the ideal body, offering users happiness in a vial: In 1996, a popular drug among many young men in their twenties was GHB—gamma hydroxybutyrate—a drug originally developed as an anesthetic but that turned out to have various other desirable qualities to some people. The drug was sold over-the-counter in the 1980s primarily to bodybuilders who say that GHB stimulates growth hormone, aids in fat metabolism, and builds muscle. Most bodybuilders took it before bed, as it apparently worked overnight and also induced sleep. But many young nightclub people in the 1980s found that if GHB was taken just prior to hitting the dance floor, it produced a euphoric, Ecstasy-like high. The FDA thus banned GHB in 1990, citing abuse.

GHB, sold in liquid form in a vial, has continued to thrive on the black market, and it is indeed the "perfect" drug for many gay men on the circuit today and is especially popular among younger gay men: Like Ecstasy, it lowers inhibitions. It is thought to stimulate growth hormone and build muscle. And it is also believed to be an aphrodisiac.

The major problem with GHB, however, according to the Libra Project, a British chemical-dependency counseling group, is that "the amount of GHB you need to take [in order] to feel the effects is very close to the amount needed for anesthesia, and this is very close to the amount that can cause seizures or coma." That is exactly what was happening in lots of places in the gay world in much of 1996, as young gay men were dropping like flies on dance floors across the country. In the San Francisco Bay Area, GHB-related emergency room admissions, according to the *New York Times*, "topped 100 [in 1996], up from 37 in 1995." The coma that GHB induces is more like a rapid sleep that makes a person totally incapacitated within minutes. Users generally wake up hours later, not remembering anything. Mixing GHB with alcohol, however, is far more dangerous and could cause respiratory collapse. At the Gay Men's Health Crisis's Morning Party in August 1996, a young man had to be revived in the first aid tent. He had stopped breathing, and one witness said doctors believed for a little while that they'd actually lost him. The man was airlifted off the island via helicopter and woke up the next day in a hospital, stunned. The incident was reported in all of New York's daily papers, fueling the controversy that had erupted shortly before the party regarding GMHC's sponsorship.

That same weekend on Fire Island there were two other GHB overdoses; one man passed out and fell off the deck of a house, crashing to the ground twenty feet below. Another young man lapsed into a coma while on the dance floor at the Pavilion, the nightclub in Fire Island Pines. Thinking he'd just had a bit too much to drink, some men carted him outside and laid him on the ground, where he stayed for hours until someone realized he had overdosed and needed help.

The other major problem with GHB is that, since it has been banned, a lot of it is now made in people's kitchens and then sold on the black market, so no one knows quite what they're getting: The recipe for homemade GHB involves using lactone—which is also used as a wood cleaner—and other toxic substances, which are put through an elaborate process of double boiling, mixing them together only when they reach precise temperatures. The pH must be measured at various times and must be just right. If it's not, you've made poison.

That's what happened to two Long Island, New York, men last August who made GHB in their kitchen, hoping to build up their muscles. Instead they were rushed to the hospital, having burned the insides of their mouths and organs.

The extremes that many will go to, it seems, to attain the ideal body, to achieve the greatest high, to elevate their self-worth, are boundless, as the cult of masculinity knows no limits.

But some men are beginning the process of deprogramming—joining others who never really got so caught up in the cult of masculinity in the first place. Deprogramming doesn't mean giving up parties, giving up beauty, giving up pleasure. Deprogramming simply means loosening the grip of the cult. To do that, many men are looking at how others are living their lives—on the outside.

PART TWO

LIFE

OUTSIDE

While the urban gay social and sexual scene, replete with its physical ideals and frenetic pace, mushroomed over the past several decades, gay life outside of it also grew at a rapid pace.

Over the years, within the urban centers, alternatives arose that in many ways have acted as a resistance to the scene. Not only have other sexual subcultures emerged that have been less rigid with regard to body type, but groups and clubs have formed around every conceivable interest and vocation. In San Francisco alone, for example, there are over two hundred gay groups focused on a vast array of activities, from gay kite fliers and gay mountaineers to gay artists and gay writers. It's true that there is some overlap, and that many gay men who are themselves caught within the overriding urban ghetto scene also cross over into its other racial, sexual, social, and vocational subcultures. But there are also a great many men within those subcultures who do not have a relationship to the scene, and in fact have often found themselves happily in opposition to it.

Gay youth groups, including high school and junior high groups, have formed in recent years in many cities also, perhaps challenging more and more young gay men to forgo joining the scene when they become of age and to become more politically aware. Similarly, groups for older gay men and for gay seniors have emerged, offering a place for many men who left the scene or who never participated in it.

For many gay men in the cities, religion has become a central part of life, as the Metropolitan Community Church and the many gay-positive Christian churches and Jewish synagogues have grown dramatically. Indeed, while some gay men in the cities over the years have found alternatives to the scene that are perhaps more bohemian, avant-garde and on the edge—such as in the diverse and eclectic art, theater, and literary communities in many cities—others have gravitated to alternatives that are more mainstream and traditional. Many gay men are settling into relationships and even raising children. And many are involved in the same-sex marriage movement, which in recent years—and particularly in 1996—rose to the forefront of the gay rights movement.

"I think there has been a great trend toward familialism among gay people from the 1970s through the 1990s," says Evan Wolfson, senior staff attorney at the Lambda Legal Defense and Education Fund in New York and a leader in the fight for same-sex marriage. He sees a great many gay men, in the cities and beyond, working within the marriage movement. "I think that in that way many gay men have been part of a larger trend in America toward domesticity and family."

All of these various alternatives outside the urban ghetto scene, as different as they are from one another, have represented the *deghettoization* of homosexuality in recent years. For many gay men, deghettoization has not necessarily meant leaving the gay ghetto or even leaving the urban areas. And it hasn't meant rejecting the ghetto's many positive attributes, including the sense of community and camaraderie that the ghetto offers. Rather, for many gay men deghettoization has often meant remaining in the thriving urban gay ghetto but breaking from the particular gay male urban lifestyle ruled by the cult of masculinity.

This phenomenon of expansion, which for years was still limited to life within the urban centers themselves, is now occurring outside the cities as well. Part II looks at a new trend, a sister trend to deghettoization that is emerging across the country, as many gay men are leaving the cities and moving out to suburban, small-town, and rural areas, or are growing up outside of the cities and are not moving to them at all: the *deurbanization* of homosexuality.

Together, deghettoization and deurbanization, compli-menting and empowering each other, are offering gay men even wider choices beyond the narrow options offered by the cult of masculinity. While this is occurring in an exhaustive variety of ways, for single men as well as for men in couples, This section focuses in particular on how these trends are influencing many gay men's choices in relationship styles both inside and outside the cities.

Part II also looks at how these trends are impacting the pro-cess of growing older in the gay world, in the cities as well as in suburban, small-town, and rural America, and how many men are once and for all putting to death the stereotype of the lonely old queen, perhaps offering a blueprint for all gay men to follow in the future.

5

THE DEURBANIZATION OF
HOMOSEXUALITY

"We have Christmas parties, with fifty to a hundred people, and ninety-eight percent of them are men, and, well, it doesn't seem to be an issue with the neighbors," Ken, a thirty-one-year-old gay man tells me, laughing. He's sitting next to his partner, Matt, also thirty-one, at the dining room table of their new home on a suburban block in Arlington, Virginia, outside of Washington, D.C. "We've not experienced anything negative. If anything, it's been a great experience. Our neighbors bring us cakes, and some other [gay male] friends of ours [who live nearby], who've been together twelve years or so, their neighbors bought them a patio furniture set. Out here, you've got neighbors lending you tools to work in your yard with, all sorts of nice things." Matt chimes in, noting that the two never really "came out" to neighbors, that folks just figured it out and let them know it was okay. "The next-door neighbors and I ran into one another at a movie theater once, and Ken was waiting outside for some friends to join us and they saw me in the lobby, and Laura [one of the neighbors] said, 'Where's your other half, Ken?'" he says. "It wasn't like, you know, *your other half*, with emphasis on that or anything. It was just very casual, just part of the conversation."

This kind of openness beyond the central neighborhoods of the urban centers is something new in America. "Historically, older gays and lesbians were very quiet in the suburbs," Jeffrey J. Vitale, president of Overlooked Opinions, a gay and lesbian market research firm, told the *New York Times* in May 1996. "What we're seeing [in the suburbs today] is the result of younger gays and lesbians who grew up proud about who they are. As they move to the suburbs they're taking that pride with them."

But the suburbs are not the only place where many gay people take that pride. In the small city of Bloomington, Illinois (population 55,000), for example, a meeting called by gay activists to start an advocacy group drew 150 people in November 1995; Bloomington, like many other towns its size, today also has a gay and lesbian bookstore and a gay nightclub, establishments that would have been unthinkable there just a few short years ago. The first generations of gay men and lesbians from small-town and rural America are not, en masse, moving to the urban meccas to settle. Yet a great many are living openly gay lives. Taking on some, but certainly not all, of the urban gay values system, they're redefining what it means to be gay.

SMALL-TOWN BOYS

"My dad worked in a meat-packing plant," thirty-three-year-old Jerry, an office temp, explains, describing his life growing up in Sioux City, Iowa, on the South Dakota–Iowa border. "Mom worked in a clerical office in the plant. They were not particularly religious, not conservative politically, in terms of being Republican. They were working-class Democrats."

When Jerry was twenty-two, home from college on Christmas break, he took out a book from the library, "something about homosexuality," he says. "My parents checked out my room, and one morning I got up and they were, like, 'We need to talk to you.'"

That winter of 1985 was when he reluctantly came out to them. "It was shocking, they were in denial," he says. "They were pretty much freaked out, they wanted me to go for psychiatric treatment. They were pretty confrontational at the beginning: My dad called me a *cocksucker*. I didn't want to talk about it. I wasn't ready to deal with it myself." Jerry decided he had to be on his own to sort things out, so he moved out and moved away from Sioux City.

Over the last ten years things have changed somewhat in Jerry's family, though they're not picture-perfect. "My mom's really accepting and very supportive and realizes what a mistake it was to feel that way," Jerry says. "She asks about my life, and boyfriends, and she does love me and accept it. My dad, we just don't talk about it. If I'm home in Sioux City I go out to the one gay bar, Three Cheers, and he just says stupid stuff to me."

Part of what helped Jerry grow and accept his sexual orientation was moving away, surrounding himself with other gay people, going to live in a place where he could be comfortable and be out. In the early 1970s, that place was likely to be far from home: San Francisco, New York, Chicago, Los Angeles, Washington, Boston, and a few other large, liberal urban centers where gay ghettos expanded dramatically shortly after Stonewall.

But Jerry moved to Iowa City: population 59,738 (1990 census) and declining. A six-hour drive across the state from the place he was born and raised, and where his family still lives, Iowa City is actually *smaller* than Sioux City in population (by 20,000 people) and is by far not the stereotypical place to which you'd expect a young gay man to migrate: It is a major retirement destination in a state with one of the largest populations over seventy-five years of age (7 percent). Sitting on the banks of the Iowa River in eastern Iowa, Iowa City is also the commercial center of an agricultural region dominated by cattle, grain, hogs, and poultry production. The town indeed prides itself on being a stone's throw from some of the country's most productive farmlands and cow pastures.

Iowa City has for much of this century also been a college town, home to Iowa's flagship state university, the University of Iowa at Iowa City, which includes a renowned writers' workshop, so it is somewhat more liberal than most of the state. Still, in the 1970s the idea of Gay Pride Day in Iowa City would have been unthinkable. Today however, as Jerry explains, Gay Pride Day tends to be a "progressive, together time" in Iowa City. "You kind of see a lot of integration [in the gay community] in Iowa City," he explains. "It depends on the time of year. During Gay Pride time in June, gay men and lesbians are more mixed. But really, in general, throughout most of the year there's a lot of mixing, you see people of different ages together. Cities of course can be much more segregated by sex, by age, by class. But in a town like Iowa City it all blends together. Because it's so small, it has to, in a way. People have to stick together."

It wasn't that Jerry hadn't tried living in a large urban ghetto; he in fact moved to San Francisco for a year in 1986, after previously having lived in Iowa City off and on (where he attended the University of Iowa). "I went to San Francisco because I had a really good friend who was out there and felt I needed to go, to do something different," he says.

But "something different," it turns out, was not necessarily what Jerry needed. "It just wasn't a place I wanted to put roots up," he says on his decision to move back to Iowa after less than a year. "California, in general, I don't know, it just wasn't for me. I'm just a naive midwestern kid," he says, laughing. "Just working and doing your thing, I felt you could not be yourself there. The gay community was okay, but the bars are different there than they are here [in Iowa City]. I didn't go out alone, wasn't up on the etiquette, not up on cruising. I went to the Metropolitan Community Church, for community, for the social groups and discussion groups. It was nice, but I was always meeting a lot of men older than I was. I wasn't meeting people my age; they were all going out to the bars."

Though it may seem the case, Jerry is not personally or politically conservative by gay standards: he's not, for example, so high on gay marriage, an idea embraced by many gay conservatives. "It's not that big of a deal to me," he says. "I'm not that worried about it. I can understand it as far as legalities, and financial aspects. But it would not make people more monogamous, no way. I think it's silly for anyone straight or gay to define it that way." He also takes pride in talking about his best friend in Iowa City, who used to be "into the raver thing," but now is "postrave," and who is a lot more sexually adventurous than Jerry is (something Jerry seems to envy in this friend). No, it's not that Jerry doesn't like the gay ghettos for any moralistic reasons. He simply likes small-town life.

Part of that, for Jerry, perhaps has to do with being the quintessential big fish in a little pond. Prior to moving to San Francisco, for example, Jerry was popular on the small-town gay night scene, working as a deejay at 620, an Iowa City gay dance club, one of the few gay bars in town. "But in San Francisco," he says, "I worked at a car rental agency, cleaning [apartments] on my days off. I was homesick for Iowa and the Midwest." Indeed there was a community, a family of friends, to go back to in Iowa City when San Francisco proved disappointing. "I had a boyfriend back here whom I missed, and a lot of friends," Jerry says. "We have a big circle of friends. In the summertime everyone is out on the pedestrian mall, strolling. I like it."

Chuck, a thirty-year-old gay man, also lives in Iowa City. He grew up in California, in Apple Valley, a small desert town in Southern California; like Jerry he also moved to the San Francisco Bay area; he lived there for several years, never quite feeling comfortable. When his boyfriend, a man he was in relationship with for a year, moved to Iowa City for work, Chuck eventually moved there too and enrolled in grad school. But when school—and his relationship—ended, he decided to stay.

"To go from San Francisco to Iowa City, it was a pretty big change," he says. "What's surprising is that [being gay] is not that big of a deal here. It's a bigger deal in San Francisco because everyone there makes it a big deal. No, it's weird, but I feel more comfortable here being gay and out, than in San Francisco." As Chuck describes it, San Francisco, for him, was somewhat polarizing precisely because there were gay ghettos and because people demarcated their territory, by both marking their spatial boundaries as well as their bodies. He says he felt a pressure to look a certain way, and to act a certain way. "There, it's so in everyone's face, it's all about the way you dress, how you look, and what neighborhood you live in. And sometimes that just sets up the differences and keeps people separate. It's crazy, but here in Iowa City it just seems like more of an acceptance and even an interest [on the part of straight people]. It's not ghettoized, it's more like here's everyone, straight and gay, living together. When I was in San Francisco, I thought to myself, I'll have to stay here for the rest of my life. I felt uncomfortable in the Castro, and I wouldn't want to live in the Castro. To me, in San Francisco, it's like you're known as either gay or straight. [Your sexual identity] is your priority and you have to choose one and [show] it. It's not that I don't love [San Francisco]. It's a great city, with a lot to offer that you don't have here. I plan to go back, actually. But I imagine I'll be more comfortable there now, having gotten out and experienced this midwestern thing."

Like Matt and Ken, who live in suburban Arlington, Jerry and Chuck represent a new phenomenon that appears to be taking root across America, evident in interviews and surveys of hundreds of gay men as well as in the research of demographers and sociologists: Many gay men who moved to the urban centers from small towns, suburbs, and rural areas are finding that big-city life is not appealing to them, and the gay ghettos are not the be-all and end-all of being gay. Some are moving back for good, others in what seems like a transitional phase. Unlike their counterparts of a generation ago, however, they increasingly don't feel pressured to stay in the cities and adapt to the urban gay ghetto if they want to lead a relatively safe, out life. These men's lives, and the way they are restructuring them, are indicative of one of several factors contributing to the deurbanization of homosexuality.

THE MARRIAGE CLOSET

Until relatively recently, perhaps no longer than the past ten years, if you were a homosexual living in a place like Sioux City, Iowa, for example—or in Iowa City, for that matter—you had for the most part three choices:

- Stay deeply closeted, perhaps marry a woman, and have sex on the sly with men at rest areas or in public rest rooms and other locales where men met for sex;

- Completely uproot yourself and move to the gay ghettos of the country's largest urban centers, the only places where you could safely live openly.

- Be one of a select few rebels who were brave enough to be out, risking your livelihood and physical well-being and safety, or lead a gay but circumspect quiet life, still punctuated by fear of physical violence and discrimination.

There have always been those who chose the last option. There have been gay and lesbian pioneers, some heroes to the cause, who lived their lives openly in rural and small-town America prior to the 1980s. Some have in fact been activists organizing in their community for decades. But their numbers were always small. There are many places in America, even today, where no one lives as an openly gay or lesbian person, places where it is still impossible to do so without physical or other danger.

There have also been many others in small-town and rural America who were not activists but who lived quiet lives. They did not broadcast their sexual orientation from the hilltops, but at the same time they did not mask themselves as heterosexuals in most aspects of their lives, and they made what they considered minor compromises.

"My parents are fundamentalist Christians," says Albert, who grew up in rural Boiling Springs, Pennsylvania, and now lives in a nearby rural town. "I told them twenty-five years ago, and my mother lamented about the Bible—and still does. But they're too important [for me to leave them]. I never thought of it any other way. Like most gay men, I idolize my mother. Why would I want her as a stranger in my life?" Albert and his lover, whom he's been with for almost twenty years, lived a quiet, partly closeted, partly out life throughout the 1970s and 1980s. Albert was out to some family and friends, but his lover was out to almost no one, and neither was out at work. They were also not out to neighbors, whom they was always afraid might suspect something. Their greatest concern was gay-bashing. But there were other concerns as well: Eventually, Albert was discriminated against at work when word of his sexuality got to his employers.

The kind of life Albert chose was decidedly not the one chosen by most gay men in rural and small-town America in decades past, who knew all too well about family rejection, gay-bashing, and discrimination and were aware about how such issue play out in a small-town environment. The choice made by perhaps the vast majority prior to gay liberation and even after its onset was in fact to remain deeply closeted, marry a woman, and have sex with men secretly, always living in fear of being found out.

"I initially got married in 1979, thinking it was the proper thing to do," says Stephen, a thirty-nine-year-old paramedic who was born in Kokomo, Indiana (1990 census population: 62,000), and lived in the smaller town of Martinsville before settling in even smaller Clarksville, where he lives today, openly gay and in a relationship. "I've felt I was gay since I was three years old. I was sexually active with two men when I was in high school. But that just wasn't an option in my mind, where I lived at that time, and in the 1970s. I married because of social pressures, parent pressures."

CLOSETS WITH BREATHING SPACE

For a great many gay men, however, neither of these options—living somewhat openly but quietly and in fear or marrying and remaining closeted—was acceptable. For these men the only choice was to move to a place both where homosexuality and difference were more tolerated, and that was far away from their hometowns, where family would not know much about their personal lives. Indeed, gay men over the past century migrated to the cities at various paces throughout the decades. The end of World War II, for example, saw a dramatic migration to the cities of both lesbians and gay men who had served in the war, individuals who, for the first time in many cases, met other gays in the service. Rather than go back to their small towns and rural areas where they were forced to live in the closet or risk their lives and livelihood, they moved to the burgeoning gay ghettos of the urban centers to be with people like themselves.

The migrations to the cities directly after Stonewall and the birth of modern gay liberation, however, perhaps saw the greatest influence on the urban gay ghettos. There was dramatic growth in the gay ghettos of America as gay men across the country in small-town and rural America moved in large numbers to the urban centers. The gay neighborhoods of New York, San Francisco, Chicago, Los Angeles, Dallas, Boston, Atlanta, Washington, and other cities burgeoned in the 1970s. The cities became havens for gays, where they could build their own communities, explore their sexuality, which had been denied them, and live relatively free from physical danger and discrimination. Gay men and lesbians began organizing politically in the early 1970s in many cities, making a presence in local party politics and getting laws passed that protected them from discrimination; they also pressured police and city officials to treat gay-bashing seriously. By 1989, for example, New York, San Francisco, Washington, Boston, and half a dozen other municipalities had laws protecting lesbians and gays against discrimination in housing and employment. And gays and lesbians became a visible group within the local media, politics, and culture.

But the cities, paradoxically, also provided another function for gay men: The gay ghettos were places where gay men could cordon themselves off, often remaining closeted to family and friends back home where they grew up. In a way, the ghettos, for those men who remained closeted to family, simply were closets with some breathing space, places they could find others like themselves who'd also escaped the small-town life and who were still closeted to friends and family back home. Many men who entered the gay subculture did not progress further in terms of coming out, in large part due to the comfort and distance of the gay ghettos.

"I didn't tell my mother until last year, a few months after my dad died," admits Ernie, a forty-six-year-old doctor who lives in Chicago and who grew up in rural Cairo, Illinois. "There was no need to, or at least that's what I kept telling myself. I always said that when it became necessary I would tell them, you know, when I got involved with someone. But none of my relationships have ever been that serious, at least not to the point of introducing them to my mother. Actually, I've been doing some soul-searching in therapy and I think one of the reasons my relationships never worked was the unconscious idea, in the back of my mind, that I'd have to come out to my parents if they got too serious. Living in Chicago, hours from home, had [kept my homosexuality] out of sight and out of mind. It made it very easy to be out in my profession and socially and, at the same time, to be totally closeted to family and others close to me. They didn't know any gay people back there, it was totally foreign to them up until very recently."

Indeed, gay life in suburban, small-town, and rural America stayed in the closet following Stonewall, untouched by gay liberation. That is, until the onslaught of the full-blown AIDS crisis unfolded across America in the mid-1980s. The fear that the AIDS crisis whipped up and instilled in millions of people, gay and straight, across America resulted in AIDS activism and its offshoot, "queer" activism, which dramatically spurred the visibility and further acceptance of homosexuality.

BACK TO WHERE I STARTED FROM

"Somewhere around 1985, I just made a decision," says Adrian, a forty-two-year-old nurse anesthetist who lives in Scappoose, Oregon. Adrian grew up in Beaverton, Oregon, a suburb of Portland, came out in the 1970s, and lived in Philadelphia, as well as Seattle and Portland. But in 1985, due to AIDS and his own personal fears (in spite of the advent of safer sex), he purposely slowed his sex life down dramatically and found that he not only did not miss what he endearingly calls the "debauchery" of previous years, but also saw less of a reason to live in the city. So he moved to Scappoose. "I bought some land, built a house, and my job demands quite a bit of time," he says. "I had to really focus on myself. I've learned to be reasonably comfortable being alone. I have a close circle of trustworthy friends. I think there's clearly an overemphasis on the whole sex scene in the gay world, and what I've done is simply filled my life. I sowed my oats back in the late 1960s and 1970s, and to be very frank I have very little sex. I dated one guy for six months, and we never slept with each other. In ten years, I've probably had sex three or four times. It's just taken the back burner. Now, at forty-two, having become self-taught in so many things, there are other things that are important to me. I've been involved in sports for a very long time, went to the Gay Games III and IV as a triathlete. I suppose [it's] very likely [I might meet someone at these activities]. But most of the single people I've met so far, they are interested in getting laid. I respect that, but that's not for me. Certainly, it's not the most important thing to me. If I meet Mr. Right, then I think it would become important. And I would like to meet someone, but the situation hasn't presented itself." Adrian and many other men his age who, in interviews and surveys, say they have taken a similar route, express their happiness with the way their lives have changed and how they have found meaning in new ways. It is clear, however, that AIDS is a factor that affected (and still affects) their social and sex lives and which spurred a change in both how and where they live.

For others, ironically, their moving back to rural and small-town areas wasn't so much due to the fear and often resulting sobriety that AIDS instilled. Often it had more to do with their being inspired by those gay activists who were in fact fighting such responses to the epidemic, responses the activists viewed as sex-negative and self-defeating. ACT UP and Queer Nation, with their proud, in-your-face, sex-positive message, captivated the media in the late 1980s and early 1990s, instilling a sense of pride in many gay men across the country. Pushed by the activists, gay and AIDS issues soon came to the forefront of American politics and culture; everywhere, it seemed, people were coming out of the closet and going public in the media. And that en masse coming out was having an effect nationwide, beyond the cities.

"I didn't like Washington, hadn't for years," says thirty-six-year-old Phil, who grew up in Wheeling, West Virginia, and moved to Washington, D.C., in 1983, only to move back to Wheeling in 1992, where he recently took a job as an auto mechanic. "But I felt stuck there, like there was nowhere else—except maybe New York, which for me was like going from the frying pan into the fire. I just don't like cities and feel out of sorts in them. But somewhere around 1990, *gay* was all over the place, *gay* this and *gay* that. The activists, ACT UP and those guys, were doing stuff. I didn't like a lot of it—it was things that got people angry and alienated people. But it made people talk. Then the military issue took center stage and then all of these other issues, lesbians having their children taken away, just heartbreaking things. You couldn't turn on the TV without seeing all of these very nice gay people talking to the country. I realized that people in Wheeling were seeing all of that too. And when I went back for the first time in two years, it really had changed a bit, more people were coming out, doing things, and a lot of straight people had changed—my family too. So I thought, all right, it's time to move back."

THE KIND OF LIFE MOM AND DAD HAD

Demographers are noting a subtle shift from the cities among gays and lesbians, particularly to the suburbs, where many adult gay men and lesbians grew up in the 1960s and 1970s. According to Overlooked Opinions, 32 percent of gays and lesbians now live in suburbs. The move to the suburbs seems to be as dramatic in the Midwest as it is anywhere else.

Jerry Kramer, a geographer at the University of Minnesota, studies the whole range of landscapes, from inner city to rural, in the upper Midwest. In Minneapolis, for example, he has been tracking a steady exodus from the city's gay ghettos of Loring Park and Powerhorn Park.

"Here in the twin cities, it's started with people moving to St. Louis Park and Edina, suburbs that are immediately adjacent to Minneapolis," he says. "People have also settled in Golden Valley. These are well-established suburbs; probably the housing dates from the 1920s." Just as gays did in neighborhoods within the inner cities, Kramer explains that gays and lesbians are tending to settle in places where the housing stock might be cheaper and where they can fix up old homes, places left behind by heterosexuals looking for newer housing stock. They are also settling in suburbs that have somewhat of a tradition of tolerance.

"These are suburbs that have a long history of being nontraditional," he points out. "St. Louis Park, for example, was the only place in Minnesota where Jews could safely live in the 1930s. Edina and Golden Valley are more upscale areas, and the people there generally are liberal.

"As gays get more statewide rights [as opposed to geographically narrow city ordinances], more gays and lesbians are moving out of the city into the inner-ring suburbs," Kramer notes. He and his colleagues noticed a significant change soon after 1991, when Minnesota passed a statewide gay rights law. "There was a big change when we got statewide rights," he says. "It was quite sudden. There's been a pretty large movement out of the city, at least that's my perception. I would say it's hard to tell how much of it is actually a movement out, and how much of it is gays and lesbians who were living in the suburbs before and [are] just coming out now because they feel more protected. It's probably a mix of both. And people are still moving to the cities. There's been a [gay and lesbian] housing boom in the past five to ten years in both the inner cities and in the suburbs. I would say that it's just a lot of movement. The borders no longer mean anything. People now have legal recourse. They have a lot of choices." He notes that as many gay men enter "new life stages," for example, entering into committed relationships and sometimes even having children, their priorities change and cities become less important. Many of the reasons they're moving in fact are similar to those of heterosexuals.

"Concern with safety is always a big one," Kramer says. "People are trying to have the kind of life their parents had. There are differences of course—they're not moving to the same suburbs, and their families are a bit different. But especially if they have children, safety is a factor."

The seemingly sudden trend among gay men to raise their own children—the Gayby Boom, as it has been called—does indeed seem to be, for some men, part of the reason to move to the suburbs. Tim Fisher, executive director of the Gay and Lesbian Parents' Coalition International, reports that there are over four million gay and lesbian parents in the United States, though a vast majority are parents from previous heterosexual relationships. And in many cases, the heterosexual parent has retained custody.

It's not known what percentage of gay parents who have custodial rights live in cities and what percentage live outside them. Fisher, who with his lover and two adopted children lives in the New Jersey suburb of Montclair, perceives that there has been a lot of movement in recent years to the suburbs by gay men settling down with children. "If you have a vision of family in your head, you often want to go to the suburbs—grass, trees, a backyard," he says. "You want to re-create your own family unit or do it better. It's not as hard as it was a while ago. Every week that goes by, more and more people talk about gay issues and it gets easier and easier. More and more, it's safer for gay parents and the children of gay parents in the suburbs. There's open space, lots of other kids on the block, and the schools are better."

Fisher says he knows gay couples in small cities and towns, suburbs, and rural areas from Alaska to Maine. "There's a lesbian moms group in Anchorage," he notes, "and a gay dads group in Colorado Springs. I know a gay male couple who have two transracial kids and who live up on the Canadian border of New York state, on a farm. One of them is the town doctor. They love the fact that their kids can get up and feed the cows."

LEATHER AND SHOPPING MALLS

Whether gay men are seeking to have children or not, there appears to be a subtle movement to the suburbs in many urban areas. Suburban areas surrounding San Francisco, San Diego, Chicago, Boston, and New York are seeing a rise in openly gay dwellers—and other former city residents—precisely because the cost of living and real estate prices in the city's center have forced many people out. Many gay men, for example, are forgoing the increasingly costly gay ghettos of Dupont Circle and Logan Circle in Washington, D.C., and heading to the surrounding suburbs of Maryland and Virginia. "We followed four other couples, friends of ours, who moved out of D.C.," says Andy, who with his lover, Chris, moved to Rockville, Maryland. Andy and Chris are young professionals, both African-Americans, both aged twenty-six, and have been together for two years. "No, it's not for reasons of having kids," Chris says, laughing. "I don't think we're ever going to do that. It's just that the city has gotten so expensive, and if you've got a car—anything with wheels—you can be in town in no time; this is all a pretty easy area in terms of traffic, more or less. And instead of being crammed in a town house we have a nice four-bedroom home. It still needs some work, but not any more than those old houses people are taking over in Logan Circle. We don't know any people in Rockville, but we've got friends in Bethesda, just close by, several couples, and we all meet one another at restaurants or visit one another's houses."

While some couples, like Andy and Chris, are moving to traditionally heterosexual bastions like Rockville, often being the only gay couple on their suburban block, other gay men, both couples and singles, are flocking to suburbs that are becoming dominated by gays and lesbians. In Royal Oak, Michigan, for example, a suburb of Detroit that over ten years ago was predominantly straight and Jewish, you will now find gay men and lesbians packing restaurants, suburban shopping malls, movie theaters, and supermarkets. In Royal Oak, there is a gay and lesbian bookstore, as well as plenty of gay bars and clubs. It is for all practical purposes a ghetto in the suburbs—except that a lot of straight families share the same space. "It's not like the gay ghettos in that the lifestyle is still suburban—*slow*, you know, the streets roll up at night," says Grant, a thirty-one-year-old store clerk. "And the families and their station wagons are all around you—but sometimes they're lesbian moms or gay dads." Many of the gay men in Royal Oak moved there from Palmer Park, which was already a kind of semisuburban ghetto of beautiful old homes (and which previously was inhabited by mostly middle-class, heterosexual Jews) on the outskirts of Detroit's city center. But Detroit underwent a massive exodus in the 1980s as the economy of the city collapsed. When you drive from the city's center on Woodward Avenue, which stretches 25 miles up to Pontiac, Michigan, you can see how the various urban neighborhoods and outlying suburbs have changed. Palmer Park, the former gay ghetto that was formerly a Jewish enclave, is now a predominantly middle-class heterosexual black area, settled by African-Americans who fled the city's now desolate center. And the more suburban Royal Oak is now mixed with gays and straights (though many of the heterosexuals moved farther out into the suburbs toward the north). The mix provides for an interesting, new kind of suburbia that will no doubt punctuate the twenty-first century, where shopping mall culture meets the leather lifestyle.

Jim Domanski, co-owner of Pronto's, a popular Royal Oak restaurant, in a statement that seemed to sum up much of the gay suburban experience, told *Out* magazine last year: "In my restaurant you can see guys in leather come in and sit down next to a family with three kids. And people are cool with that."

"I KNOW THIS TOWN"

The deurbanization of homosexuality seems to be influenced by several sociological trends, each of which is in turn influenced by the overall greater acceptance of homosexuality in America. There are those gay men like Jerry in Iowa City who move out of their hometowns (in his case, Sioux City), desiring to live away from parents and family. But they move to a town not too far away that is roughly the same size, rather than moving to the urban ghettos. There are also those gay men like Phil who are going back to the towns and rural areas they grew up in after having lived away for many years. He moved from Washington back to his hometown, Wheeling, West Virginia. And there are the many gay men settling into relationships and moving to the suburbs as well as to small-town and rural areas, perhaps desiring to raise children outside the urban environment, because the cost of living in the cities is too high or simply because they enjoy life outside the cities and now can take advantage of it.

But perhaps the greatest influence on the deurbanization of homosexuality is the many gay men of younger generations, those in their late teens and early twenties, who are coming out at such early ages to family and friends and not moving out of their hometowns at all. A great many of these gay men, in interviews and surveys, say they like the places they grew up in and want very much to live close to their families but out of the closet. And for the first time in history, it appears many of them can. Unlike their predecessors, they have at their disposal a record number of gay community centers, support groups, and high school and college gay groups encouraging them to come out at a young age and offering them places to turn to for support. There are now gay community centers in towns and cities as small as Scotts Bluff, Nebraska; Lubbock, Texas; and Cedar Rapids, Iowa. In many places, the institution that men increasingly turn to is the gay-founded Metropolitan Community Church (MCC), as there are now over two hundred MCC churches around the country. With a budget of $10 million, MCC is the largest nonprofit organization in the country serving the gay community; it is often *the* place that offers many gay men a sense of community in cities such as Augusta, Georgia; Biloxi, Mississippi; and Eureka Springs, Arkansas. Parents, Families and Friends of Lesbians and Gays (P-FLAG), often the first place a young person turns for guidance and counseling, now has over 425 chapters across the country, in urban, suburban, small-town and rural locales. And the Gay, Lesbian, and Straight Teachers Network, founded in 1990 as a support and advocacy group for teachers, students, and parents organizing in schools, has over sixty chapters in urban centers as well as smaller towns.

For gay men to come out of the closet at all at a young age, no matter where they lived, was extremely rare only ten years ago. And being out in high school and college while living in a small town, and having gay friends to turn to, was almost unheard of by most people. But that is quickly changing.

"When I was eighteen and I was a senior in high school, I had a good friend who was gay too," says John, a twenty-one-year-old college student who lives in the coal-mining town of New Castle, Pennsylvania (population 12,000), talking about the year 1992. "He's out now to his family too. We actually came out right about that time, a couple of years ago." John is actually somewhat embarrassed that he did not come out sooner. "I was denying it for a long time. I never wanted to say it, that I was 'gay.' But that's what I was feeling. Around my senior year in high school, I hung out with a couple of people in the Christian society. The Inner Varsity Christian Club. But the main motivation for hanging out with these people was this one guy, this friend who turned out to be gay, who I liked. Pretty ironic, huh?"

Soon enough John started meeting other gay people in New Castle, and unlike perhaps most gay men who move to the urban centers, he at first made more gay female friends than male. "Well, through the one guy who I saw in the Christian club, I met some of his friends, and they were out, and then just met more. I started hanging out with them in high school. I met a clique of gay people, mostly lesbians and a few gay men. They were out. They didn't switch pronouns [when they talked in public]. It felt good but it was also scary because they would talk openly."

Upon graduating, John enrolled in college in nearby

Clarion, Pennsylvania, where he lived on campus and made even more friends. "We had a whole gay family. A couple of them were from Virginia, most were from eastern Pennsylvania, rural and small-town areas. I would say that they were pretty much out. I told my family six months after [school started]. It wasn't as good as I wish it would have been. I came out to my mom on the phone. I was talking to her one Saturday night and she was just going on and on, and I was depressed at the time. She was just asking me why I was depressed. I told her I was in love with someone I couldn't have, a straight guy. She just kind of paused. It was very upsetting. I felt I had to keep explaining things and proving things. She was pretty much in denial about that and still is. Me and my mom have always been pretty close. I've always been able to tell her anything. I really felt like I wanted some support and some comforting words. I was leading a double life, and it was not comfortable for me. But she was not as understanding as I had hoped. I told my brother [about my being gay]. He was cool with it for a while. But then he told me I'm ruining the family. My dad? I think my dad knows. I haven't officially told him. But I plan to. My father is really hard to read. I'm close to my father, but he's not just cut-and-dried. He can be liberal and he can be conservative, so I don't know how it would fly. I know he wouldn't disown me. I guess the immediate thing I'm afraid of is the anger. My mother told me not to tell him, but I plan to. And I think they're all going to get it in time. They have to understand that I need to be out to everyone, and I will be."

During the college break last summer, John lived in Clarion with his friends rather than live at home. "We had a really large family of so many different people, people of different ages who lived or worked in the school, or worked at the glass factory," he says. "Nothing ever takes place in Clarion.

We go to Indiana [a small town in Pennsylvania], which [has] a bigger school, and there are more people there, and a lot more out people. People go to these parties and they meet people in town, a lot of gay people who've lived in the area a long time. And one of the professors is gay."

John's two best friends are a lesbian and a gay man, both his age, though they have friends of various ages. Sometimes they all pile in a car and go to Pittsburgh, an hour and a half away, the nearest big city. "There are some discotheques there, and we go and hit on people," he says, laughing. But John has no interest in living in Pittsburgh, or even in Indiana or Clarion, for that matter. Even with all of the problems he's having at the moment with his parents, he's confident that it will all work out. And he'd like to settle down in New Castle—maybe even right down the block.

He sounds much like William, a twenty-two-year-old college student who lives in Abilene, Texas: "I feel like I've come this far, come out to my family, dealt with their emotional upset, and gotten past it. And I have a few friends who are gay. I'd like to now see if I can just live in this community and lead a life that doesn't have to be so different from my family's even though I'm gay." Or Alex, who is twenty years old, currently unemployed, and lives thirty miles outside Carson City, Nevada. "I didn't get the education that I think is probably necessary to move to a big city and get a high-paying job," he says. "I know this town, and I know people here, and there are people who will help me out—family, friends, and neighbors. And the fact that I'm gay would have mattered a lot before, but it just doesn't now as much. If they're willing to accept me, then I'm willing to accept them—and take their help rather than move somewhere where I don't know what might happen. I may leave here someday, but the truth is, I really like it here."

Ryan, a twenty-two-year-old Eugene, Oregon, student says he likes visiting Portland once in a while and really enjoyed San Francisco when he visited, but things are "cool enough" in Eugene for him.

"I'm involved in a gay and lesbian youth group, and a campus group," he says. "I'm vice president of a gay fraternity. Over the summer I'm going to facilitate a discussion group made up of young gay and bisexual men. I feel totally comfortable in Eugene. Yeah, Eugene is totally cool. We have a feminist bookstore, a lot of gay people. It's totally cool. In another time I think I would have moved, but I know I wouldn't have liked that. I visited San Francisco, and boys were approaching wanting to do coke. I was in a club, and I was, like, floored when I was standing there and when this guy came up and said, 'Come in the bathroom and snort.' It was great to visit, a neat feeling to go to the Castro, but I think it would get old really fast. I would want to leave. I suppose I could see myself getting wound up in that scene very easily if I stayed. I could see myself going out and just over time acclimating to what the standard is there, so I'm glad I don't have to."

In discussing the pressure in much of the urban gay world to look like the pumped-up physical ideals, Ryan notes, "There's a lot of pretty, pumped-up boys, especially in Portland [75 miles to the north]. But it's not the dominant thing," he says. "It's not like in San Francisco, where you see all these fliers with beautiful men and stuff. That's just not as visible here. Definitely not. And where I'm at, in Eugene, people are just laid-back and it's 'be who you are.' It's not artificial. I work out at the gym, but it's a personal thing for me. Most of my friends actually don't. I don't want to be a cookie-cutter gay boy, and that's not why I work out. I just want to stay in shape. And I feel confident that I have a nice body."

REWRITING THE STORYBOOK

Of course, the same ills that plague people in cities often plague those outside of them. Drug and alcohol abuse are prevalent in suburbs, small towns, and rural America, including among gay men, and it would be foolish to believe otherwise. AIDS has also reached far beyond the urban centers in America, and one study conducted by Medical College of Wisconsin in the early 1990s found that as much as 31 percent of gay men outside of big cities reported that they had recently engaged in unprotected anal sex. Statewide antigay ballot initiatives as well as campaigns to institute local antigay ordinances have also raged in small towns and in rural areas in recent years. While for a great many gay men and lesbians these right-wing campaigns have energized them and brought them out, for others the hateful atmosphere has done the opposite, driving them deeper into the closet.

The deurbanization of homosexuality is of course still very uneven, not occurring in every nook and cranny of America at the same pace, and in some places seemingly not all. Many men I interviewed and surveyed, for example, told horror stories about where they lived and the amount of homophobia and antigay violence they have endured, and they expressed their desires to leave such places as soon as possible, although more often than not they wanted to move to another town or a small city nearby rather than the traditional urban gay meccas. Much of this depends on individuals' personalities: What some gay men might see as an unlivable situation, others might see as perfectly reasonable.

Still, what appears to be an overwhelming number of gay men seem to desire staying in the relatively small cities and towns they grew up in, living openly and honestly. This perhaps portends a shift that will continue well into the next century. The deurbanization of homosexuality has perhaps only just begun. And many of these men express needs and desires in life that are just as simple and traditional as the heterosexual people they grew up with: In interviews and surveys, many of these men said their main priority was to meet someone, fall in love, and settle down.

"I would love to be able to, right now, bring home somebody, a guy I was kind of chasing after for a year, who just last night gave me his ring," John, the New Castle, Pennsylvania, student says, of a relationship that began in the spring of 1996. "It's naive, maybe, and I know nothing is really storybook, but that's what I'd really like to do, if I could have my perfect scenario."

Actually, John and many others *are*, slowly but surely, having their perfect scenario—directly as a result of the gay rights movement that began in the cities and burgeoned because of the concentration of gay people in the gay ghettos. The nearly thirty years since Stonewall has seen the gay movement reach goals it might have thought unattainable, and indeed might not have ever imagined: As gay men in small-town, rural, and suburban America are now coming out, rather than take on the lifestyle of the gay ghettos, many are staying in their hometowns and keeping their small-town values while living their lives out of the closet. While the urban gay ghettos are in no danger of dying out—as many gay men are choosing to live a quieter life in small towns, a great many are still flocking to the ghettos and expanding them further—gay men in suburban, small-town, and rural America are now offering yet another alternative to the gay urban circuit scene, in addition to the many alternatives that had arisen inside the cities themselves.

It was the political and cultural power of the urban gay

ghettos that in time made life outside the cities better for gay men. Now, those gay men will perhaps offer back to the gay ghetto new ways to cope with issues that have vexed gay men for decades.

One area, in fact, where the deurbanization of homosexuality, accompanied by its sister trend within the cities, the deghettoization of homosexuality, now offers gay men a new way is in that of love and relationships.

6

POSTMODERN MONOGAMY

"We have friends who have, you know, different arrangements," Ken says. "But we're, well, monogamous." Matt, Ken's
partner, adds, "It's interesting though that, almost across the
board, the people we know who are also in monogamous relationships say there's no way any other way could work for
them. They're convinced that other arrangements, for them,
would be doomed to failure or would be unfulfilling in the
end."

Both now thirty-one years old, Ken and Matt met seven
years ago on the beach at Rehoboth, Delaware, a popular
beach resort for gay men from the Washington, D.C., area.
Matt was living in a town house in Alexandria, Virginia, and
Ken was living in Washington, D.C., in Dupont Circle.
They'd both been out for a few years and dated a bit, did the
bar and club scene, and had lots of friends. After meeting, they
dated casually for six months or so, gradually became more
serious, and moved in together after a year.

"Even when we were still just dating, I wasn't convinced I
was ready," Matt says. "But then once we decided, it did happen pretty fast. I was moving out of my town house in
Alexandria and needed to find a place to live and I said, 'Why
don't we just move in together as roommates?' Ken said, 'No,

if we move in we're going to be lovers.' And I took that to heart and realized, This is going to be a big step. And I thought about it and was prepared for it."

"We didn't do it just because it was convenient," Ken adds. "I actually talked to a lot of couples who'd been together a long time and asked them what it was like to move in together. I wanted to be sure."

Ken and Matt first lived together in Alexandria, in a town house; even there, though it was quiet, they had "a whole gay house" around the corner, as Alexandria is perhaps the most liberal place in Virginia and is home to many gay people. But when they moved to Arlington, to a quiet, woodsy street of big trees and old brick homes, they became the only gay people in the area they knew of.

"This was a big move," says Matt. "We were removing ourselves [from a gay environment], moving into the suburbs." Ken nods in agreement, noting what he sees as perhaps a mark of the seriousness of what they did: "What we did was, we bought a piece of land together." Their plot of land is small, encompassing the typical-size driveway and yard to be found in the suburbs. The house is a quaint, small, three-bedroom brick cottage, dating back to the 1930s; it needs a lot of work, and slowly but surely, they're fixing it up.

Soon after Matt and Ken moved, several of their friends, also couples, made the move into the suburbs too, settling in areas within a short drive from them. "We've all bought in areas we wanted to live in, that we each thought were perfect for us," says Ken. Along with the other couples Matt and Ken seem for now to be doing a juggling act between the life in the suburbs, which for them is mostly about socializing with gay couples, and life back in the gay ghetto in Washington, which they see as focused on gay singles. They still go out with single friends to bars in the city once in a while—it's ten to fifteen minutes away by car, a hop over the Potomac—but they also spend a lot of time in the suburbs with their coupled friends, visiting one another's homes. It's not that they don't want to spend more time with friends in town, they say, but they see—at least in their lives, if not in general—a kind of disconnectedness in the urban gay ghetto between singles and couples.

"I think there is a kind of a support for couples, but it's more on a personal level, like on a friendship level, not one that's more visible within the gay culture," Ken notes. "What you do see is mostly single people having fun. In general, in [the larger] society, you can't really see [gay] couples in the way you see straight couples because society doesn't allow you to be holding hands and stuff a lot. You see gay couples in stores or something and you kind of figure each other out, but it's not visible. And what is most visible in the gay world itself is what's most commercialized, the circuit events, the clubs. It's more sexual and single-oriented than about relationships."

"There are more institutions or structures available for couples in the straight world," Matt says. "The gay community is very much structured for a singles environment: The attitude is, 'Oh, couples are welcome if you guys *really* feel comfortable going to a bar, even though it is very singles-oriented.' But it's never the other way around, where it's a couples-oriented thing, and the singles are the ones trying to fit in." For that reason, perhaps, Matt and Ken find themselves gradually spending more and more time in Arlington and the suburbs and less time in the city, even if it means having single friends come visit them rather than meet them in bars in town. That is not to say, of course, that there aren't plenty of gay couples in the city, or that gay life in the city is not fulfilling for couples. Rather, in Matt and Ken's case, their coupled friends happen to be leaving the city, and it appears it is mostly their single friends who remain.

On the surface, Matt and Ken perhaps defy most gay men's view of gay couples, or at least the more traditional (for lack of a better word) view of gay couples that the urban ghettos have promulgated: Most of us (particularly of the age groups over thirty-five), weaned on the books, articles, images, and culture of the urban gay world, perhaps don't think of two gay men in their mid-twenties who settle into a long-term (more than a couple of years) relationship and move to the suburbs as the slightest bit *typical* of gay men. And we might even think it impossible for a gay couple in their thirties, who are together for seven years and counting, to remain intent on being sexually monogamous.

Matt and Ken in fact answer questions about monogamy in a way that many gay men in surveys and interviews who said they were in sexually monogamous relationships for more than two years responded: half-apologizing for not being in a *non*monogamous relationship, and being careful not to stigmatize others. They're neither moralistic, nor condescending. Quite simply, an open relationship wouldn't work for them. These men tend to be of younger generations, but they include many men of older generations as well. They represent a growing trend both inside and outside the cities. For several reasons, however, it appears that men outside the cities find it easier to be sexually monogamous, and thus this trend might be greater outside the urban centers. These men outside the urban centers may in turn be serving as examples for others, perhaps influencing still more men in the cities.

Defying everything both the straight and gay worlds have said about gay men and their relationships, many of these men seem to stay true to their intentions of sexual monogamy, perhaps many more than we might believe. Of course, gay men striving to be monogamous—just as lesbians, heterosexuals, and others trying to do the same—may find themselves or their lovers "cheating," and in those cases they either break up or vow, often successfully, not to allow the situation to arise again. Others may be having sex on the outside covertly without their partner ever finding out, but these men say that such instances are few and far between; those who have done so more often generally report having been found out and facing the consequences.

Another trend, one toward near but not complete sexual exclusivity, also seems evident among many gay men today inside and outside the cities. These men have an understanding between them that they will be emotionally monogamous but will allow for a once-in-a-blue-moon outside sexual encounter—or rather understand that it may happen—and have decided that there is no reason to discuss it and thus dredge up jealousies. These men accept that either they or their partner might have sex outside the relationship, perhaps while on a business trip or while the other is away from home, but that, unless such outside sex becomes too frequent, it is not a problem, and that acknowledging and discussing these activities might do more harm than good. Understanding and accepting the realities of jealousy and resentment, these men desire, as therapist Rosemary Caggiano calls it, "the illusion of monogamy," something she and other therapists believe is, for these men, healthy and comfortable.

While these might seem to be two distinct relationship agreements—one to be sexually monogamous, the other *technically* not—what they together represent is a trend to reject what has over the years come to be defined as the 1970s-inspired gay "open relationship." Though there are in actuality different kinds of open relationships—a spectrum, perhaps, from the most open to the least open—the term "open relationship" has for a great many gay men come to have one specific definition, one associated with the most open end of the spectrum: A relationship in which the partners have sex on the outside often, put away their resentment and jealousy, and discuss their outside sex with each other, or share sex partners.

Certainly, the men described above who allow for sex outside the relationship on occasion are in a form of an open relationship, even though it lies at the less open end of the spectrum. And yet, perhaps because of what the terms "monogamy" and "open relationship" have both come to represent, these men do not classify themselves as being in open relationships. Critics might have a point when they suggest that these men, in using the term "monogamy" to describe their relationships, have been influenced by the conservative tenor of the times. But it appears the reason is more so that for these men the term "monogamy" simply doesn't necessarily mean sexual exclusivity as much as it means bonding, commitment, and closeness. And that the term "open relationship," as it has come to be defined, simply does not describe their relationship.

I have placed both of these trends in relationship styles—an agreement for sexually exclusivity (or an agreement to strive for sexual exclusivity) and an agreement to accept sexual nonexclusiveness on occasion but to agree to keep it unacknowledged—under the umbrella term of "postmodern monogamy." It might be said that I could just as well have termed the latter relationship style, which is, after all, technically a form of an open relationship, as a "postmodern open relationship." But because these men do not define their relationships as open, I'm letting them use the term they wish to use, based on the constantly shifting definitions of these terms.

BUCKING CONVENTIONAL WISDOM

In the six hundred responses to informal surveys I'd posted in various places on the Internet, a strikingly large number of gay male respondents said they were in long-term relationships, and a large number of those said their relationships were sexually monogamous for over a period of more than two years. Equally striking was the number of similar responses I'd received from several hundred interviews I conducted in my travels over a two-year period through cities, small towns, and suburbs, and in telephone interviews with men who'd written me letters or sent me E-mail responding to various topics on which I'd written.

These surveys and interviews were not done scientifically; still, the fact that just under half (48 percent) of these men reported being in a committed relationship for more than a year was in line with some polls of gay voters, for example, done by professional pollsters. These polls, however, included lesbians as well as gay men. The results of the *Advocate*'s sex survey of gay men, again not a random sample, but with a sample perhaps large enough (over thirteen thousand) to draw some basic conclusions, also reported similar high percentages of gay men in long-term relationships. Seventy-one percent of those surveyed by the *Advocate* said they preferred long-term monogamous relationships to other arrangements. Of those men who reported they were in a relationship, 77 percent reported that it has lasted more than a year, and 26 percent reported the relationship has lasted more than ten.

Fifty-two percent in the *Advocate* survey reported that in "either their current or last relationship" they "are or were monogamous as far as they know." Another 28 percent are "supposed to be monogamous" but one or both partners has had sex outside the relationship. Of those men in my surveys who reported that they were in relationships for more than two years, 59 percent said these relationships were sexually monogamous. If you expand this group to include those men who reported they were in monogamous relationships of less than two years and those men who were not in relationships but said they had a desire for a monogamous relationship, the figure jumps to 84 percent of the total of more than six hundred surveyed. Even accounting for the facts that some men might simply lie, that the sample was too small and not demographically drawn, and that there are other built-in problems with informal surveys, these percentages are large enough to take note of and to challenge some of our basic assumptions about gay men and relationships. In tabulating the survey responses, for example, I had expected to find that, as the conventional wisdom of the urban gay ghetto had told me, the vast majority of gay men in relationships, even if they started out sexually monogamous, within a year or so either opened up their relationships or had much more circumspect sexual activity outside the relationship.

That conventional wisdom is of course in part a product of our own experiences with the urban scene: Many of us in the urban gay world, looking to ourselves as well as friends and acquaintances, see many gay male relationships starting out with heated passion and sexual exclusivity and often breaking up within a matter of months. We may even view the vast majority of those that last longer as perhaps in the classic open relationship. There is an overriding belief among us that this is simply the gay condition. We have come to expect and accept that this is the "lifestyle" of gay men, something inevitable—perhaps even *natural*. The deurbanization of homosexuality—as well as the deghettoization of many men inside the cities—demonstrates that such a "lifestyle," though established in the urban ghettos, is not necessarily inevitable whether or not it is *natural* for men, an idea that is the subject of much debate these days. After all, we do many things that conflict with our natural instincts in order to maintain our lives and live with one another.

The non-monogamous lifestyle was, in fact, carefully if often unconsciously constructed shortly after Stonewall in response to political and social realties. And it has come to define what many gay men in the urban centers perhaps expect of one another and what they promote to one another. Until recently, that is, as a new choice has begun to emerge, influenced by men outside the cities as well as the many men in the cities looking beyond the ghetto mentality.

THE "MEN ARE PIGS" MYTH

In books, films, plays, magazines, and the media of the urban gay culture of the 1970s, sexual monogamy was not only frowned on from a political perspective, but it was also seen as behaviorally impossible. In the absence of women, men were seen as being sexually unstoppable. Gay culture as well as gay politics was about sexual liberation as an antidote to combat sexual repression. Sexual monogamy, even if it might have been a choice that some or many men might desire, simply did not fit into the equation.

"Gay romance was condemned as nothing but an imitation of straight marriage," Ian Young recalls of the 1970s urban ghetto ideology in *The Stonewall Experiment*. He quotes the influential Toronto-based gay liberationist newspaper, the *Body Politic*. "Having a lover—or wanting one—had nothing to do with the heart's desire; you were merely 'identifying with oppressors' . . .

'a sell-out to the straight establishment' . . . 'embarrassingly unliberated.'"

Thus, the very essence of being gay, what defined *gay*, was wrapped up in sexual adventurism at the time. Those men who did couple, more often than not, did it the "liberated" way—the "open relationship." Otherwise they might feel "embarrassed," thought of as somehow less than gay. The gay commercial sexual culture was exploding and beckoning gay men everywhere in the new and open ghettos. Indeed, the sexual culture became the very center of gay life. Not partaking of it took an enormous amount of willpower. Not partaking of it meant rejecting the newfound freedom of openly gay life. It became understood among gay men that they simply would not and could not be monogamous. Promiscuity became a kind of inside joke as well as a source of pride among gay men when they gathered in their favorite spots in the ghetto. Proudly, we accepted the "men are pigs" description. This belief took hold and continued well into the 1980s, even with the onset of AIDS. Although gay men slowed down their sexual activity momentarily, until the safer sex message put out by AIDS organizations and the sex-positive missives of direct action groups like ACT UP and Queer Nation got out, the prevailing disdainful attitude about monogamy continued. If anything, it solidified into more of an ideology and an orthodoxy with the onset of AIDS activism, as activists—rightly—felt that gay sexual liberation was fiercely under attack and that they had to fight back by promoting safer sexual freedom.

That ideology still exists today throughout much of the urban gay world. Even if monogamy is not so looked down upon in many urban circles, particularly among some younger men coming into the urban centers, as well as among some older men who have found alternatives to the urban scene, and even if it is seen by some as something even desirable, sexual monogamy among a great many gay men in the urban centers is still viewed as utopian and unrealistic. This belief has been validated over the years by the work of experts in the gay world itself, from social scientists to self-help gurus, further solidifying this ideology and helping to perpetuate a self-fulfilling prophecy that gay men are incapable of any relationship style but the classic open one.

THE BIBLE OF THE OPEN RELATIONSHIP

It was in 1984 that David P. McWhirter, M.D., and Andrew M. Mattison, M.S.W., Ph.D., produced *The Male Couple: How Relationships Develop*, which was considered a landmark study and was published in book form by Prentice-Hall. In the several years prior to publication, the two had been traveling the country lecturing about their findings. Some of their conclusions had been printed in the *Advocate* in 1980 and in the *Journal of Homosexuality* in 1981 and 1982. The highly respected researchers were both board-certified sexologists with the Clinical Institute for Human Relationships in San Diego. (McWhirter is also a psychiatrist, and Mattison holds a Ph.D. in psychology, and both had been treating men in clinical private practice.) They did ground-breaking work, studying 156 gay male couples over a five-year period. The fact that they themselves were gay men in a long-term relationship was seen at the time as a positive break from the usual kind of scientific study of gay men, where straight and often homophobic researchers might bias their results.

Perhaps the greatest contribution McWhirter and Mattison brought to the understanding of gay male coupling was the idea of breaking down long-term male relationships into six stages: Blending (first year); Nesting (second and third year); Maintaining (fourth and fifth year); Building (years six through year ten); Releasing (year eleven through year twenty); and Renewing (beyond twenty years). Whether they agreed or disagreed with other findings of *The Male Couple*, therapists in private practice, as well as writers on the subject of gay coupling, found the usage of stage theory, as it is known, and particularly the specific stages that *The Male Couple* outlined, to be immensely valuable and useful in discussing gay relationships.

Among the many other findings that McWhirter and Mattison considered significant in their study was their conclusion that "many of the practices that are cornerstones of heterosexual relationships are absent in male couples." One of these was sexual monogamy:

> Indeed, it was startling to find that some of the qualities identified with stability and intimacy between opposite sex partners can be detrimental to homosexual relationships. As an example, although most gay couples begin their relationships with implicit or explicit commitment to sexual exclusivity, only seven couples in this study considered themselves to have been sexually monogamous throughout the years of their relationship. Sexual exclusivity is not an ongoing expectation among most male couples. In fact, some couples report that outside sexual contacts have contributed to the stability and longevity of their relationships.

In other words, the researchers were saying—or could be interpreted as saying—gay male relationships work *better* if they are sexually open. In another part of the book, the researchers clarify their findings regarding the seven supposedly monogamous couples even further, concluding that in actuality *none* of the couples were monogamous in the long term:

> Only seven couples [of the 156 studied] have a totally exclusive sexual relationship, and these men have been together for less than five years. Stated in another way, all couples with a relationship lasting more than five years have incorporated some provision for outside sexual activity in their relationship. . . . Because gay men are automatically placed outside mainstream values anyway, some find it easier to explore nontraditional sexual patterns.

There were other highly respected researchers, such as sociologists Pepper Schwartz and Phillip Blumstein, authors of the influential *American Couples: Money, Work and Sex* (their study began in the 1970s and was published in 1983), who showed that some—albeit a "minority"—of gay male couples were intent on being monogamous, and they noted the difficulties the men had living within a gay culture that "encourages sexual variety." Bell and Weinberg even showed in their study, published in 1978, that some gay men were in "close-coupled" relationships and were quite content with their arrangement. Over the years some lesbian and gay psychotherapists and journalists too, drawing conclusions from clinical practices or interviews with a cross section of men, have written about gay male couples in sexually monogamous, long-term relationships and certainly have discussed gay men as being capable of such relationships; psychotherapist Betty Berzon, author of the 1988 book *Permanent Partners*, is an obvious example, as is journalist Eric Marcus, author of the 1992 book *The Male Couples' Guide*.

But the McWhirter and Mattison study has, over the years, been held up and pointed to in much of the urban gay world. It's often been put forth as some kind of definitive proof that gay men in couples are and always will be nonmonogamous. Perhaps that is not such a coincidence because their findings neatly fit into—and further bolstered—the prevailing political and cultural ideology within the gay world at the time about gay coupling and sexual exclusivity. Soon after *The Male Couple* was published, the research was drawn upon—and continues to be drawn upon—by countless gay psychotherapists, gay couples' counselors, gay doctors, gay journalists, HIV-prevention groups, gay activists, and even politicians. All use it as evidence that gay men do not desire or expect—and are, for all practical purposes, incapable of—sexually monogamous relationships.

That is not to mention the influence the research has had on perhaps the hundreds of thousands of men who have either read *The Male Couple* over the years or had the information (and the ideology it has been used to bolster) filtered down to them by counselors and friends who have read it. Even thirteen years after *The Male Couple* was first published, its influence is still apparent.

At the White Party in Palm Springs over Easter weekend, for example, Joe and Pete, a young couple (both in their midtwenties) from San Francisco newly on the circuit, tell me that they went through a rough patch six months earlier, and they explain to me how *The Male Couple* influenced them. They were previously sexually monogamous, in a relationship that had just reached the two-year mark. But they were both getting "antsy," Joe says, and began arguing a lot more, until it became almost unbearable. "We were getting sick of each other," is how Pete puts it, giggling. A friend gave them *The*

Male Couple and told them to read it. "We read *The Male Couple*, and it, like, opened up a whole new world for us," Joe tells me while we casually chat, sitting on a couch in the hotel room he's staying in. "We saw that it wasn't right, what we were doing, it was kind of unnatural. It was like, gay men have a whole different thing. We can really have intimate relationships and still, you know, do all of this." He laughs heartily, gesturing with his hands. "All of this is good for a relationship."

What Joe meant by "all of this" was, presumably, spending the weekend in Palm Springs, sleeping in a room with a man the two had met a couple of days earlier in San Francisco, and whom they've both been having sex with all weekend (as well as with many of the man's friends), and whom they're snorting coke with at the moment.

COPING PATTERNS

Of course, *The Male Couple* does not encourage or promote the circuit, drugs, or even necessarily sex outside of relationships. But *The Male Couple* has certainly led readers to believe that the "norm" for gay men is an "open" relationship, and that monogamy not only is unachievable but that it might just be the source of a problem in the relationship.

"As much as I respect what David McWhirter and Andrew Mattison did write in *The Male Couple*—and they are truly pioneers—I wonder, since they are in a long-term, *open* relationship, and the fact that out of all the couples they interviewed—156 couples—*none* were monogamous [over the long term], isn't there the possibility of some self-selection going on?" asks a skeptical Michael Shernoff, a New York psychotherapist whose clients are almost exclusively gay men, regarding how the men for the study were selected. Shernoff himself published a paper in the *Journal of Gay and Lesbian Social Services* in 1995, entitled, "Male Couples and Their Relationship Styles," which focused in part on the fact that many gay men are in sexually monogamous relationships, among several other relationship styles.

With regard to his own relationship, Andrew Mattison, still in private practice in San Diego and celebrating his twenty-fifth anniversary with David McWhirter in 1996, tells me that the two were "not in an open relationship" when they did the study, but then adds, "we *have* publicly discussed that each of us were [at the time] having a relationship with a person [outside the relationship] who we were very emotionally bonded with."

"Were those relationships sexual ones?" I ask.

"Well, yes," he responds.

"So, doesn't that mean that your relationship [with McWhirter] was open?"

"Well," Mattison replies. "I guess I think of an open relationship as one where you have a series of various partners, at will."

McWhirter and Mattison readily admitted in their book that they used what is known as the friendship network method to obtain research subjects, a valid and respected method, not uncommon in scientific research. But it's clear that in this case using such a method—rather than, for example, randomly reaching out to couples by placing newspaper ads—might bias the sample, since friends tend to have similar philosophical beliefs. The study subjects might recommend other study subjects they met through sexual liaisons, men whom they had sex with and who had sex with other men who then became study subjects, ensuring further that the couples were nonmonogamous.

The two greatest problems with *The Male Couple* that seriously call into question applying the findings regarding monogamy to gay men today have to do with time and place: Though the book was published in 1984, the study began in the mid-1970s, and the last interviews were done in late 1979. Perhaps even more significant is the simple fact that all 156 couples lived in one city: San Diego, which, at the time, already had more than forty bars, as well as gay restaurants, bathhouses, gyms, and other establishments. In other words, it was an urban gay ghetto.

What McWhirter and Mattison were actually charting then were the coupling patterns of gay men in an American urban ghetto at the height of the post-Stonewall, pre-AIDS sexual revolution—patterns that could not possibly have been the same outside the cities, patterns that would change dramatically in the cities themselves by 1984 (when their book was published) simply because of the impact of a cataclysmic epidemic that no one could have imagined at the time the study was conducted.

To their credit, McWhirter and Mattison warned against using *The Male Couple* to generalize about gay male couples. "We clearly recognize the risks of having our findings etched in stone as *the* way male couples should and must be, setting new standards, as it were, against which others will measure themselves." Perhaps foreseeing sociological phenomena like the deurbanization of homosexuality, they noted that "we anticipate the development of a still young gay culture to influence male couples in the future." The researchers took note too of the emerging AIDS epidemic, putting forth their belief in the probability of "a trend toward sexual exclusivity in the future" which would be "propelled by the fear of Acquired Immune Deficiency Syndrome." And they clearly were also aware of the unfortunate possibility of their work being used for political purposes, though they were probably thinking more about the right wing than of gay sex radicals: "We did not intend or want a new typology for male couples to emerge from these hypotheses. The dangers of creating new myths about male relationships through studies like this are to be avoided."

But as with many such studies, those who wanted to use the findings for their own purposes did not include the authors' caveats. Andrew Mattison sees a difference today that might call into question applying his study to gay men now. "One of the things we see is that men in couple relationships are being more restrictive, some being more sexually exclusive," he says.

THAT MAN-EAT-MAN BOOK

More than fifteen years since the study was completed—a period of time in which the American gay community has undergone unforeseen changes—the McWhirter and Mattison study is still quite powerful, still often used to bolster beliefs about gay men and monogamy. In 1996, for example, a popular self-help book on dating and romance, *Finding True Love in a Man-Eat-Man-World*, swept the urban gay ghettos, remaining on gay best-seller lists for months. It was the kind of book many gay men, looking for answers and direction, were waiting for: a breezy and generally informative and useful guidebook to navigating sex and love. When it came to relationship style, however, author Craig Nelson seemed intent on steering gay men in one direction.

In the humorous style he employed throughout the book, Nelson titled one chapter, "Fidelity? What's Fidelity?" In this chapter, Nelson tells readers that two studies "done in the mid-1980s . . . found that for gay couples together longer than five years, *all* of them had made some kind of special arrangement for sex with outsiders." Nelson does not cite the studies, tell readers where the studies took place, or offer the number of couples that were studied. It is safe to assume, however, that one of the studies Nelson is referring to is the McWhirter and Mattison study, since he quotes the two researchers a sentence later saying that "sexual exclusivity is not an ongoing expectation" among gay men. (The other study Nelson was referring to, judging from the reference list in the back of the book, was probably Joseph Harry's *Gay Couples*, published in 1984, which also studied a small urban sample similar to McWhirter and Mattison's.)

Nelson goes on to quote a Darwinian theorist saying the natural role of men is to spread their seed. He explains to readers for the remainder of the chapter just how wonderful an open relationship is, and how it can be mastered, with a slight nod toward those who might want to choose monogamy: He mentions that there seems to be an "upswing of monogamy," quoting the *Advocate*'s 52 percent figure, and observes that "being monogamous and faithful to each other, against all the odds, can give the two of you an immensely strong bond.

"Sex with outsiders can boost self-esteem and can even integrate you more into the gay community," he writes. "We want casual sex as something novel and fresh for ourselves; to do something we can't do with our lover; to reassure ourselves of our attractiveness. . . . Sometimes a guy we couldn't have screwed in the past for whatever reason is suddenly available, and we've gotta have it. . . . If you're a gay man in urban America, you're living in a sexual Disneyland, and many think of random sex just like Dad thought of bowling."

Some (though not all) of the therapists I have spoken with in the urban centers, while noting that for some couples open relationships work quite well, agree that using sex to validate oneself—i.e., to feel "attractive" or "boost self-esteem"—is indicative of a deeper emotional issue that the sex does little to resolve, whether one is in a relationship or not. The myth of the cult of masculinity, however, is that validation and self-worth *are* achieved through physical adoration. The cult encourages single gay men to believe they can achieve self-worth through sex, and it encourages men in relationships to believe they can boost self-esteem by having sex outside the relationship. The implicit message is that without sex outside the relationship, without actively participating in the cult of masculinity even while in a relationship, one is unattractive, worthless, and doomed to suffer from low self-esteem.

THE QUEER PICKET FENCE

Attributing what Nelson calls an "upswing in monogamy" to supposed behavioral changes that the AIDS crisis spurred, as Nelson does, is perhaps inaccurate if the implication is that the 52 percent in the *Advocate* survey who said they were in a monogamous relationship are typical of a great many men in the urban gay ghettos. Certainly, many gay men in the urban ghettos were affected in this way by AIDS and settled into relationships, monogamous and otherwise. But cohort studies tracking the epidemic show that significant numbers of gay men in the major cities appear not only to be engaging in sex with multiple partners, but are doing so frequently and often unsafely: Epidemiologists are still seeing a 30 percent to 50 percent HIV seroprevalance rate among gay men in many urban centers, and it appears that enough men of younger generations are engaging in unprotected sex with enough partners to keep the epidemic's threshold almost the same as it was for the previous generation in the 1980s. And from our own experiences, again, we all know that multiple-partner sex and non-monogamous relationships among gay men are alive and well in the urban centers.

So it appears that the 52 percent figure in the *Advocate* study—a sharp contrast to the McWhirter and Mattison study's 0 percent—does not necessarily mean monogamy has taken hold on some grand scale in the urban centers. The figure is more than likely a result of both the many men in the cities who deghettoized and, perhaps more profoundly, the deurbanization of homosexuality: "Rural Americans and those who live in small towns—6 percent and 16 percent of our sample, respectively—are better represented here than in AIDS studies," the *Advocate* researcher, Janet Lever, Ph.D., reported. "No one has ever done a nationally representative study of gay men, and while this survey is not representative either, we believe it includes men who have been underrepresented in previous studies."

A significant number of gay men surveyed in the *Advocate* sex survey then—22 percent—live in small towns and rural areas; the survey does not say how many of the remaining 78 percent live in suburbs, presuming that the 78 percent included those who live in both cities and the suburbs surrounding them. The *Advocate* survey also does not give a ratio of monogamous couples outside the cities as compared to inside the cities. My own informal surveys, however, suggest that, almost by a three-to-one ratio, those in small-town, suburban, and rural areas who said they were in relationships were more likely to be in sexually monogamous ones. I found similar results in interviews I conducted over a two-year period.

Interviewing men in my travels of course or on the telephone provides an impressionistic rather than scientific view; still, having lived for years in the urban center of New York, it seems to me that sexual monogamy among gay men is perhaps a greater trend outside the city, in smaller cities and towns where homosexuality is now more accepted.

New York therapist Michael Shernoff has some insight into this as well. During the 1980s, he designed among the first safer sex intervention programs, known as "Eroticizing Safer Sex," through Gay Men's Health Crisis as well as through various AIDS service organizations around the country. "My experience, both clinically, and in traveling all over North America, speaking to over fifteen thousand gay men, allowed me to talk to a lot of gay men about sex and relationships," he says. "What surprised me, being a consummate third-generation New Yorker, was that gay men outside of New York City, San Francisco, Los Angeles—the large, large urban centers— were virtually indistinguishable from their heterosexual neighbors in a way that most of us in the urban gay ghettos are not. They were more like Middle Americans, in their values, in the way they chose to live life. And there was, unfortunately, a myopic view from so much of the gay movement on the two coasts: that there was something less worthy, something less valuable, something almost homophobic about people choosing to do white picket fences and maintain connections with families, but still do their own gay identity in suburban, small-town, and smaller urban America. I've really come to understand that where there isn't the ghetto, more and more people are living their lives like the rest of Americans, but they just happen to be homosexual. And they will have gay cultural identity, and gay political identity, but how they choose to live their lives and make their relationships is going to look less like a group of circuit queens in Chelsea, West Hollywood, or the Castro."

Having a gay identity and being out, while at the same time not taking on the value system of the urban gay scene, is what the deurbanization of homosexuality in particular is all about. It's not that gay men in suburban, small-town, and rural America are necessarily moralistic or politically conservative when it comes to sex and relationships. Certainly, there were those whom I interviewed who were clearly struggling with a lot of internalized homophobia and who made religious and moralistic judgments about sexual behavior. (I have, however, also interviewed many men in the urban centers who are wrestling with the same demons—even men on the circuit, torn about their own sexual behavior.) But many more men, the majority of those I interviewed, had been out for some time, had been reading the national gay press—not to mention gay porn—had read a lot of gay fiction as well as gay nonfiction, had seen all the prerequisite gay films, were well informed about many of the cultural and political trends within the urban gay world, and espoused a generally sex-positive viewpoint and a rather progressive political perspective. Their personal lives are often simply quieter than those of a lot of men who live in the urban centers, as they are for their heterosexual neighbors.

"I'm ready to settle down, have a one-on-one monogamous relationship," says twenty-nine-year-old Michael, as if his life thus far has been rather wild. He grew up in the towns of Columbus and Crofton in Nebraska, and in Fort Peck, Montana, and is currently living temporarily in Lincoln, Nebraska, attending school. But he plans to either move back to a smaller town, perhaps Scotts Bluff, Nebraska, or spend some time in an urban center first, such as Seattle, before moving back to a smaller town. "Well, after my first two-year relationship ended in 1992, I've actually had sex only twice," he says, explaining what single life has been like. "The first one is someone I went on several dates with and someone I've known socially. I've dated a whole lot, but with that one guy we had sex too. The second one was anonymous sex. I was experimenting to see whether or not I would like it. I went to the Loop, this place where people cruise with their cars. So, I proved to myself I could do it, and, well, it was nice, I guess, but not so exciting for me. I think it was because there were no feelings involved other than the physical. That actually was my one foray into anonymous sex. I had read a lot of stuff about anonymous sex. I don't look down on people who do that— pushing the boundaries of whatever it is that is considered 'normal' sex is great. Maybe it's just the setting I'm in—it's not like there are tons of places around here to have anonymous sex. And it's not like everyone you know is talking about it, so you don't feel you've got to do it. It's not something I'm particularly dying to do."

"I don't have much time to give right now, although I am open to occasional dates," says twenty-one-year-old Brian, a college student living in Emporia, Kansas, where he grew up. Brian, a strawberry blond, rosy-cheeked young man, espouses the same simple desires for his future that many other gay men in small-town and rural America espouse, desires that are not much different from those of their straight counterparts. "I've been sexually active, but lately not," he says. "I'm looking to settle down, not just yet, but soon. Someday, I would like a long-term relationship, living together after a while of living apart. I'm looking for someone who doesn't shower me with gifts, someone simple, sort of like a best friend, someone I can trust and talk to. I'm definitely someone who likes to cuddle, someone who likes to be intimate. I've thought about adoption. I've enjoyed children. I'd like to have a child with someone, adopt a child. Gay marriage? Well, yes. Just because I'm gay doesn't mean that I do not want a traditional wedding. It's the kind of thing that would, you know, unite everyone, walking down the aisle, both families together."

"EVERY FAGGOT FROM HERE TO GRANT'S PASS"

Beyond the fact that life is simply quieter and slower outside the urban centers, one reason gay men in small towns might tend to be more monogamous is that small-town America for gays, just as for straights, is the quintessential Peyton Place, where gossip can be biting, particularly around sexual indiscretions. Whereas in the urban center someone might simply go to another neighborhood for sex outside his relationship, choosing from literally tens of thousands to hundreds of thousands of men in bars, on phone sex lines, or over the Internet, in small towns and rural areas, where everyone tends to know one another, things can get too close for comfort.

"Well, one thing is, every faggot from here to Grant's Pass knows your business," remarks Walter, a thirty-six-year-old delivery man who lives just outside of Newport, Oregon, giggling over every line. "And Lord have mercy on you if you're caught with someone else's lover! We're talking about a major scandal. No, unless you have some open arrangement—and I mean *really* open, where it's no big deal if your lover sees and meets and knows the people you sleep with, and I do know couples like that, though they are small in number—or unless you're willing to drive a bit, to another town or to the city, you can't be fooling around behind your boyfriend's back."

Even at the places where anonymous sex occurs in small-town and rural America, such as parks, parking lots, and rest stops on the highway, there tends to be a direct line to the queer gossip network—more so if one is *out* of the closet rather than *in*. "In terms of rest stops, your secret is actually safer if you're closeted and married [to a woman], which is what most of those guys are," says Dwayne, a twenty-eight-year-old farmhand who lives just outside of Plattsburgh, New York, near the Canadian border, and who expressed a sentiment common among gay men outside the urban areas about anonymous sex. "The married guys' secret is safe because, you know, their wives aren't going to find out, they're not plugged into that, and there's still that code where you don't out people like that no matter what. But among the people who are more out, leading a gay life with gay friends—even if they're still closeted to family—well, I think people think of rest-stop sex as all so closeted, because it's seen as being so secretive. It's got that stigma attached to it, the self-loathing, all of those scared, married men. There are a few guys who are out, who get off on the married guys at the rest stops, and so if you go there, those guys kind of gossip, and then it gets around and people are like, 'Why are you going there when you can just meet people out and about? You're only gonna meet a married, closeted, scared guy there—and who wants that?' And you can imagine the problems then if you have a boyfriend and he doesn't know. People talk around here, *especially* queer folks."

For many gay men outside the ghettos of the cities, monogamy is not so much something they agree to as much as it is something that occurs by default. As Michael, the twenty-nine-year-old Nebraska student, alluded to, in many areas there are simply fewer opportunities for sex than there are in the urban ghetto, even for men who might not necessarily want to be monogamous. There are rarely more than a few bars, if any at all, let alone bathhouses or sex clubs. Jerry, the man who moved to Iowa City, having grown up in Sioux City, Iowa, says that between him and his lover, monogamy is not a set-in-stone agreement—it just happens, often despite Jerry's best efforts.

"My friend Eddie doesn't believe in monogamy, and I see his idealism in his nonmonogamy views, and when he wants sex he goes and gets it," he says. "Then again, I think all sex for me has an emotional level, so there's always a cost and you think before acting. Still, on the weekends these days I want a release of some sort since my lover, Chris, has been away. I go out with my friends, party a lot, but not much happens." He chuckles, and adds, "I don't know if I turn off people or what, but it's pretty hard to get it around here."

By contrast, the urban gay ghetto offers a multitude of opportunities for sex and is so centered around the single and sex-filled life, that even men who want and agree to be monogamous sometimes find it difficult to do so within such surroundings. This is perhaps the single greatest environmental factor that distinguishes the urban centers from the outside areas with regard to sexually monogamous relationships.

"Not inconsequential . . . are the perils that the gay male [urban] subculture can present to a relationship," Betty Berzon notes in *The Intimacy Dance*. "In a long-term partnership one or both people will sometimes need the freedom to be away from the other—spend the evening with a friend. Typically, with gay men, this does not involve visiting the neighborhood bowling alley or playing poker with the guys. Dinner with a friend might well be in a gay restaurant, perhaps followed by a drink at a gay bar or time spent dancing at a gay club. In all of these environments, the air is somewhat charged; the hunt is on for at least some of the people present. This does not mean that a night out will necessarily result in a sexual escapade. People do have control of their behavior. It does mean, however, that temptation is built into these experiences."

Andrew, a thirty-eight-year-old lawyer, and Carl, a thirty-five-year-old journalist, live in Boston and have been together over ten years, having met while in college.

Over the years, the two rarely had sex outside the relationship; they both point to a couple of incidents, one separately and one together, in which they had sex with others, and these encounters were not particularly threatening to their relationship. Most of their friends were straight couples, though they had some gay friends, couples as well as singles. They led a quiet life, going out to dinner, to the movies, and visiting friends.

"Occasionally we would go out, more so in the first two years out of college," says Carl. "We never went to Saint parties or anything like that. There wasn't an appeal. I wasn't particularly drawn to it. It was fun to go out dancing in college, but I never really participated in that way [in the gay scene]."

Roughly two summers ago, however, Andrew's and Carl's lives changed dramatically: They went to Fire Island Pines for a weekend, for the first time.

"A friend of mine from high school had a house there," says Andrew. "We loved being out of Boston, being in a gay environment, and just loved the beauty of it. We went there four weekends that first summer as guests."

Carl says soon after those first few visits to the Pines, he started to feel "caged in. I felt as if I'd gone through my twenties and hadn't explored," he says, "and now blinders started to be taken off, and I felt like there was something I couldn't have because of my relationship."

Andrew was not having the same feelings, but he began to notice that Carl was feeling differently. "Carl can't hide anything," he says. "Things became tense."

Carl observes that the sexually charged Pines scene, awash with muscle men, both on the beach and dancing the night away at the local nightclub, was having an effect on him.

"A lot of it was a product of starting to go to Fire Island and being more aware of things like that—just sort of changing in that environment," he says. "Fire Island is very sexual, very—"

"Very vanity-filled," Andrew interrupts. "It's all about who you are, based on how you look. All the myths about Fire Island are true."

And yet, they decided to get a share in the Pines the following year.

"From when we first started going to Fire Island and for the next year and a half," Carl notes, "well, once you enter that arena you change. I started working out harder, instead of just swimming and running. I started working out harder and put on fifteen pounds. I started trimming my hair shorter and shorter. One day I finally looked in the mirror and I had shaved hair, and a shaved torso, and visually I was pretty much a whole different person."

Andrew notes that soon after their first few visits to Fire Island the two had started having "anxious conversations, and the tension level started to rise."

"I wanted to have sex with other men," Carl says. "There were certain men I wanted to have sex with whom I'd met [on Fire Island]."

"We fought about it, and we had a very difficult time," Andrew says. They decided to open the relationship. But that seemed, at least for a time, to make things more tense.

"It absolutely had a change on us," Carl says. "There were

some out-of-control weekends on Fire Island, and afterward you think, What are we doing?"

"There was this one kind of major out-of-control weekend about a year ago," Andrew says. "I was at a conference in California, and I was about to give a big speech, and two hours before that, Carl calls up from Fire Island. He tells me about this really wild Friday night he had, and about this wild Saturday night he had, and about all of the people he'd slept with."

"They were people we'd both slept with the previous weekend," Carl says.

"But this was the first time he'd slept with people outside the relationship [without me included]," says Andrew. "Things were rocky after that."

"I knew, going out, that it was bound to happen," says Carl, with a smile.

Carl and Andrew went through a year of rough patches. "We just weren't on the same path together," Andrew observes. "He was off being fabulous—I was off being fabulous, but less so. We just didn't seem to have a common goal together. We were not really a couple *emotionally*, in the way we were before. We had gone into a huge gulf."

Andrew and Carl in time began to accept the changes in their relationship. After a troubling and painful period—including separating for a short time—they say that they are learning how to navigate an open relationship more successfully.

AT THE POST OFFICE

Andrew and Carl underscore how there are many gay male couples in the cities who are monogamous for long periods of time—they in fact lived in a city together for over ten years and were for the most part monogamous—and that urban life in and of itself doesn't foster nonmongamous relationships. The urban gay scene, however, is only a stone's throw away, and a couple can for a variety of reasons find themselves falling into the gay fast crowd.

For men in small-town and rural America, unlike the case with Andrew and Carl, however, there is no fast crowd to fall into. It's not that relationships don't go through changes; ten years is, after all, a long time, and whether they lived in or outside of the city, Andrew and Carl would probably have experienced some upheavals. The sexual underground in and of itself was not the cause of problems between them. Rather, their relationship was going through natural changes for which the sexual underground provided a backdrop. At best, it was something new and interesting to explore together, and at worst, it was a debilitating distraction.

Though those in small-town, rural, and suburban America lack such a sophisticated sexual underground to facilitate a more open relationship, more often than not if after ten years there are some problems in the relationship, a couple seems to either resolve them or end the relationship. And it also seems likely, if they end the relationship, that both men will soon be seeking another relationship, simply because there is no vast sexual playground for singles to spend years exploring.

Of course, that is not the rule; there are many couples in rural and small-town America who navigate open relationships. But while in the urban centers couples have to work hard in order to keep a relationship monogamous if they've made that choice, it seems that in small-town and rural America, as Jerry from Iowa City alluded to, the difficulties and the pressure are often on those who are trying to keep a relationship open.

"We both date outside the relationship," says Josh, a thirty-two-year-old carpenter who lives in Manhattan, Kansas, and who reiterates what Jerry states. "But it's not the easiest thing to do around here. For us, we believe it enhances our relationship by allowing us to explore and then come back to each other. But you can't really just have anonymous sex outside, because it's harder to find. It happens once in a while, and I consider it a hot blessing. But it's not like it is in Chicago or New York, where you can meet someone walking down the street. You need to go out, meet people, have dates, little minirelationships, minicrushes. And of course that can be a problem. We both tell the men, going in, that we're in a committed, eight-year relationship, and for some of them that's cool. But for a lot, it's not, and I get turned down quite a bit because of that. They're often looking for someone themselves, and they want something more permanent. If they're single and they want just sex, or a friendship that's sexual, then they'll do it. But I'm honest with them about the fact that I also don't want it becoming long and drawn out—for both Fred [his lover] and I, if it gets long and drawn out, that can get tense. So, that scares them away too. Usually, I find, I have sex with men who are also in open relationships, but that's not so easy to find too. There are a lot of open couples, but I would not say they're the majority, and if they're people you've known for a while—friends—you don't want to have sex with them.

"Sometimes when there's jealousy between Fred and me over the men we date, we'll break it off, but then, since they might live in town, you see them a lot and it gets awkward. We have threeways sometimes too. When one of the guys falls in love with one of us and not the other, there again is that problem that you're going to see them a lot, sometimes for years, every day at the bank or the post office. That's a little weird. In general I find it difficult and a lot of work to keep having sex outside the relationship, but it's what I want, so I do work at it."

Many men outside the cities who are in relationships, fearing that they'd get caught up in the fast life of the urban ghettos and fearing that they might not be able to handle it, are glad it is not accessible to them.

"I have often thought, that if we lived in the city, hell, yes, we'd be fooling around like crazy," says Albert, the man who lives in a rural area with his lover near Boiling Springs, Pennsylvania, and who has sex outside the relationship maybe once a year. "And I can't imagine what our relationship would be like. I suppose we'd come to terms with it somehow, but I honestly can't imagine it." Mark, a thirty-one-year-old bank teller who lives in Albany, Georgia, notes that he has "the kind of personality that would get real involved and stuck in all that real quick. I'm glad," he says, "that I live right here. When I go to Atlanta, every year or so, that's enough for me. I know I'd be having a lot of sex, and maybe doing drugs more, beyond the little bit of pot I smoke once in a while, and getting involved in the competitive body culture, and I'd just lose myself. And I think it would without a doubt be the end of my relationship. My partner is not like me in that way, he'd probably not get caught up. I think he'd lose me to it, 'cause he wouldn't stand for it. As it is here, there's really no one worth it to fool around with. It has happened—once in ten years. But in the city it probably would happen once every ten days. And I don't think I would be happy with that in the long run."

A DEEPER LOVE

Clearly, the logistics and environmental constraints of life outside the cities contribute to some couples' decisions to be sexually monogamous, or to remain mostly sexually monogamous whether they make an agreement to do so or not. But for a great many men I interviewed who live in small-town and rural America—as well as in urban America—it was neither a lack of a large and tempting sexual underground nor the fear of gossip that influenced their decision to choose monogamy. It was something much deeper.

"We came here to build a home, and to raise a family, and to really bond and connect, and as far as we're concerned there's no room for a connection with anyone else, not in a physical way," says Martin, a thirty-nine-year-old landscaper who, with his lover, George, a thirty-six-year-old former investment banker, moved four years ago from New York to the mountains just outside of Worcester, Massachusetts. They built their own home and recently adopted a baby girl.

"I lived in New York for fifteen years and was immersed in the whole scene. I had two long-term, open relationships, one that lasted four years, another that lasted five years. One was very problematic in being open. The other was, more or less, okay, but I think it did affect our relationship in terms of how intimate we really were. It kept a distance between us, which we both probably needed at the time, so in that sense it was good. But now, in this relationship, I feel a bond I've never felt with anyone else. And I believe, for us, a lot of that has to do with our being sexually exclusive. You know, I did all of that. I did it. I got it out of my system. I think it's, for me, boring now. Now I want to do this. You know, having an open relationship is not for everyone, particularly throughout one's entire life. We have to stop setting a standard that says that's the way you're supposed to be. For some people it's good for a period of time. And for others it's never good. They're too jealous, whatever. What's wrong with saying this?"

Even as far back as 1981, it was recognized that some gay

men might choose sexual monogamy not for moral reasons but simply because it was less stressful, and that some of these men might in fact even have had open relationships previously. "Most often this kind of person has had a good many of these experiences," noted the pioneering Dr. Charles Silverstein in his 1981 book *Man to Man: Gay Couples in America*, outlining a reason that still rings true today for Martin and many other men who choose monogamy.

> Some men, particularly the experienced, have come to believe that "arrangements" interfere with the quality of their love relationship. They maintain that they have worked out any potential problems of jealousy and competition with a lover, that their arrangements are acceptable to both parties, but that the energy required to find third parties and to coordinate them with the relationship destroys the intimacy. They reject outside sex for this reason. For them, it isn't a moral issue but a practical one.

Many such men, young and old, who are in sexually monogamous relationships, who either spent some time immersed in the urban gay fast scene, like Martin and his lover, or grew up outside of them and never moved to the cities, resent the viewpoint they see as emanating from within the gay urban scene that valorizes the successful "open" relationship and deems monogamy (sexual and sometimes even emotional) as "square" and unrealistic at best, oppressive at worst. The same sentiments are expressed by many living in the urban centers who, rejecting the ghetto ideologies, are leading their lives in new and different ways.

Many monogamously coupled men who, like Martin and his lover, have entered their thirties and forties and say they have lived the fast life long enough to satisfy themselves, have retreated from it but without moving out of the cities. There have of course always been gay men in the urban centers who even while in their twenties and thirties did not follow in the rituals of the gay subculture, and there certainly have been many who've coupled, some monogamously. But many of these men, many of them now in their fifties, sixties, and seventies, say that in the past they not only felt they were few and far between, but that also they were often made to feel they were doing something awfully atypical.

"I thought we'd landed from Mars," chuckles Herb, a fifty-seven-year-old Los Angeles Realtor who has been in a sexually monogamous relationship for almost thirty years. "And I think everyone else thought the same thing about us. A lot of the time, I would not even discuss it, the fact that we were sexually exclusive, because it would really push buttons for people. Some would laugh you off. Others would challenge you. We kept quiet about it mostly."

Today, however, those men of the middle generations—men in their thirties and forties—who in the urban centers are beginning to choose paths similar to Herb's seem sturdier, bolder, more confident about the choices they've made. As therapist Michael Shernoff notes, echoing other therapists, "Don't forget that many of these men came to the city from small towns and the suburbs." Now that they're getting older, they are rejecting the urban ghetto mentality they'd adopted, or at least rejecting it in part, and many are drawing upon those small-town values they grew up with and settling down.

"I dropped out of it all five years ago," Randy, a thirty-six-year-old Chicago telephone salesperson, tells me. He'd grown up in the suburbs of Omaha, Nebraska, and moved to Chicago when he was twenty-two. "First off, as you get older *it* dumps *you* before *you* dump *it,* and I wanted to dump *it* before *it* dumped *me,*" he says of the gay urban ghetto sexual culture. "The bar and party scene is ruthless when it comes to telling you that you are no longer valued. Suddenly, people aren't looking at you as much, and you're standing there at the mercy of these twenty-three-year-olds. *Please.* I was brought up to think a lot more of myself and others, to have some self-respect. I have more integrity than that, than to allow myself to do that."

"There are so many other options available for living," Randy continues. "People need to open their eyes instead of just following like zombies. I look at a lot of the older men trying to keep up, men in their forties and fifties, dressing like they're twenty-five, going to the parties. It's so desperate and pathetic. I also have too much integrity—and just am smarter now that I'm a bit older—[than to] be seeking *validation* by running around and having sex outside my relationship. Because, for me, that's what sex outside the relationship was mostly about—validation. It wasn't just once in a while. I [had sex outside the relationship] a lot, even though I didn't want to in the larger picture. It was an obsession at times, and it was really affecting me and the relationship. I guess for other people it's about something else, but for me that was it. I could tell myself all the rationalizations I wanted—I was being 'modern,' 'living the city life,' etc., etc. But really it was the thirst for validation. In my current relationship, which I've been in for two years, I decided that when I needed to feel validated, it meant there was something we needed to talk about."

DEGHETTOIZATION MARCHES ON

Slowly but surely more gay men of younger generations also, men who haven't previously experienced the fast life of the ghetto at all and who are either growing up within the cities or are moving to the cities from small towns, suburbs, and rural areas, are choosing a new path. These men seem not to be joining in the frenzied young, gay urban scene, like so many of their peers, sometimes withstanding enormous pressure but perhaps seeing, as Randy said, that there are more "options." It's hard to know for sure, but from what we see around us as well as in the scant data we have available, they are perhaps not the majority or even a substantial minority of young gay men in the cities big enough to, say, make a major dent in the HIV transmission rates. But perhaps they are the beginning of a trend, the continuing effect of deghettoization of homosexuality within the cities.

Chris is a twenty-four-year-old, handsome six-footer with blond hair and blue eyes, the quintessential all-American boy. He lives in L.A. and is a student at the University of California, Los Angeles. He grew up in a military family, living on bases around the world, including, for quite some time, living in Alaska. He came out to family and friends, as well as into the gay community, while living in L.A. several years ago, with the West Hollywood scene right in his backyard. Yet he hasn't really hung out there at all. He has gay and straight friends, mostly his age, and hangs out at school a lot, in gay groups on campus and in other organizations.

"I don't go to bars, and, no, I don't have one-night stands," he says, when asked. "This guy that I dated two years ago, I fooled around just for the fun of fooling around, but it wasn't that much for me in terms of excitement. There needs to be something substantial, otherwise it's boring. If I look at my friends, generally they're the same way in terms of sex. I feel like I've sampled from both sides of the pie—the physical with the emotional, and then the physical just to do it, just for the physical. And I just like the physical with the emotional. I'm very emotionally based. If I'm feeling really horny, I can take care of it myself. It doesn't really appeal to me to go and meet someone just for that. My friends, yes, I'd say they are very relationship minded too. They're all about the same age, sort of a mix, gay and straight. Some of them are in relationships."

Talking about a gay roommate he had a couple of years ago, Chris describes the subtle and not-so-subtle pressure that someone his age undergoes in the urban center today. "We've had a couple of discussions where he doesn't think that I'm gay because I don't go to West Hollywood and am not into the gay scene," Chris tells me. "He asked me why I don't go and said, 'You don't seem to like guys.' We kind of didn't really understand where the other was coming from. But you do see what he is saying. The mentality, I mean. It's all around: To be gay means that you have to go to West Hollywood. Sometimes I feel I'm not doing that enough, that I should get out more and go to West Hollywood. But then I realize that I do meet gay people at school. I'm in the music club, places like that. I meet a lot of gay people. I think maybe, for a lot of people who go to West Hollywood, it's kind of maybe they've held it in [being gay] so long and then they went to the other extreme. There's a wide range of people, and so you can't generalize. But for some, well, in some ways they're finally being gay, in their minds, and so they go to the extreme. I know a lot of people that, when they came out, they started wearing the tight shirts and trying to fit in, and even though they were going to the bars, they were still looking for relationships. They were settling for tricking because it was easier. It seemed to me that there was something more to being gay than tricking. Someone told me I should give up looking and stop being so picky about monogamy because quality gay men are hard to find, and that I'd never find what I want. That just screamed internalized homophobia to me."

The deghettoization of homosexuality coupled with the deurbanization of homosexuality is perhaps a state of mind, something that defies geography. What the many men outside the cities as well as Chris and many other men living in the cities talk about when they discuss sexual monogamy is their desire to make a different choice, a choice that they see as not visibly offered by the urban gay scene that is highly promoted in the urban ghettos. Many are careful to note that they are not labeling this choice as the right one for everyone — just for them. But they are pointed in their criticism of the ghetto scene for both pressuring many to choose the "open relationship," setting it up as the ideal lifestyle for gay men, and for deeming their choice of monogamy as unrealistic. In the extreme, these gay men, according to some lesbian and gay psychotherapists and counselors in the urban centers, actually think they are emotionally or psychologically disturbed because they deviate from what the ghetto often considers the norm. In an odd twist, a political movement that has rather successfully fought attempts to pathologize multiple-partner gay sex has now perhaps pathologized gay monogamy.

"I have had patients come to me who say to me, 'I didn't feel properly queer, because I didn't like the fast-food sex track,'" says therapist Michael Shernoff. "This one man said, 'All I always wanted was a steady supply of good old-fashioned vanilla sex, preferably with the same man. I was ashamed to tell my friends about it while they were going to all the sex parties — as I wasn't properly queer.' Have we in fact, confusing *sexual* liberation with *gay* liberation, allowed a kind of *sexual fascism* to come in, where if you don't want to do it in esoteric ways with lots of people you are less queer than the happily married queens down the block with the white picket fence?"

TO MONOGAMIZE, OR NOT

The decision to choose sexual monogamy, near monogamy, or an even more open arrangement is one that gay and lesbian psychotherapists are grappling with more and more in the urban centers and beyond. Many, though not all, don't want to appear to favor one way or another. They are, on a personal level, as varied in their choices of relationship style as the gay community itself. They generally seem to agree that whether to make a relationship open or monogamous is up to each couple, and there is no standard to follow.

"I think different things work for different people," says Los Angeles psychologist Jim Babl, a gay man in private practice who has also treated many young gay men at UCLA since 1979. "I've seen very successful open relationships and very successful monogamous relationships." Yet Babl and other therapists also seem to agree that many men in the urban ghettos believe not only that the quintessential open relationship — in which they have sex outside the relationship and discuss it with each other and share sexual partners — is inevitable for them, but also that it is far easier than other options, and that it is the best way to structure their relationships, even though it might not be so in their individual case.

"I think it is easier for two gay men to have an open relationship than, say, for a heterosexual couple," Babl says. "On the other hand, men have not been very well trained in dealing with feelings, and that is true of gay men in particular, often having been cut off. It's threatening to know that your lover is fucking around and so forth. There are a lot of intense

feelings there. For gay men [in a couple] who are having problems, running around on the side is not going to help."

"Men seem to be more sex driven than women," says
Duane McWaine, an African-American gay man and Los
Angeles psychiatrist who treats primarily many gay men and
people infected with HIV. "And so there is more tension
around sex. So when men have relationships, and have sex
outside the relationships, there's a wider variety of things that
can happen. For some, it's no big deal. For a lot of men, it's an
absolute bash in the face with a brick."

"I really think that we have brought something on an
unexamined level that I see as potentially damaging to our intimate relationships," says Shernoff, remarking strongly about
what he views as the pressure that has often been prevalent
within the gay urban ghetto to have and master an open relationship. He notes that he too, now forty-four years old, was in
a fifteen-year open relationship, and so he speaks not only as a
therapist who treats many gay men but also as someone with
firsthand experience. "There is the unexamined assumption
that open relationships are great," he says. "Well, I think they
always have a cost. I think they never are without some level of
problems. And there is also an unexamined assumption that
two men can't be monogamous, and that if they're not, it won't
have any negative attributes on the relationship. I think that is
a crock of shit, quite frankly. I think that there can be some
open relationships where it's not an escape from intimacy,
where it's not an avoidance problem. But too much of the
time, there's something else going on. When I hear about it
either socially or in my consulting rooms, it's like 'Oh I was
really angry with him, so I went out and picked someone up.'
As opposed to talking to him about being angry."

A growing number of therapists in fact see gay men in relationships rushing to have sex on the outside, openly or clandestinely, as a sort of cure-all for what might ail a relationship. But the problems in the relationship may have little or nothing to do with sex itself, even though sex is then made the cause of the problem.

"I think more often than not what it's about is not knowing how to be in a relationship," Betty Berzon says about sex outside the relationship. "When problems emerge, sex is often looked at as the problem, defined in terms of 'I just have more of a sexual drive than he does,' for example. It gets translated into something else, something sexual, rather than that they have not developed other things in their relationship. And going outside for sex is seen as some kind of answer." As a therapist, Berzon says she supports and counsels couples in any decision they make regarding sex outside the relationship. "I have to be nonjudgmental," she says. "There's a great deal involved. When the subject of sex comes up, I say to a couple, 'What is your agreement?' They're each absolutely certain they know what the agreement is and that they think the other accepts it. Often, however, it turns out that the agreement isn't clear, or it turns out that one really wants to have an open relationship and the other doesn't and he just goes along. One is sexy and friendly [with other men], and an open relationship appeals to him. The other one is settling for something that he doesn't really want. What I try to do is say, 'Why are you or aren't you interested in each other? What kind of a relationship do you want?'"

Berzon describes a scenario that plays out often among gay men: One partner wants an open relationship while the other doesn't but simply goes along. In my interviews with couples in open relationships, even among those who did not readily admit it, I sensed in many instances that one of the men was not happy with the situation but was so in love with the other, and so afraid of losing him, that he simply accepted the open relationship and subverted his own happiness, hoping that the open period would fade—as it sometimes does. As therapists like Berzon point out, that can be a recipe for disaster down the line. Perhaps that is why many single men now report that early on—perhaps on the first or second date—they establish what they and their potential partner want and don't even allow a relationship to begin if their goals are at odds.

"I used to just go along with guys who wanted open relationships," says Robert, a thirty-seven-year-old Milwaukee sales manager. "I thought, Oh, maybe he'll change—or maybe I will. But ultimately, I was always hurt, and it was always a dreadful situation. I feel I lowered myself, allowing myself to do something that I didn't want to do—including threeways—simply because I loved the men, or thought I did. And I don't mean by saying I 'lowered myself' that I did something dirty. If people want to do threeways or have open relationships that's fine. I mean by that that I did something I really didn't want to do, that just wasn't right for me, that I wasn't comfortable with, that wasn't about sex with emotion, which is important to me. But I did all of that because I thought there truly weren't men like me. I've had friends who were pretty much like me at one time and who eventually accepted the open relationship, got used to it, and even came to love it. That's fine, but it didn't happen with me. Now, I'm finding there are a lot of men like me. It's like we're coming out of the closet—the closet in this community, it never ends. My feeling now is—and I tell this to young gay people when I do counseling at a gay youth group—you need to establish early on what you want in a relationship. If, for example, you really are committed to an open relationship and can't see yourself doing it another way, and the other person doesn't want it, do not fool yourself into thinking that you can accept their ways or that they can accept yours, or that you can change them, or that you can change yourself. Sometimes, it's true, people really want to change. They want to explore something different, and then it's fine. But in most cases that is not so. I tell people, don't fall in love with someone if you do not want the same kind of relationship that they do, because the results will often be tense and ultimately heartbreaking."

NEGOTIATED SAFETY

While many men are rethinking just how involved they should get with someone who wants a different relationship style, others have been rethinking how their relationship style relates to safer sex and what ways it can enhance or detract from their abilities to remain safe. Many men who are in relationships in which both partners are HIV-negative, for example, say that being monogamous has also had the added bonus of allowing them to engage in unprotected sex, anal as well as oral. Some of these men say that this has been a major factor among several in their decision to be sexually exclusive in a relationship.

This strategy of HIV prevention with regard to relationship style is the subject of much controversy and disagreement. It is actually a form of safer sex promoted in other countries, such as Australia, known as "negotiated safety." (See Appendix II.) It has not been promoted in the United States by AIDS organizations, primarily, it appears, because of what some critics have charged is a paternalistic attitude on the part of many AIDS organizations, a refusal to treat gay men as adults and accept that some men can have—and are having—sexually monogamous relationships (or attempting to do so) and discarding their condoms. Other critics charge that in the case of some AIDS organizations at least, the ideological tenets of early sexual liberation have clouded their judgment: They refuse to advance a form of prevention that might in any way be seen as "promoting" monogamy.

Whatever their motivations, AIDS organizations' concerns are legitimate with regard to HIV prevention and negotiated safety: Too many men in couples will *say* to each other they are and will be monogamous, or that they will not use condoms with each other but make sure always to use condoms when they have sex on the side, and they will perhaps even try to stick to these rules. Then, in the heat of passion, they will fool around on the side, perhaps unsafely. Many will then find themselves in a dilemma, and some, so fearful of offending their partners and perhaps risking the relationship, will decide it would be worse to tell partners of their unsafe sex outside the relationship than to put the partners at risk of HIV infection. And so, there is the danger of HIV transmission. AIDS prevention caseworkers as well as psychotherapists have certainly seen this scenario play out.

The truth is, however, many gay men *are* practicing their own (often uninformed) versions of negotiated safety, whether AIDS organizations like it or not, and it behooves HIV prevention leaders to at least educate these men as to how to do it properly, after first helping them to assess if negotiated safety is indeed right for them. All too often, the reason many men in couples in fact become infected with HIV is that they attempted their own version of negotiated safety, and they were not aware of the ground rules that have been advised. As the Australian AIDS organization, Gay Men's Health Centre advises, for example, couples shouldn't even attempt this form of safer sex unless they can be completely honest with each other, able to discuss the issue without fear of damage to the relationship when and if one partner has sex on the outside and if that sex is unsafe. It also means playing safe for a period of months in the beginning of the relationship, then testing repeatedly to be sure that neither one is HIV infected before forgoing condoms.

"I thought, since we were both in a relationship, and we were in love, and we weren't fooling around, that it was okay," says Andy, a twenty-three-year-old San Francisco student. He and his lover, George, also twenty-three, recently tested positive. "I had tested negative a year before and hadn't really done anything unsafe, beyond oral sex. And he had tested negative two years before we met. He now says that there were two times where he was unsafe, where he allowed the guys to fuck him without a condom, but he didn't think it was a big deal because one guy didn't come, and the other one did, but said he was negative. Within a few weeks of dating, we decided to stop using rubbers and promised each other there would be no one else. On my part there wasn't. I don't know about him. But it didn't matter anyway. One or both of us had it already, I figure. To tell the truth, we can't figure out which one of us gave it to the other, or if we both already were infected. Looking back, we just went about the whole thing the wrong way."

While Andy and his lover were uninformed and made uneducated and life-threatening decisions, other couples have thought out the issue a bit more. Despite the AIDS organizations, they have devised forms of negotiated safety that work for them.

"It wasn't as if having sex without condoms was an incentive to being in a monogamous relationship," notes Roger, a twenty-nine-year-old Houston airline ticket agent who has

254

been in a relationship for four years. "But it was certainly a fantastic fringe benefit. We waited for, like, a year before we stopped using condoms, and we both tested twice within that year, both times negative. We were totally safe throughout and committed to each other. We were monogamous, and as we came to really know each other, we trusted each other more. But we're both pretty low-key, in that if something [such as a sexual infidelity] happened, we could handle it. There would certainly not be a blowup. We're not really that jealous, and I think we both know that if something happened, it would be just sexual, not a major threat to our relationship. Still, I've not been interested in anyone else: Even when I'm turned on by someone, the thought of the hassle of condoms and all, and then you know, just my commitment and all—it would be wrong for me, and I'd be too conscious of it. It's not come up. I know it's the same for [my lover]. We do talk about it once in a while, remind each other that we've been monogamous and remind each other that it's okay if something happens, and it's okay if we need to tell each other, and if we need to start having [protected] sex again."

Other couples I interviewed have other, nonmonogamous arrangements that, by the Australian Gay Men's Health Centre definition, are a form of negotiated safety. Some, for example, have unprotected oral and anal sex with each other and limit sex outside the relationship to nonpenetrative sex (both anal and oral), and discuss it if and when anything else occurs. Others decide that they will have anal sex only with each other and limit any penetrative sex outside the relationship to oral sex. And still others decide that they will have anal sex on the outside, but always protected, and they will discuss it if and when one of them engages in unsafe sex.

All of these scenarios, of course, are variously difficult to maintain, and they do not insure that those who engage in them will not be infected with HIV. Any sex on the outside is risky in that there is the possibility that they'll slip up or the condom will break, and couples practicing negotiated safety should not be seduced by a false sense of security: Their chances of getting infected if they are having sex on the outside are just as great as anyone else's. Couples who practice negotiated safety also need to define what safe sex is for them. Despite some AIDS organizations' efforts to portray oral sex as relatively risk-free, for example, several studies have shown that oral sex does carry a risk, and men have been infected through oral sex. The decision about how "relative" that risk is should be up to each individual, based not on the urgings of activists or prevention groups but on carefully looking at the facts about transmission, understanding that there is risk involved, and, in the case of couples attempting negotiated safety, deciding upon a course of action together.

EMOTIONAL MONOGAMY

When it comes to HIV transmission, sexual monogamy is only an option for those who truly want it and who can be successful at it. It also does not necessarily offer the promise of unprotected sex for those couples in which both men are not HIV-negative.

For men in relationships in which both men are HIV-positive, for example, there are other concerns that impact their decision to continue using condoms, at least for anal sex. Many men who are HIV-positive said that they have sex with others who are positive without concern for the risks, while many others—including several in monogamous relationships—report they always protect themselves during anal sex (and sometimes avoid unprotected oral sex), afraid of being infected with new and different strains of HIV as well as with a host of opportunistic infections and other sexually transmitted diseases.

For men in serodiscordant monogamous relationships—that is, where one man is HIV-positive and the other is HIV-negative—unprotected sex is *never* an option, not even once, no matter how monogamous and in love the couple is. For some, that reality can perhaps be unbearable.

"I was always looking for something special," says twenty-four-year-old Demetri, who lives in Washington, D.C., and works for an AIDS agency. "When I came out [a few years ago], I wanted a relationship, a monogamous relationship. It was, like, you were either single and doing the one-night-stand thing, dating casually, or doing a monogamous relationship." After several short-lived relationships, Demetri met Bart, who was twenty-two years old and was HIV-positive, and they had a relationship that lasted for several months. Demetri believed that being in what he thought was a monogamous relationship, even though his lover was HIV-positive, made him *safe*—safe not necessarily or only in terms of HIV, but in the larger sense of what monogamy has come to mean in the larger culture: having one person who looks after you and takes care of you. Though the couple used condoms for anal sex (though not oral), in fact they rarely had anal sex. One night, things just got carried away, Demetri says. He acknowledges he knew that Bart was having sex on the side and sneaking around, but he was somewhat in denial about it. This made Demetri insecure, afraid he might lose Bart, afraid that if he offended him or got him angry, Bart might dump him. That fear apparently played into his decisions around safer sex.

"It just spontaneously happened during sex," he recalls of

what he believes was a fateful incident. "He just was suddenly inside of me. I wasn't expecting him to do that. He didn't stay in me very long. He didn't come. I thought during it that there was something wrong and I should say something. But in this case I had more of an investment, thinking he doesn't want to hurt me. I felt that if I say no, he won't love me." Demetri says he now hears similar stories from other young gay men. "We value love and affection more than we value our own health," he observes, "enough so that we put ourselves and each other at risk for HIV." Not long after their relationship ended, Demetri tested positive for HIV. "When I told [Bart], all he had to say, very nonchalantly, was 'Wow, that's too bad,'" Demetri recalls. "Then he said, 'Well, you had half the responsibility too.'"

Clearly, the fairy tale notion of love and sexual monogamy as "good" and "pure" and as something that might keep us "clean" and take care of us no matter what can create a false sense of security in many people and can be dangerous when it comes to safer sex. Perhaps this is why some AIDS organizations are cautious about talking about monogamy. That notion of monogamy, promulgated for centuries as a way of keeping the prevailing order in place, is not something that many gay men in the urban centers feel is right for them. Having made the break from society's prescriptions around sexuality merely by coming out of the closet, many gay men also feel unburdened from what they view as the rules of traditional heterosexual coupling, most visibly the rule of sexual monogamy.

And yet, there seems to be a duality operating in many if not most of us, a conflict that tears away at us: Many men interviewed in the urban centers said that *sexual* monogamy in the strictest sense of the word—complete sexual exclusivity—is difficult if not impossible for them, or that they simply didn't desire it even if it were possible for them. And yet, most of these same men said not only that they desired *emotional* monogamy—being emotionally bonded in a deep and committed way with only one partner—but also that they did not want to know about their partner's *sexual* infidelities and didn't want to discuss their own with their partner, afraid that they and their partner couldn't in either of their minds separate the sexual from the emotional. So they're constructing a kind of monogamy with a little breathing room: within the spectrum of postmodern monogamy, this is at the opposite end from complete sexual monogamy.

NEAR MONOGAMY

"Many men can easily separate sex and love, have sex without the emotional side," says New York psychotherapist Rosemary Caggiano, noting that for these men strict sexual monogamy might not be appealing or possible. "And there are some people who can deal with [an open relationship], people who feel more secure if they know [about their partners' outside sexual activities]," she says. But for what Caggiano believes is the majority of gay men in the urban centers—and, for that matter, she believes, the majority of straight men, and even many straight women and lesbians—what works best is adhering to and preferably verbally agreeing to this arrangement, which is not quite the classic open relationship but not quite a strictly monogamous one. These couples accept that sex outside the relationship will occur once in a great while and that there's no reason to discuss it and thus dredge up jealousy and resentment. Of course, they agree to always have protected sex with each other and with those whom they may have sex with on the outside.

"For many, it threatens their security, threatens the emotional aspects of the relationship, if they know about sexual infidelities," she says. "If the sex doesn't matter and it's not very often, there is no need for them to know. [This arrangement] allows us to follow through on the physical once in a while, while still following the cultural norm [of having a committed relationship]. And that cultural norm does have a basis in logic. If we were all bouncing around from partner to partner, the society would be one hell of a mess. There would be a subtle form of anarchy going on.

"I have worked with men who, for long periods of time, are absolutely faithful to their partners," she continues, "but then something happens, somebody goes away, whatever, the opportunity presents itself. That doesn't necessarily harm the relationship."

Michael Shernoff, in a paper in the *Journal of Lesbian and Gay Social Services*, terms this arrangement the "Sexually Nonexclusive But Unacknowledged Open Relationship." It is one of several relationship styles he outlines, including: "Nonsexual Lovers," where the "couples are still quite romantic" but "for a variety of reasons are no longer sexually active with each other," and may or may not be sexually active with others; "Primarily Sexually Exclusive Relationships (Menages)," in which couples have sex with each other as well as "go out together seeking a third person with whom to have sex," but generally follow "the rule that neither member of the couple sees the third person alone, to minimize jealousy"; "Acknowledged 'Open' Relationships," the classic open relationship, in which the partners have sex with each other and sometimes with a third person and "openly discuss outside sexual experiences" that they have separately, and "even introduce their lover to their other sexual partners"; and the

"Sexually Exclusive Male Couple," in which the men, even if they think about "either having sex outside the relationship or having an affair," decide "for a variety of motivations . . . not [to] act on those feelings."

Some couples spend various amounts of times in two or more of these relationship styles, being monogamous for a period of time, for example, and then opening the relationship, or even becoming monogamous after many years of an open relationship. And many men today, in their second, third, or fourth long-term relationship, are choosing different relationship styles from those they'd utilized previously, though they didn't ever think they would.

"I have found that, after thirteen years of having an open relationship, I'd like to have a monogamous relationship, or at least a near monogamous one, where we aren't running around with people and talking about it all the time and pointing guys out to each other that we had sex with," says David, a fifty-four-year-old Dallas doctor who six months ago met Chuck, a thirty-six-year-old who is also a doctor. "He's had open relationships too and says that he would never have thought he'd ever want a monogamous one. I felt that way too. I just didn't think it was natural for men, and I always said, you know, that straight men were all fooling around behind their wives' backs too anyway—which I've come to realize, however, just from my experiences with colleagues, is a lot more exaggerated a condition than we think. Anyway, I used to laugh when I'd hear about [monogamy between two men], and I'd make a judgment immediately about these men, like they were in denial. But now there's a real sigh of relief when I'm thinking about it. All that competition, constantly feeling you had to keep up, not just trying to pick people up but competing with your lover, always afraid he was going to find someone cuter than the guys you did. It was exasperating. This, so far, has been really, really nice. You know, if it happens once in a while, while traveling or whatever, big deal? I don't consider that anything and neither would he. But that's not like actively seeking it out, planning out your weekends with other people, and sticking it in each other's faces. Some of my friends my age have been doing the same thing that we're doing—after years of open arrangements—and they're finding it just as stress-free as I am."

A MUTUAL CHILD

There clearly are then many choices—perhaps more even than Shernoff and others outline—that gay men are making today in terms of relationship styles, both inside and outside the urban ghettos; these relationship styles are shattering myths promoted inside and outside the gay world about how gay men live. And many therapists agree that, in particular, for the first generations of out-of-the-closet gay men growing older, more monogamous relationships are an increasingly appealing choice for a reason that Randy, the thirty-six-year-old Chicagoan, alluded to, and David, the fifty-four-year-old Dallas doctor, perhaps touched on: They simply can no longer compete in the gay sexual marketplace, a marketplace that, ironically, many of them helped create many years ago but which now does not include them.

"The difference in gay [male] life and straight life," therapist Rosemary Caggiano observes, "is that straight men can always be validated by sex, no matter how old they get, because women are attracted to more than just their looks. But for many gay men, because much of the gay culture is all about physical beauty, that passes. The physical beauty after a certain point just can't be maintained, though many will try as hard as they can to maintain it for as long as possible. For those who don't maintain it, they sublimate it, as you're supposed to do. They find it equally as satisfying to validate themselves through other activities."

For many gay men today, that means burying themselves in other important and rewarding activities related to their relationship and their gay "family." When you're over forty, peaking in your career, living with your lover, puttering around the house, entertaining lots of friends and other couples, and maybe have just adopted a child, there is "not very much time" for an affair, or for sex on the side, says Caggiano. "Your energies and your focus are on something else," she notes. "It might be about your kid going to school, and doing parent-teacher meetings, and taking the kid to Disneyland, and all of that stuff. But it doesn't have to be an *actual* child. In the past, some gay people who have stayed together for a long time created a 'child' in terms of being involved in the same work, or buying and selling old houses and fixing them up, or being, say, the actor and the manager—being a team. When a couple does not have a mutual 'child,' there's very little to keep them together except for their indulgences."

Those men who have opted for settling down in a relationship and nurturing a "child"—real or surrogate—say they sometimes receive subtle and not-so-subtle criticism from friends who have chosen the fast lane of the urban ghetto. Martin, the thirty-nine-year-old landscaper who with his lover moved several years ago from New York to the mountains of Massachusetts, built a house, and adopted a child, observes that some of his friends, men in New York whom he was on the circuit with, have been disdainful toward him and his lover.

"I honestly think that some of my friends from the city—

not all, but some—are critical of what we're doing," he notes. "It's not because they really believe we're dull and that we're 'conforming' to the straight world, as they have said to some other friends of ours, sometimes mocking us and laughing at us. No, these are the kinds of queens who would be the last to talk about politics, or about 'conforming to the straight world,' or who even care about that—and besides that, they do conform quite a bit in their nine-to-five lives, holding down very straitlaced jobs. No, it's because, I think, they're enormously conflicted much of the time about what they're doing, the drugs, the whole thing, and they need to tell themselves that they're doing the 'right' thing and I'm doing the 'wrong' thing. It's more about them and their lives, and what they're afraid of. I truly believe that they need to look down on me now, as a way to put a stamp of approval on themselves, because they are ambivalent about their own behavior. I try to be supportive and show an interest in what they're doing, but I think they really believe that I'm passing judgment on them simply by choosing a different way, and by getting out of all that. And that's not the case at all. I really don't care what they're doing. I just think— for me—all of that is completely boring. I want to do this now. And because of how far things have come, I *can* do this now."

Reiterating Martin's last point, many gay men like him and his lover believe in fact that the choice they have made is a direct result of the nearly thirty years of gay liberation and queer activism; in other words, they view the success of gay liberation itself as allowing them to now choose postmodern monogamy.

"It's like, maybe twenty years ago you had to be the sexual rebel, almost as a political statement," says Keith, a twenty-seven-year-old furniture salesman who lives in Royal Oak, Michigan, with his partner of five years. "You had to put everything out there in people's faces. We're a sexual minority, and this is a conventional, repressive country—the only way to rile [people] was to assert that sexual liberty, put it out there. You had to tell the world that there was not one way to be, that sexual desire and sexuality were really complicated. That had to be driven home over and over. But now, I think so much has been won; there's a lot to go, but we've entered the mainstream. There is so much more acceptance. The message has gotten through. Now it's all about choosing different ways of living our lives—some, yes, quite traditional. But we're living it all so openly, as gay people, which I think always adds a new twist to it. We're still, you know, 'in your face,' but now we're on Main Street and at the local shopping mall."

In that way, for many gay men, the next step in gay liberation is to move beyond the boundaries that have penned us in—the physical ones that have kept us cordoned off in the urban gay scene as well as the psychological ones that have kept us chained to destructive behaviors, ugly myths, and hateful stereotypes.

And that means finally taking on one of the most enduring and powerful stereotypes we know, one that has haunted gay men for decades and has wreaked havoc on every gay generation. Many gay men have come to realize that now is the time to kill off the stereotype of the lonely old queen.

7

THE DEATH OF THE LONELY OLD QUEEN

*I understand exactly who I was destined to be . . . the
graying head of an English department in a second-
rate boys' school, say, in the Berkshires. . . . I'd look out
over the deserted campus, the green of the hills beyond,
and the silent sobs would heave my shoulders. No
relief till the pitch of midnight, and then my fumbling
hands would guiltily lift the shoe box from the back of
the closet. My stash of muscle porn, mail-ordered to a
PO Box in Great Barrington. I jerk myself to sleep. The
cry I make when I'm coming is like an animal caught
in a trap, or a vampire's groan at the first light of the
day. . . . For I had become the thing that heteros
secretly believe about everyone gay—a predator, a
recruiter, an indoctrinator of boys into acts of darkness.
Sullying my mission as teacher and guide.*

–Paul Monette, Becoming a Man

"This has gone on all my life, and certainly became more
acute in my fifties and sixties," says Arthur, a seventy-three-

THE DEATH OF THE LONELY OLD QUEEN

year-old retiree who has spent much of his life picking up younger men on the streets, in bars, and in other locales. As we sit in his comfortable condominium apartment, he laments about the gay world and his own relationship to it.

"I just want to surround myself with these young guys," he says. "I love watching them, and I love their bodies. But then, even if they do want me to give them a blow job, I think that's kind of freakish and weird because I can't believe someone would be attracted to men my own age. I think I'm, well, quite honestly, *grotesque*. I think all older men are. I'm in no way even remotely attracted to men my own age, and I don't like to hang around people my age."

Though he was having furtive gay sex since his teen years, Arthur didn't come out to family, friends, and colleagues until he was sixty-seven. For most of his life he played the role of a heterosexual, dating women but picking up men on the side. He says that for many years he'd have sex every night with men he'd meet on the street or in bars and believes in fact that his "compulsiveness" was spurred by his having to remain so secretive.

"When I was living in L.A. many years ago, I was picking up guys on Hollywood Boulevard every night," he says. "Then in New York, on Forty-second Street, in dirty movies, in bars. It was the only intimacy I knew, the only way I could be close to a man. I couldn't have a relationship, but I wanted to be close to men. And I hated gays, hated myself. So I went out of my way never to pick up another gay person—no, I was grossly homophobic, hated myself for doing this, and hated men who seemed gay or said they were gay. I only picked on people who were perceived as straight men, men who wanted a blow job. It wasn't until the instant I came out at the age of sixty-seven that I suddenly found gay men attractive—beautiful, even. I began right at that moment to deal with all of this homophobia I have built up over the years. But there's too much. It's all still there. I was too closeted and have hated myself for too long for it to all go away."

Arthur says he is sometimes intensely angry with himself for not coming out sooner. "I feel it was a great tragedy in my life that I wasn't out and that I've never had a relationship with a man." Now, I just couldn't do it. I don't know anything else but this furtive sex I have had and this cult of youth. I look at these young couples today, and I see that the world will be different for them. They're not living like I did, with this closet sexuality."

When I point out to Arthur that it's never too late, that there are men his age living their lives in happy and productive ways, men who are proud of being gay and who are sexually active and are often in loving relationships, he insists that it is too late. "Youth is power and money is power," he says, "and I don't have youth and I don't have any more money. A rich old queen can still survive. A poor old queen is dead meat."

Arthur is representative of a small but not insignificant number of men in their late fifties, sixties, and seventies whom I interviewed and surveyed who are unhappy with their lives and who see some salvation in hanging around solely with younger people. Some of them go to bars, meet young gay men, get rejected quite a bit, and often are laughed at, they say. Sometimes they find young men who will have sex with them and who even befriend them, thus becoming the only older role models for these young men. Men like Arthur are different from others who have young lovers and life partners, who are not unhappy and are well adjusted to their sexuality and to aging. A desire for sex or relationships with younger men is not a "symptom" of some kind of a pathology, or indicative necessarily of a problem. A proclivity for rejection, though, is indicative of deep unhappiness.

Men like Arthur are unhappy about their lives for a variety of reasons, often stemming from their not having fully accepted their homosexuality or at least not beginning to do so until very late in life. Considering the times Arthur grew up in, the fact that he is even out of the closet after all these years is an enormous achievement. Men like Arthur, it must be realized, are coming out in a gay world that is quite segmented and can be isolating, particularly if one is not a member of its most visible crowd: the young and buff bar and nightclub world.

In many cases in fact men like Arthur are drawn to that world despite its exclusiveness, seeking the company of young people because it's in some respects actually easier, because young people (or at least those who will pay them any attention whatsoever) will not challenge their thoughts and ideas in the way older men who are out and confident about their lives might. In other cases they may feel trapped because they have become so conditioned to the cult of masculinity's focus on youth. And more often than not, it's a mix of both.

These men epitomize the stereotype of "the lonely old queen." The cult of masculinity cannot survive without keeping the stereotype of the lonely old queen alive. But it seems as if the deghettoization and deurbanization of homosexuality, for a variety of reasons, may very well kill the stereotype of the lonely old queen once and for all.

CRIMINALS, SINNERS, PSYCHOPATHS, AND PREDATORS

The image of the lonely and lecherous old queen has been around since the idea of the "homosexual" has been around.

Unlike every other stereotype about gay men, it has endured in a relatively unchanged state throughout the decades, despite gay liberation and beyond. Its origins are rooted in homophobia, as homosexuals historically have often been portrayed as lonely and often desperate older men, pedophiles seducing young boys in order to recruit them into the "homosexual lifestyle."

A 1961 best-selling sociological-psychological tract about homosexual life, *The Sixth Man* by Jess Stern, is one of many examples, noting "the oddities of older gays" whose fate is to live "in the Bowery, seeking oblivion in handouts and cheap wine . . . regressing to a point where [they] prey on small children." Norman Mailer went one better in an interview in 1962: " I think one of the reasons, that homosexuals go through such agony when they're around forty or fifty is that their lives have nothing to do with procreation. . . . They're used up their being."

"Such characterizations were universal," says seventy-one-year-old veteran activist Frank Kameny, who founded the Mattachine Society in Washington in the 1960s. "Along with all the other forms of demonization—that we were criminals, sinners, psychopaths—we were lonely and old and predatory."

That kind of demonization reached high points in the 1950s during the McCarthy era, in the 1970s during Anita Bryant's antigay "Save the Children" crusades, and even in the 1990s among Christian Right leaders, who mass-produced slick propaganda videos that described gays as "recruiting" children. The image of the lonely old queen in particular has always worked well for homophobic religious leaders and antigay politicians as a deterrent to young people who might act on their homosexuality, a warning that, should they "choose" the "homosexual lifestyle," they would be destined to lead lives of sadness and loneliness.

The stereotype, however, has been debunked since the 1960s in study after study, which show that older gay men—men over forty—once out of the closet, are comparatively content with the quality of their lives. In 1982, Raymond M. Berger, Ph.D., published one of the most important works in the field, *Gay and Gray: The Older Homosexual Man.* It was the result of a comprehensive study he and other researchers had done of 112 gay men—aged forty-one to seventy-seven—in a four-county area that encompassed urban, suburban, and semirural locales. Berger's research went a step further than previous studies: He showed that, contrary to popular belief, aging was perhaps even *less* stressful for gay men and lesbians than for heterosexuals, precisely because gays were often forced to come to terms with life crises—for example, the various traumas associated with accepting one's homosexuality—early on in life.

> For the most part we found striking similarities between the problems of our respondents and the problems of older individuals in general. . . . The older person must adapt to the loss of physical attractiveness and to the limitations of poor health often associated with advanced age. Inability to accept these changes may lead to depression and denial for some older people, both heterosexual and homosexual. . . . [But a] difference between older homosexuals and older heterosexuals is embodied in the "mastery of crisis" hypothesis. Many heterosexuals experience their first "crisis of independence" in old age. In earlier years they are integrated into their family of origin; when they leave this family, they move quickly into a family of procreation. Not until old age,

when children have left home, work associates and friends have dwindled due to retirement and death, and the spouse has died, is the older person left alone. Old age is not the best time to develop the where-withal to negotiate these changes. The older homo-sexual typically faces the crisis of independence much earlier, and he cannot usually look to a family of procreation for support. . . . Because the crisis of independence must be resolved in young adulthood, his transition to old age and retirement is often less severe.

Like previous studies, Berger also found that older gay men were not any more likely to be lonely and isolated than younger gay men; they tended to have a wide range of friends, to date and have relationships, and have active sex lives, with almost 75 percent content with the quality of their sex lives. Most in fact preferred men within their age range.

"Anything I might have imagined about the sex drive mer-cifully burning out with the passing of time has proved all wrong so far," says Alan, a forty-seven-year-old singer who lives in Queens, New York, and who is single and relatively satisfied with the quality of his life. "I've always liked older men, and it seldom occurs to me—until in some way it manifests itself obviously—that a younger man might *not* like me. But I'm black. So rude awakenings are nothing new to me. How do I feel about it? It makes me sad to lose an opportunity to share."

Alan has been in several relationships over his lifetime; having one now would be nice, he says, but he's content being single and has a lot of friends—whom he calls his "family"—and has no urgency to have a relationship. At this point, he says, it would have to be on his own terms. "I've never been sold on the idea of the so-called open relationship," he says. "Being blunt, I say it's bullshit. It's been my experience in such cases to watch one guy who wants to have a life of play, leaping in and out of the sack with people, but also continually wanting a shoulder to cry on when he has to go to the doctor for shots. His counterpart is usually one so deluded—he'll swear it's love every time—that he'll hold on by feigning agreeability when in his heart the idea of other hands on his heartthrob's goodies is in no way something he wants. For me, now, it's all or nothing. My bottom-line feeling on this is that after the making of a mutual commitment, if I did not find that I was satisfied with the total of what a man's got to give me or I've got to give to him, then it's time to close up shop and go look elsewhere."

Unlike Alan, Bob, a retired schoolteacher who lives in Arcadia, Washington, has a lot of sex with two different men he's been involved with for several years. He describes himself as a "decent-looking Scotch-Irishman, reasonably good-looking, a wholesome smile, in-shape body from working out." He says that younger men are attracted to him, but for the most part he's not really interested. "I'm quite sexually fulfilled by my two current sex-sharing men [both older]. I have no problems whatsoever growing older for I have never disassociated sexuality from my mind. My sexual experience is never 'anatomized' or 'bodily secularized'—I'm 'in it' body, mind, and spirit. Otherwise, sex would be about as interesting and stimulating as watching paint dry."

Bob, at sixty-five, breaks a few molds. He's not the stereotype of the retiree who has little or no sex drive, and who we have become conditioned to believe is alone and depressed. He also doesn't fit perhaps the most widespread stereotype in the gay world of older men who might still desire sex: the wealthy old queen who is "keeping" a young and attractive man, paying his way and giving him a good life in return for what little bit of sex he'll offer now and then. He's not particularly interested in younger men—again, defying the stereotype—and he certainly doesn't have time for any who might have hang-ups about older men.

At seventy-two, Dubose, also a retiree, doesn't have much sex at all and not nearly as much as he had "from 1950 to 1980," he says. But he's busy with a lot of other things. He moved to State College, Pennsylvania, home of Penn State University, after having lived in New York City for thirty-six years. Yet he seems to have met more gay friends of various ages, and more straight friends, than he ever had in New York.

"At this point in my life, I'm not looking for a long-term relationship, but I have quite a large number of gay friends, and I am grateful that I have a lot of much younger friends," he says. "As I'm retired, I can give more time to gay causes, and trying to help younger gays and lesbians. For instance, I am on the board of directors of our local chapter of P-FLAG [Parents, Families and Friends of Lesbians and Gays], with a special outreach to university students here, as well as high school students. I also help with the local AIDS project. I moved here just five years ago and I'm living in a continuing care retirement community, and enjoying it, even though I am the only gay [man] out of 250 people. There is one lesbian too! But both of us are fully accepted into the life of this community without prejudice from residents or management. Older people seem to be far more accepting of gays and lesbians in my judgment. I have not felt any prejudice of any kind. On the contrary, I'm very busy running the library, the sound system, slide shows, the weekly movies, on the program committee, and volunteer for many jobs that help the residents. It's fun and very rewarding."

KILLING MYSELF AT FIFTY

And yet, despite the testimonies of older men, as well as the work done by gerontologists and others in the field over the last few decades, the myth of the lonely old queen persists. The same fears expressed by Paul Monette in the passage at the beginning of the chapter are still shared by a great many young gay men today, particularly in the urban ghettos. In interviews and surveys, it is clear that many younger gay men view aging in the gay world as a fate worse, sometimes, even than early death.

"Growing older in the gay community is scary," says George, a twenty-nine-year-old Long Beach, California, student (who, ironically, is working toward his master's degree in social work). "I often have tremendous fear that I will be lonely. It seems that when you do get older in the gay community, you are kind of shunned. How then do you meet anyone? These are the thoughts that I have when I'm depressed."

"I have a fair amount of fear of [growing older]," says Jay, also twenty-nine, a massage therapist who lives in Madison, Wisconsin. "I already feel like an older man in the gay community. I feel that with the focus of most men on wanting someone eighteen, that I am 'over the hill' and that it will become more and more difficult to find a romantic relationship."

Some younger gay men nervously laugh off growing older, mocking older men, and often even laughing at their own aging process while still expressing revulsion and horror.

"I already feel ancient at the clubs," says Sean, a thirty-two-year-old New York entertainer. "I am mostly concerned about being lonely when I'm old. I know that being one of the last of the boomers, there will be a lot of us when I'm a SAGE [Senior Action in a Gay Environment] member. We'll probably still find each other for Donna Summer sing-alongs! Of course, the truth is that older men are actually our mirrors, and the picture can be a frightening one. 'If you think I am old, know that I am your future.' Yikes! Who wants to deal with that reality when there's [partying] to do?"

"When gay men reach a certain age, they are slapped with the label 'troll' on their foreheads," cracks twenty-eight-year-old Andy, another New Yorker. "The gay community might as well find an island where men over forty should be whisked off, sparing them any of the humiliation the younger gay population subjects them to."

It might be true that in an American culture so youth-obsessed, all young people, gay and straight, fear growing older. But many young gay men often identify a different timetable in the gay world and the straight world when it comes to aging.

"The joke when I turned twenty-six was that I was 'over the hill'—twenty-six for most hets is at least fifty in 'gay years,'" observes Bryan, a student who is still twenty-six and lives in Austin, Texas. "And when I stop to think about it, twenty-six is not old anyway, even though it certainly feels like it is. I do dread thirty-five. Gay culture is definitely youth-oriented. It is strange to think that in a couple of years the whole business may just pass me by."

The different timetable around aging has many younger gay men seeing even middle-aged men as being desperate to fight aging.

"When I see these men in the gym in their forties and fifties just knocking themselves out, it's just unbelievable to me," observes Jose, a twenty-five-year-old Mexican-American student who lives in Houston. "I keep saying to myself, No, Jose, you are not going to do that. Don't let that happen to you.

But when you really study why they're doing it, because they're so afraid to get old, and you look at your own body now and other guys' bodies who are your age, and you realize that you don't want to lose it or you'll be worthless. Those men are working so hard to look young, going to all of these bars and the clubs at their age, the clubs where all the people in their twenties go. I know some of them and I like them and respect them and consider them friends. But I sometimes want to say to them, 'What the hell are you doing on this scene? What are you doing to yourself?'"

Tragically, quite a few young men even say that growing older as a gay man is one of the things, in addition to the fear of becoming infected with HIV, that makes them sometimes wish they were heterosexual. "I really love being gay and I love gay men," says Joseph, a twenty-four-year-old unemployed Minneapolis musician. "I think I have come to terms with it a great deal in the last few years since coming out, and I feel a great affinity for this community. But getting old in this community is the one thing that makes me sometimes, in my deepest thoughts, wish I were straight—something I haven't dared to tell anyone. And because I'm Asian I feel it even more. I think for men of color, it's like, if you're young, you're cute, exotic, whatever. But when you're older, you're dirty, ugly. The way I have seen old gay men treated in the bars, and the loneliness that you can see that they endure—it's just really hopeless. Older people who are heterosexual aren't doing that stuff, going out to bars and trying to meet young people, since they don't have to, and they're not treated as terribly by young people. I had a friend who died of AIDS, an older guy—well, older than me, thirty-five—and he said to me once, when he wasn't feeling so good, 'I guess I should look at the bright side. I've lived a lot, had a great time, and now I don't ever have to be an old troll, which is what I have always feared. Maybe this is really a blessing.' That stuck in my mind and comes back to haunt, you know, when I'm feeling dejected or something. It's not that I'd rather have AIDS than grow old. But between the two of them, sometimes you do think maybe being straight is better off."

Tony, a twenty-one-year-old San Diego student, describes the even more extreme feelings that his own fears of aging in the gay community dredge up, and alarmingly, his response was not uncommon, expressed by far too many younger gay men in interviews and surveys who dreaded the idea of being the lonely old queen: "I feel threatened and unsure about growing old. Several times, I've thought about killing myself at age fifty, no matter how prosperous I was."

It's not hard to imagine then how the fear of growing older in the gay world plays into young gay men's decisions about safer sex—and it is among young gay men in particular that epidemiologists have in recent years noted a difficulty in maintaining safer sex practices. In a study conducted of young gay men in 1992 in San Francisco, for example, one HIV-positive twentysomething young gay man, reiterating an all-too-common sentiment, told researchers: "My boyfriend [who is negative] is willing to have unsafe sex with me. . . . He doesn't want to be another aging queen, being jeered at by people like himself, being laughed at."

These views underscore that, though the stereotype of the lonely old queen may have originated within heterosexual culture, the gay world itself has done a great deal to vigorously promote it. Many gay men today still buy into the stereotype. The cult of masculinity demands of its members that they fear and hate the lonely old queen.

LIPOSUCTION, TUMMY TUCKS, AND BUTT LIFTS

Focused obsessively and solely on youthful physical looks, the cult offers to younger men only a very narrow, negative image of older men. And many men, as they enter middle age, fulfill the prophecy for younger men, sometimes going to ridiculous extremes to appear young as the cult of masculinity begins its insidious process of rejecting them, stamping them with the old queen label.

"I can't say I never thought it would get to this, because I always knew it would—the idea of not being attractive anymore is downright frightening to me," Peter, a forty-six-year-old Boston attorney, tells me. Peter has a deep, dark tan—always— as he goes to the tanning salon twice a week and has done so, on and off, for almost ten years. But the artificial sun—combined with the real sun on Fire Island and other gay summer vacation destinations over the years—has taken its toll. Peter had a dermabrasion a few years ago to battle wrinkles, but now he says he needs something more. He's going for his first facelift, taking off a month from work. "Actually, I wanted to get it done years ago, but I never had the time," he says. "So I walked around looking a little like a prune for a while. That's why I went to the tanning salon a lot because, believe it or not, you look better with a wrinkled face when it's tan, even though the tan gives you further wrinkles! I have had liposuction on my tummy area. It was pretty painful—but yes, I'd do it again, and I'm sure I will. What is the alternative? Sitting around while all the good-looking and gorgeous men are playing? Going to church socials? Playing mah-jongg? That's not me. I want to stretch out this life I have as long as I can, and then I'll just roll over and die—in a few years they can cart me off to the old-age home. I go to a lot of parties. I travel quite a bit. I do Fire Island in the summer when I can. I had a share for a few years, but it's a trip from here. I'm going to Mardi Gras in Sydney next year — biggest gay party ever. It may be the last time I can go to that kind of grand, fabulous event. I want to look my best and I should." He cracks a smile, and then says, only half-jokingly, "I'm going to be forty-seven in three months, and in three years, fifty — and that's it man, you're dead then. I'm already living on borrowed time as it is."

When Peter says he looks at fifty as the year he'll be "dead" and talks about already having lived on "borrowed time," one might think he has AIDS or is HIV-positive. Quite to the contrary, he's HIV-negative. He simply means that there's nothing worth living for. He sees this time in his life as his last great hurrah, before he's packed away for good. He is like a great many men in their forties, still trying to be active on the party circuit, who told me of extraordinary lengths they've gone to in order to look young. Many men over forty, for example, feeling that they must compete with increasingly buff twenty-four-year-olds, are using steroids precisely because it is very difficult for the body to bulk up on its own after forty. Growth hormone is not produced in the body as it was in years earlier. Yet at the same time, because of their age, they are much more susceptible to liver damage, particularly if they have had hepatitis in years gone by, and a great many men over forty have had one form of hepatitis or another, which is most often sexually transmitted. But steroids are the least of the cosmetic enhancements some gay men over forty in the urban centers discussed when relating the various ways they are trying to both compete with and attract younger men.

In terms of surgery and other cosmetic procedures, beyond face-lifts and liposuction, many gay men who are in their forties and on the circuit (or who come on and off of the circuit for different intervals of time) talk of tummy tucks, pectoral implants, calf implants, laser treatments, chemical peels, cheek surgery, jaw surgery, eyelid surgery, chin augmentation, dermabrasion, collagen implants, hair transplants, butt lifts, and, of course, nose jobs (complaining, for example, that their noses are "dipping" as they grow older).

"I have had more work than most people know or suspect," says Richard, a fifty-one-year-old dentist. Richard looks remarkable, not a day over thirty-eight, and like a *Men's Health* model, rugged and sturdy, although there is a waxy texture to him that betrays the work that has been done on him. He estimates that he has spent over $35,000 on cosmetic enhancements.

Richard has had a face-lift, a nose job, eyelid surgery, cheek surgery, a chin augmentation, liposuction (once on his thighs, twice on his lower back, abdomen, and side), ear surgery (to pull his ears back), a breast reduction (his breasts had become enlarged through steroids use ten years ago because his body had produced too much estrogen). Of course, he also has perfect teeth. But after all of that, Richard has recently developed skin cancer on his face and on his back, a product perhaps of years of sitting on beaches as well as weekly sessions at the tanning salon. "Now I don't know what to do," he says. "I'm, you know, saying to the doctor, 'Come on, there has to be some surgery, something we can do.' And he just keeps saying, you know, with a firm look on his face, 'What you have to do is stay out of the sun. Period.' And I'm saying back to him, 'Doc, that is *not* an option here.'"

Ironically, by trying desperately to escape the image of the lonely old queen, these and other men instead perpetuate it— and eventually simply become it.

Whether they are middle-aged men in a futile battle with aging, trying to appear youthful and stay on the scene, or even older men like Arthur, who are disdainful of themselves and all older men and who go out to the bars, attempting to connect with any younger man who will give them the time of day, these older men are often the most visible image of older gay men that many younger men see: desperate and fearful.

Some of these older men even sometimes lament that younger men are too focused on the physical, and they complain that younger men refuse to see other, nonphysical qualities they have to offer. And yet, these men over forty seem not to see the inherent contradiction in their thinking: They too are only attracted to younger men and are as much concerned with the physical body as the younger men they accuse of being shallow. How can they expect younger men to break from the cult of masculinity when they themselves refuse to?

And though there are so many other older gay men—perhaps the majority, according to the studies—who are not wasting their time on the scene but are leading productive lives, having coped with aging perhaps better than most heterosexuals, they are invisible to most younger gay men in the urban gay ghettos, where gay life is so segmented and compartmentalized.

But both the deghettoization of homosexuality within the cities and the deurbanization of homosexuality across the country are perhaps slowly changing that.

KILLING OFF THE LONELY OLD QUEEN

"This is a small community—seventy thousand total population," says Michael, a forty-two-year-old librarian who lives in Menasha, Wisconsin. "Since there are so few places for gay men and lesbians to socialize, there's very little room for segregation. You see a lot of mixing and socializing between the generations. Sometimes I go out to bars—there are two bars here in Fox Valley, but I'm not fond of bars. I've met people through the reading club I belong to. I think there's a lot of attention given to youth, beauty, and muscles in the gay press. I don't think that's the reality of most of the men I've met."

As more and more gay men come out of the closet at younger ages and push families to accept them—many coming out in their teens—in both the urban centers as well as in rural, suburban, and small-town areas, the gay bar is no longer the first place where they meet other gays. With community centers sprouting up in even small towns, gay churches such as MCC in many cities and towns, and gay youth groups and gay groups for seniors abounding, more and more young gay men and older gay men are meeting one another in these locales.

"Most of the older men I know are associated with my [gay] youth group," says Matt, a nineteen-year-old student who lives in Indianapolis, discussing a gay-support group he belongs to, where older men and younger men interact. "I look up to them immensely. I want to know what it was like back when they were younger, and they add an interesting perspective to all the issues that us younger gays and lesbians deal with. They've been through it all—and then some."

More and more younger gay men in the cities and beyond are beginning to meet a wider variety of older gay men. These tend to be the men who are not necessarily scouring the bars and doing the circuit. In organized settings and support groups too, more and more younger gay men are meeting many lesbians, young and old, who often have a profound impact on them, an experience that the male-focused cult of masculinity does not offer.

"Most of the older gay men I know, who are my good friends, are university professors and teachers," says George, a twenty-one-year-old student in Hartford, Connecticut. "I guess that's because most of the people I know who are gay are from school. I don't go out much to clubs and bars. Actually I don't go at all. I'm just now legal, so maybe I'll go but I'm not really in a rush. I have some friends who are into the clubs and some who aren't — younger friends I mean. But I have a lot of older gay and lesbian friends, and none of them are out at clubs or anything. I met them in groups I belonged to at school, and I met two of my dearest friends when I was in high school, when I first came out. I went to a meeting for lesbian and gay and bisexual youth, and these two men — they're life partners, both high school teachers, and they're both forty-four — were like lifesavers for me. We've been friends ever since. We do the movies, I go to parties at their house — on Halloween they have a really campy drag party. All the queens come, of every age, and it's a hoot. Another one of my closest friends is Ellen, a sixty-three-year-old lesbian friend who I visit once a week. I know more about lesbians at this point than even some of my younger lesbian friends. I never really knew the two cultures were so different, but I think gay men could learn a lot from lesbians."

In some ways there is a subtle conflict between the two forces — the cult of masculinity and the deghettoization of homosexuality. It is a battle not only over control of whether or not *young* men will buy into the stereotype of the lonely old queen; it is also very much over control of older men's relationship to the stereotype as well.

Under the influence of deghettoization, many older men, having spent years in the cult, are now backing away from it a bit as they reach forty (or sometime thereafter), rather than buy into the stereotype of the lonely old queen. For many of them that realization is a moment of truth, a period of crisis that requires adjustment but which is followed by a sense of resolve.

"I had a panic attack," says Drew, a thirty-eight-year-old Philadelphia chiropractor, discussing a change he has been experiencing in his life. "That was before a trip to San Francisco that [my lover] and I went on. I was never afraid of flying, but on the plane, we're sitting in first class, having gotten an upgrade, and I just had a panic attack. Then on the way back it was this low-level anxiety that stuck with me. I was very confused. I was asking myself, Where was this coming from? Why was I depressed? Why was I frightened or scared? The more I started to delve into the issues, I started looking at it, realizing I was going through a change. I was dealing with growing older, realizing the vulnerabilities. I think because of AIDS, seeing death and dying all around you, it comes earlier. I always saw myself as never afraid of death, never afraid of getting older. Then all of a sudden, here you are, and it's so quick."

Drew notes too that, even for gay men and even considering AIDS, he was perhaps having his midlife crisis a bit early. "I've always been, like a little older than I am," he says. "I was losing my hair at nineteen. I always looked older than I was. I was a daddy when I was still a kid."

Instead of responding to this passage in his life by frantically trying to look young, by running to the gym, by forcing himself on the scene, by feeling that was the only choice, Drew decided to break free. A dark, handsome man, Drew had for many years been on the Fire Island scene, renting a share every season. But he decided this year to give that up; instead, he decided to rent a home in upstate New York, in the country, year-round.

"You realize that there are certain things that come with

age," he says. "There are certain things you're going to lose, one of them being physical attributes, and you have more health problems. But there are other valuable things that you gain. I see myself in that transition now and focusing a lot on things I never focused on before. Other things become less important. I don't work out at the gym as cosmetically as I did—it's now more health-oriented. And I kind of feel liberated, or rather I see a liberation coming. I'm just making that separation from the narcissism. I haven't participated in [the party scene] for a while. That whole Chelsea thing, the party thing, everything that's out there right now, I don't feel I'm the ideal at this point. Rather than try to fit in, I'd rather do other things."

Thinking the transition would be difficult, Drew says it's not been as bad as he thought it would be, perhaps because being gay has taught him a lot about adversity. "All of the things I've been through in my life, well I've always gotten to the other side," he says. "I mean, with family, which I'm very close with now, and other different hurdles I've gone through a lot and I'll get through this. I'm starting to observe what other people are doing, how they handle it. I have had a client for ten years who is a cop, and he was always a really macho guy, and I've been watching him deal with growing older. As he's gotten older, he's just gotten kinder, gentler. Fatherly, in a way. And I like that, and see myself in that way now. I've always had the capacity to mentor [young people]. That's something I'd like to do now."

A GENERATION OF MENTORS

Drew hits upon something that seems crucial if gay men are truly to put to death the stereotype of the lonely old queen: We must create a generation of mentors, not simply to offer to those men who are growing older a sense of meaning and purpose in their lives beyond the cult, but so that younger men will interact with older men outside of the bars, nightclubs, and other sexual venues. We must begin the process of passing down the truth to young gay men so that they don't make the same mistakes, so that they learn from the rest of us about the emptiness of the cult, and so that they see there is a future for them and that the lonely old queen is not inevitable.

In creating mentors, we educate ourselves not just about aging and growing older, however, but also about a variety of important issues that many of us are searching for answers to, even issues as seemingly simple as maintaining friendships and relationships.

"Too many of us subscribe to the myth that we are neither capable nor inclined to achieve long-term happiness in same-sex relationships," writes lesbian psychotherapist Betty Berzon in *The Intimacy Dance.* "That is a myth, because there are quite enough long-term couples around to debunk the notion that gay and lesbian relationships *can't* have a long life. The problem is that there is so little cross-generational socializing in the gay community that the real-life evidence of longevity isn't easily visible and accessible."

The lack of mentoring also affects us in more dramatic ways. It seems that even the life-and-death lessons of the AIDS crisis are not passed down adequately, and this is certainly ringing true in studies that show a breakdown in safer sex among young men. Beyond the often cold and impersonal communication of safer sex campaigns, many young gay men are not having the safer sex message solidly instilled in them. Part of the problem is that they are not experiencing firsthand mentoring from older people about issues such as safer sex.

Too many adult gay men, it is evident in interviews and surveys, are reeling from their own internalized homophobia with regard to dealing with young men. They are fearful of being close to gay men in their teens and early twenties, often because of society's stigma about gay men "recruiting" youth. Many of these older men say they are afraid of being tarred with an ugly stereotype, or are truly afraid of their own quite normal but controllable sexual attractions. In other cases, older gay men say they don't want to be with younger gay men because it reminds them of how old they are in a subculture that values youth and beauty so intensely; some say they actually feel depressed around young people for this reason.

At worst, some older gay men actually do feed into the ugly stereotypes, engaging in consensual sex with gay youth, often in their midteens, who might not yet have come to terms with their sexuality and are still confused and easily manipulated. Even though the youth consents to the sex, he might be doing so simply because he wants some guidance and trusts the older man. The older man is often (but not always) having sex with the younger man because it's emotionally less demanding than dealing with a grown-up. Sadly, but nonetheless true, sometimes older men seek out younger men because they want to have unprotected sex and know that younger men might not demand it.

It's impossible to know how prevalent such cases are. Still they should not be used to make generalizations about all sex between older and younger men. There have always been young men who are more equipped than others to deal with sex: I, for example, had sex at thirteen with a thirty-year-old man, not because I was coerced or was seeking guidance but because I was actively seeking sex, knew the man would oblige, and was, I believe, mature enough to handle it. There are, of course, older men who in such situations are very responsible when it comes to safer sex. Whether or not such sexual partnering is morally wrong—and the gay and lesbian community has heatedly debated this issue for decades—it should be assumed that the younger male is not aware enough to deal with the responsibilities of safer sex, and the older gay man should act responsibly.

"One side of it I believe is low self-esteem—on both sides," says Gregory Hutchings, prevention coordinator at the Agency for HIV and AIDS in Washington, D.C. A forty-year-old HIV-positive African-American gay man, Hutchings came out at thirty-one, after having been married (and later divorced) and after having had children. He has both a teenage son and a teenage daughter, but he has lots of other "children," as he calls them—young, mostly black, gay men in Washington, D.C., between the ages of fifteen and twenty-two whom he mentors.

"For a lot of these kids today, there is a lack of mentoring," he says. "They're into their 'lifestyle.' They're more out, more comfortable with their sexuality, but it doesn't mean they're more comfortable with themselves. They're interacting with older people who are not insisting on safer sex. [Older gay men] can be very persuasive, particularly if you know people don't have self-esteem. You can intimidate them very easily to a point where they actually feel ashamed [to ask for] a condom. You're the adult. You're the grown-up, and they don't think enough of themselves to ask for it. The other side of it is that a lot of older men are in denial themselves, in the closet. And these younger people are sitting here looking and saying, 'None of these older folks are using [condoms] so why should we?'"

By both allowing and encouraging young gay men to inter-act with him and observe his life, Hutchings provides young gay men with some insight that they probably won't get else-where about the epidemic. "What I try to do with young kids is instill in them—and they know that I'm [HIV] positive and some of them are positive too–the idea of talking about being positive, about AIDS, about using condoms. We talk about protecting yourself. We talk about unsafe sex. They have not known a lot of people who've died. But they [hear about] the people that *I know* who have died. And they watch my reac-tions, and they watch the relationships I have, and they watch all of the people they've met through me, and it's brought a reality to them. That mentoring part is very important. If these kids are coming out in the world with their sexuality, and they have no one to look up to, and their visualization of someone to look up to is just older men who just want to get in bed with them, then they have nothing to show them some type of prin-ciples, some type of esteem, and some type of direction."

A lack of nonsexual intergenerational mixing and bond-ing, Hutchings observes, is pervasive throughout all age groups in the gay world. "Particularly even in my generation," he says, noting men in their thirties and forties. "We should know the sixty- or seventy-year-olds and be the bridge that in turn links the kids that we may know to the older folks. But a lot of us don't know men in either group, above or below us. It's because of the fragmentation of the [gay] culture. We've got our closet folks, we've got transgender versus gay, white versus black, butch versus queen. Nobody comes together. There is no unity. That's why I try to get them all together. That's my biggest mission, to network them. We've got to start sharing it with smaller groups and hoping to build it into larger groups."

Before taking on mentoring, however, many gay men have to deal with a lot of issues on their own. Hutchings notes that older gay men have not been allowed to view themselves as mentors: They're often instilled with the idea, still dominant in the larger culture, that they are sexual predators, lonely old queens preying on the young. Getting past that, and rejecting the lies and distortions, is crucial in order for mentoring to exist. While a lot of gay men will feign a disinterest in mentoring, stating they simply don't like being around young people, Hutchings believes it is really the fear of the ugly stereotype that is operating in their desire to distance themselves from gay youth.

"One of the biggest problems in mentoring that I hear from a lot of older men is dealing with their own issues," Hutchings says. "It brings back those issues of sexual abuse, so they feel they can't have a relationship from a mentoring point of view. So they run from it. People have actually come to my house and have refused to stay at my house because there are too many young kids. And I don't mean stay overnight—I mean they won't stay more than five minutes. They're like, 'There are too many young kids here, I'm not going to be in this situation.' They feel old, but it's more than that—it's bringing back the memories of putting them in this [negative] category. And they're like, 'I'm getting away from here.' I have a big birthday party every year, and I've actually had folks come up to me at the party and say, 'This is unacceptable. You shouldn't have these kids here.' And a lot of these kids are over eighteen! One person called me and said, 'I refuse to come to your parties.' We're talking about probably two hundred people at this party, and ten or fifteen of them were kids and young adults. But that is enough to scare them.

"So these are some of those issues involved around mentoring. That's why we really need to get involved in kind of mentoring ourselves first, the people in our own generations, to teach people how to mentor into other generations. We've got to talk about it and bring out some of these issues that are there."

Encouraging mentoring in the gay male community, Hutchings notes, does not in actuality mean introducing something new but rather drawing upon something that has gone on in the larger culture for centuries. "I think that if older men have a responsibility to mentor younger men in the straight society, and in the culture as a whole, or in being Italian, or being a Jew, or being a Catholic, then you should have the same responsibility if you're gay," he says. "It shouldn't be any different."

Hutchings sees mentoring as crucial to gay survival right now, particularly among men in their thirties and forties. His vision of how AIDS will continue its course unless more of us begin mentoring is frightening. In many ways, he makes a call to action to us all. "I think a lot of the responsibility now [is] with the middle generation," Hutchings observes. "This [acceptance by the larger culture] of the freedom of sexuality has kind of appeared in the generation of the kids that are now twenty, twenty-one, twenty-two. I mean, when they were coming up it was much more open and freer. But they don't have a real link to anything that went before them. It's up to the thirty- and forty-year-olds to start mending these bridges between older generations and the younger people. A lot the older people, like everyone else, they're afraid of HIV. Because truly, in this world, if you're fifty or sixty years old and you're gay, well, you consider yourself blessed even to be alive. So you're scared of that, and you're automatically going to cut yourself off— from everything, in a lot of senses. And I think that's one of the problems that we have also with HIV, that if we don't stop it soon, we're losing a whole lot of the middle generation— *again*—and the younger generation is getting infected—

again. And of the people in their thirties and forties who actually do make it to be the elders in ten or twenty years, they may cut themselves off, *again*. Where does this community go? There's not going to be any direction for any of the young people. The situation just keeps repeating itself.

"That's why we've got to start now. We're the ones who have the foresight and hindsight, the people between thirty and fifty. The people who are in their fifties and sixties, they don't have a clue as to what these younger kids are dealing with, with this newfound freedom. We are the ones who do. We are close enough in age to the older ones to know what it was like for those who are older, and we also know what these kids are like coming up. We can kind of paint the picture for them about what they should do, and about developing that respect for older people. This is about personal responsibility. True, it's about each *individual*. But when the numbers connect, then it gets better. I tell people all the time, considering the number of people we have, if each person taught one younger person, took them in, we could do so much better. We could do so much."

As Gregory Hutchings so movingly puts it, if each of us does his part, if each of us mentors just one gay kid, if we all reach out to the people of the generations both below us and above us, there is no telling what we could achieve.

We could loosen the grip of the cult of masculinity.

We could encourage the growth of the deghettoization and deurbanization of homosexuality.

And we could, finally, put to the death the ugly and debilitating stereotype of the sad and lonely old queen.

EPILOGUE

Traveling the gay male world, through the urban scene in the gay ghettos and beyond, I experienced the boundless possibilities available to gay men. I also saw, more so than ever before, the limitations that so many of us put on ourselves.

Once a vital part of overthrowing oppression, the particular scene in the urban ghettos that I studied for this book today seems, ironically, to be having the opposite effect on so many men: It keeps them perpetually locked in one, highly superficial, ghetto lifestyle, chained to what they know best, keeping them from expanding their lives. The indulgences that this lifestyle encourages and the insecurities that it exploits provide these men with all of the highs and lows in their lives, offering them none of the richness of queer life that abounds both within the gay ghettos and beyond.

Even as a great many other gay men do experience that richness, much of what the scene promotes filters down to them to varying degrees. This occurs in tangible ways that are easier to chart, such as the persistence of the AIDS epidemic, due in part to unsafe sex that continues in many of the scene's circles, often exacerbated or even encouraged by the scene lifestyle. But as this book noted in great detail, it also affects them in less tangible ways, generating a cultural influence that impacts how we all perceive ourselves and one another.

But while all of this might seem depressing and hopeless to many, particularly when we look at how AIDS has ravaged the gay population, gay men in America are at the threshold of great and positive change. If we can in particular lessen the influence of the scene, and loosen the grip of the cult of masculinity, a brighter future awaits us. The new drugs that have emerged and continue to be developed for the treatment of people infected with HIV, for example, have put us at the very beginning of a road to ending the plague. If we can at this crucial moment contain the epidemic by increasing the uptake of safer sex, we might see the end of AIDS more quickly than we had imagined.

Beyond seeing a hope in ending AIDS, we are on the brink of perhaps the greatest political gains the lesbian and gay community has ever seen. As of January 1997, lesbians and gay men were at the dawn of legalized same-sex marriage, as Hawaii was about to legalize same-sex marriage, beginning a years-long battle for marriage rights in other states. Whether or not Hawaii does follow through on its intentions remains to be seen. But the debate alone has caused much of America to think more carefully about our lives, our relationships, and our uniquely gay families. In 1996, for the first time ever, Congress debated both gay marriage and legal protections for gays and lesbians in employment in this country. And while we lost both fights, simply having American legislators discussing such issues was a major win. We in fact only came within one vote of Senate approval of employment protections, so it appears that that is something we will see in the very near future.

The visibility of gays and lesbians has exploded throughout the media as even small-town newspapers across the country daily cover gay and lesbian issues, and often have their letters pages overrun with debates about topics ranging from same-sex marriage to the surge of lesbian and gay characters in television sitcoms. For gay teenagers alone, this visibility opens enormous possibilities. Indeed, a queer youth movement has formed in cities, suburbs, and small towns across the country, as gay teens are coming out, asserting themselves, and defining themselves as gay before getting drawn in to the gay ghetto scene.

There is a responsibility on all of us right now to make sure all young gay men know of all the varied possibilities, and to make them aware that there's much more to queer life beyond the cult of masculinity.

And there is also a responsibility on us all to make sure that the many other gay men we know, young and old, who are submerged within the cult—indeed, including ourselves—are aware of what lies beyond it, and are encouraged to take a fresh look at life outside.

AFTERWORD

December 16, 1997

Touring the country with *Life Outside*, visiting book-stores, coffee shops, bars, college campuses, gay pride festivals, and gay community centers has been a profound experience, as I witnessed many gay men's openness, honesty, and determination to move forward with their lives. Many spoke with me about their sexual lives, their relationships, their steroid abuse, their use of recreational drugs, their family lives, their dilemmas about growing older, their activism, their self-images, and their perceptions of the community as a whole.

I held public discussions in the biggest cities such as New York, Chicago, Boston, Washington, Atlanta, Philadelphia, Seattle, Minneapolis, San Francisco, and Los Angeles, meeting many of the men who populate the urban gay world who had read *Life Outside*. I also traveled to places big and small outside the most familiar urban gay ghettos, including Corvallis, Oregon; Bloomington, Illinois; Orono, Maine; Rochester, New York; Nashville, Tennessee; Birmingham,

Alabama; Madison, Wisconsin; Gainesville, Florida; and Las Vegas, Nevada.

In particular, I was often impressed by the age range of the audiences of men that turned out to speak about these important issues. Often in my travels, men in their fifties, sixties, and seventies came together and spoke about these heartfelt topics with men in their twenties, thirties, and forties, and often a renewed sense of unity seemed to be forged, something that would last far beyond the particular event.

Within days of *Life Outside*'s publication in April of 1997, I also began to receive hundreds of e-mail messages from men across the United States and around the world who had noticed my e-mail address in *Out* magazine. I'd received cards and letters in response to my previous books and to articles I've written, but this was different. The often lengthy, often passionate, and introspective notes were quite remarkable.

As I stated in the introduction to this book, I did not write *Life Outside* as an attack on masculinity, male beauty, gay sexual culture, sex in general, going to the gym, or partying and celebration. Rather, *Life Outside* was written for those of us who have experienced problems navigating those areas of our lives, gay men who have at some time or another allowed the urban gay scene and its values to consume them and to define their self-worth in ways they recognized as emotionally, psychologically, and physically unhealthy. *Life Outside* was also written for those gay men who have been coping more successfully with aspects of life that have troubled others. The book was meant to explore and reflect some of these men's lives, offering both visibility for them and insightful examples for others.

Many of the e-mail writers, particularly those in the

urban gay world, discussed how they recognized themselves and their own friends in *Life Outside*. Some of these men said they began a transformation. They made changes in their lives regarding their relationship to the party scene, for example, or their devotion to a particular body ideal.

"I am a thirty-year-old gay white male living in the conservative, but ever plastic and pretentious city of Dallas, Texas," one man wrote with humor. "I was working out religiously, partying till dawn, wearing the right clothes, driving the right car, knew all the right people, and in a nutshell was doing whatever it took to be 'in.' It ate up most of my time and money to keep up this pace. But hey, 'It was worth it, right?'

"Wrong! I came to realize that all of the things I was doing to be 'grand and gorgeous' were simply meaningless. I was literally selling my soul to be part of the 'cult.' Thanks for helping to wake me up. I almost lost my heart, soul, and a really great man (my boyfriend). I have started volunteering, spending more time with my friends, less time at the gym, and generally have decided that I am 'OK' the way I am."

"My ex-boyfriend gave the book to me and it's helped bring us together again," another man happily reported. "To make a long story short, I was one of those party boys who thought he had everything under control, did it in moderation—and didn't realize how the lifestyle can actually control you without your knowing it. Anyway, thanks for analyzing the scene for me and making suggestions on how to get out of it."

While some of these men said they'd decided to explore life outside the scene a bit more, others talked about how, for them, it wasn't necessarily about getting off the urban scene or even off the circuit but rather about approaching these social landscapes with a new and different perspective. Some discussed how they became more prepared for their own further explorations of the urban scene and how that was a good thing for them.

"I recognized myself on the cusp of 'falling into' the cult of masculinity," a Denver man wrote. "After reading the book, [I found myself] asking myself piercing questions about who I am and what I want out of life. I am a thirty-five-year-old gay Asian male. I work out. I take care of myself. I have a creative—and hard—job. I'm finally coming out of my shell and finding out what it's like to be popular and sexy and wanted. I feel the urge to experiment, and I have wanted to go to a circuit party. I still may go to a circuit party, but I don't think I'll need the drugs nor will I feel the desperation that comes from not 'fitting in' in the party boy clique. I guess the book reaffirmed what I already knew, and what I was almost ready to forget: I have a good life. I have good friends. I am attractive and desirable, even if I don't go to circuit parties. I can be hot and sexy in my own world, and pity the poor bastards who can't see me in that light."

Many men who'd previously felt invisible within gay culture, particularly those outside the cities, wrote to say they were quite happy to see themselves reflected. "I am thrilled to see my life and the lives of so many of my friends who live in small towns and suburbs and rural areas affirmed," a thirty-two-year-old man from Decatur, Illinois wrote. "We are often happy and thriving, and yet we are stereotyped as misleadingly as the urban gay world is often stereotyped, just in a different way." A thirty-nine-year-old Seattle man wrote, "As someone who has lived in big cities—New York, Los Angeles, Dallas, now Seattle—but has always been outside of the 'scene,' I'm grateful to see that I am far from alone. There is a whole big gay world out there, outside the narrow and commercial sexual culture that dominates the big cities. Truth is, we are the majority of gay men while we're often wrongly shown to be the minority."

Many older men too wrote to say they felt freshly empowered. "It's not often that the issues of aging in the gay community are addressed in books, or that the cult of youth is criticized and revealed to be so shallow," a sixty-four-year-old Westchester, New York man wrote me. "It's hard for me, sometimes, to tell myself that I'm still valued, that just because I don't have my youthful looks I'm still worth a lot in the gay community and elsewhere in the world. The book confronted the painful issues we don't want to face, and is helping me to plot a course and renew my sense of purpose."

Many young gay men also wrote to say that the book confirmed their first glimpses of some aspects of gay culture, and for them this seemed to have created a lot of soul-searching and self-reflection. "I live in Southern California," one nineteen-year-old man wrote. "I just recently came out of the closet and I started reading *Life Outside* and it impacted me. I have been tossing and turning since I began reading the book.

"I unfortunately have fallen into the same pattern you describe. Spending Saturday nights in West Hollywood, spending countless hours at the gym. My first excursion to West Hollywood was only seven months ago. And in those seven months I have trimmed sixty pounds, completely changed my wardrobe, and developed an eating disorder. I am at six feet four genetically able to achieve the 'ideal.' I read through your book and I see what all these other men are thinking, and these are the same men that look at me (my youth) when I am out. I love to see all those muscle men, and I like it when they look back. I know that steroids are at my gym, and I know I could get them. I also know it's wrong. I am at the larva stage of every 'Stepford Homo' you described. This scares the hell out of me. I'm glad that I now understand the 'cult,' as you put it."

A great many other men, young and old, sent me similarly detailed reflections on gay life and on their own startling, painful, and personal experiences. Many of them raised important questions about how we are to proceed as a people and how we are to grapple with the issues that plague us. "I don't fit what people like to think of as a 'loner' in gay society," a Los Angeles man wrote. "People like me go to A list parties and hit the circuit. But the catch is, I've never liked the nightlife, and I find huge crowds boring and disorienting. I look at the crowds in the gym (where I used to go to feel centered and enjoy the feel of being so physical), and I feel alienated.

"And now we've got the bareback crowd. Imagine my surprise when a guy I was having a hot afternoon of sex with last year told me that he wanted me to fuck him without a condom. It was such a hot situation, I was so turned on, that I turned off my internal 'warning signal' and went for it. You know what I'm talking about—losing years worth of control and finally having sex without that damned latex barrier. Then I stopped and freaked out. I had made a mistake, my first in all those years. But what was going on with this hot number in my bed? He said he was negative, but didn't really care what my status was. He felt that hot sex was more important than protection. Hot sex was worth more than his life.

"So that's where we're at now, eh? Have we put sex on such a pedestal that it is now worth losing your life over? Of losing your job, your self-respect, your friends? How did it come to this? I don't want to be cast into the role of the moralist, but can we have some sort of discussion about morality (much less mortality), ethics—whatever—in the gay community?"

As the Los Angeles man implied, *Life Outside* examines some very sensitive issues and raises the kinds of questions that make a lot of people uncomfortable. The book became highly controversial soon after it was published and was embroiled in often heated media debates throughout 1997. Some gay men disagreed with some or all of the views and findings in *Life Outside* and were quite critical of the book for a variety of reasons. Some men who travel the circuit protested *Life Outside*'s analysis of the circuit. Other men said they believed the impact of the commercialized urban gay culture on the larger gay community was not as great as I'd found it to be. Still other men believed there should have been more coverage in *Life Outside* of the many men outside the scene, both inside and outside the cities.

Some criticisms of *Life Outside* were rather harsh and even quite angry. Some men felt, quite strongly, that *Life Outside* was much too critical of gay sexual culture. Others were angered by my discussing sexual and/or emotional monogamy as an option for some men, claiming that by merely focusing on monogamy I was trying to steer all gay men in that direction. As opinionated and emotional as some critics were, however, they often articulated thoughtful and reasoned criticisms. I took all of these criticisms seriously and considered them to be constructive. Open and honest expressions of viewpoints are immensely important if we are to have a healthy discussion in the gay world about, as the Los Angeles man above put it, "morality (much less mortality), ethics—whatever."

Unfortunately, however, too often the criticism of *Life Outside* was polarizing and ugly. And it was enough to prevent us from truly embarking on that healthy discussion. Rather than fostering expression of divergent viewpoints, much of the criticism of *Life Outside* devolved into silly and unproductive name-calling—even if it was sometimes quite amusing. Online, in the gay press, and elsewhere, I was called everything from a "tabloid media slut whore" and "a sex-negative fascist pig" to "the Nancy Reagan of the gay community" and "the gay community's own little Gladys Kravitz."

Life Outside also came under attack by a small but vocal group that formed in New York and called itself Sex Panic. The group began a campaign in New York—which it later took national, garnering much media attention—apparently aimed at discrediting me and other writers who offered self-criticism of gay culture. In articles that its members wrote in national magazines, as well as on fliers the group slapped on telephone poles and stuffed inside copies of *Life Outside* in bookstores, Sex Panic called me and other writers with whom they disagreed "anti-sex," "neoconservative," and—in the group's least creative moment—"TURDZ!"

Rather than hearing the voices of the many gay men who have reasoned differences of opinion about *Life Outside* and the issues it addressed, the gay and mainstream media became dominated throughout much of 1997 by the critiques that Sex Panic offered.

"Those who speak out are automatically accused of assimilationist views: we want to be like straights; we want marriage and monogamy and white picket fenced-in homes," Larry Kramer wrote on the op-ed page of the *New York Times* on December 12. "It is particularly moronic that Sex Panic considers these desires so sweepingly offensive. But even gay people who don't want to be like straights, don't want to be assimilated, and don't even want to marry or have a relationship still want to live their lives as social equals and responsible citizens."

That was an important point. Our lives are not black and white. And this vital discussion we are embarking on is not about monogamy vs. nonmonogamy, celibacy vs. recklessness, or assimilation vs. radical queerness. Some of *Life Outside*'s critics have created these polarized choices because they are actually afraid to look at the real complexities of gay men's lives, afraid to see that we are leading our lives in so many different ways, some of which might not suit them. And they are also afraid to face this truth: While some of gay sexual culture may be healthy, some of it is destructive, not only to individuals but to the entire community.

As we continue to try to have this important discussion, we should expect that some people will continue to attempt to divert us, making noise and creating distractions. So we must make sure that the discussion is loud enough and powerful enough to overcome those diversions.

That is now the challenge for all of you who have read this book. We must help to foster a dialogue and create a space for people to speak their minds freely, no matter what they may have to say. And we must now begin to bravely make the changes in gay culture that are necessary if we are to survive as a movement, as a community, and as a people.

Michelangelo Signorile receives e-mail at Signorile@ aol.com. You may also visit his web site at http://www.gaywired. com/signorile.

APPENDIX I

SIX WAYS TO DEPROGRAM FROM THE CULT

1. Shake Up the Cult.

Deprogramming doesn't mean rejecting all the notions of male beauty. It doesn't mean giving up gym memberships and ceasing to pay attention to physical appearances. Being proud about how we look and how we present ourselves to others, as opposed to being obsessed, can often in fact be a boost to our self-esteem as individuals.

Deprogramming rather means refusing to allow the cult to consume us and to control our lives, forcing us to go to extremes, exploiting our deep-seated anxieties. We need to follow the path of many American women, heterosexual as well as lesbian, who began making dramatic and still-occurring changes in their lives. Many women have empowered themselves not to view physical beauty as a measure of their self-worth and to stop going to dangerous extremes in trying to fit a physical ideal. They can celebrate physical beauty for its own sake, have fun with it, play with it, use it to their advantage, but they no longer allow it to solely define their value to men. While many women, like many gay men, are no doubt still overwhelmed and exploited by what Naomi Wolf calls the Rites of Beauty, many others have expanded their lives dramatically since feminism's first calls for liberation. They today view their self-worth as affected by many qualities beyond simply their physical appearance. Gay men similarly must get past valuing each other solely upon very rigid, standardized notions of male beauty, in the process oppressing one another in the way men have oppressed women for ages.

The "men are pigs" argument gets gay men off the hook too easily: Whether or not men are genetically programmed to objectify others physically and become sexual "hunters," the fact is that straight women are telling straight men that they *must* change if we are to live in a fair and just society, and straight men are, slowly but surely, changing. If straight men can reevaluate how they treat women and begin to make changes, then certainly we as gay men can reevaluate our own behavior and make similar changes in how we treat one another.

Awareness of the cult of masculinity's power and pull helps to loosen its grip on us. Awareness allows us to look at masculinity as something in large part that is constructed within our culture and as something that many straight men have always been enormously anxious about. But instead of letting it control us as gay men, *we* can control *it*, using it when we want. We may use it for sex, as something to get off on, for example. But we must stop allowing masculinity to define who we are: We must reject the use of terms like "straight-acting" in describing ourselves and others, privileging those among us whom we deem as more "masculine," and thus more "straight." The term "straight-acting" began to be used more only after gay liberation, and particularly since cyberspace. All over the Internet, gay men, caught within the cult of masculinity, are describing themselves as "straight-acting." And many of us who don't use such terminology ourselves blindly accept others' use of it. We should look to other groups in America that have had to battle both political oppression and a low self-esteem instilled from above. As Duane McWaine, the Los Angeles psychiatrist asked, Would African-Americans, for example, today accept the usage of the term "white-acting"?

We must begin loosening up the rigid definitions of gender and sexual orientation in general that we have become so wedded to, and begin to look at them as categories that have been delineated because of political realities, categories that don't necessarily define us in totality or have any value beyond the political.

We must understand that what was considered our preferred "sexual type" was in all likelihood actually formed soon after we entered the gay ghettos and saw what the cult of masculinity deemed as "hot." We can each remember a time when we liked older men or thinner men or heavier men or men whose bodies didn't fit so rigidly to the standard, men whose bodies weren't the first or only thing we noticed.

One way to lessen the cult's influence in your own life is to literally remove yourself from the places you find exclusive and oppressive. Often, for example, a man in his forties or fifties who goes to the ghetto bars where twenty-five-year-olds hang out will complain that he can't meet anyone, and that no one even looks at him. The same is true of younger men who have nice, natural-looking bodies but who go to places where all of the steroid-pumped men go. Of course we feel inadequate if we put ourselves in situations where we are made to feel inferior. But by pulling yourself out of those environments, you put an end to those negative feelings immediately.

Make an effort to go to other places that interest you, beyond the bar scene, where, particularly in the urban areas, other gay men who share similar interests might be: museums, jazz clubs, galleries, theaters, community centers, or wherever else people are gathering. Often, the first step in shaking up the cult is realizing how much we aid in our oppression by keeping ourselves locked in certain environments.

2. Explore Intimacy.

For many gay men, one underlying factor that is exploited by the cult of masculinity is a desire for and yet a fear of intimacy and bonding. As gay men, we often faced rejection as children and later as teenagers. We spend a lot of our lives trying to correct that past, trying to feel valuable. Deprogramming means facing the fear head on and achieving intimacy.

"What is happening in our community is primarily an outcome of a huge battle to gain intimacy in life, one of the most important life achievements," observes New York psychiatrist Ron Winchel. "The capacity to achieve intimacy, for a large number of gay men—not all gay men, and perhaps not most, but a large number—hit a huge obstacle. That is because they are gay, and it was put there very early in life. There are a lot of gay men out there dealing with . . . a great difficulty in achieving that intimacy. Often, these gay men want to look beautiful because their baseline assumption is that they won't be loved for themselves. One of the most curative experiences for that problem is getting into an intimate relationship. It doesn't

even have to be what we call a primary dyadic spousal relationship—it could be a close, wonderful friend. It's about
[developing] the capacity to feel that other people value you."

As Winchel alludes to, that does not necessarily mean following in a heterosexual paradigm: The intimate relationship
we're talking about here need not be a sexually monogamous
one, or even sexual at all. Many gay men, including many gay
men on the circuit and in the urban gay subculture, have
warm, intimate friendships that do allow them to grow and to
feel valued. But many others on the circuit and beyond, perhaps too many to ignore, have sporadic and superficial relationships. We "bond" with someone on a dance floor while
high on Ecstasy and convince ourselves that it is something
deep and profound. We consider as our "friends" people
whom we touch base with no more than a few times a year, or
with whom we simply party.

A truly intimate, deep relationship gives us strength and
support and is an example to us that we are valued beyond the
superficial qualities we tend to elevate. As gay men, we have a
lot of creative options to choose from in terms of nurturing
relationships. We have the possibility of developing the kinds
of close friendships straight men can't, precisely because of
their fear of homoeroticism.

Perhaps in part because they have deep and intimate
friendships, many men who identify themselves as single say
they are very happy being single. Throughout their lives most
gay men in fact spend time alternately single and coupled and
many are happy and content when they are in a relationship as
well as when they are not.

But a great many gay men who are single are not so happy;
they lament in interviews that they'd like to be coupled and yet
can't seem to make that a reality. These men sometimes say—

sometimes jokingly, other times not—that they are "chronically single." Michael Shernoff, the New York psychotherapist, is careful to make it clear that many people are content and emotionally satisfied being single.

"It's important that neither therapists nor lay people look on single people—gay or otherwise—as necessarily having a problem because they're not in a relationship," he says. "I use the term 'chronically single' to refer to those who actively seek a long-term relationship yet never seem to be able to find the right person."

Shernoff sees this problem as perhaps more acute among gay men than straight men, noting that "heterosexual men often receive assistance in expressing, or at least tolerating, emotional intimacy from their women partners, who have been socialized to recognize and prioritize their needs for emotional closeness." Shernoff and many other therapists note that men, socialized without the tools of intimacy, are unprepared when it come to developing a serious relationship when it turns out they are gay. "When two men are interested in pursuing an emotional relationship, very often neither has the faintest idea of what it means to relate in an intimate and noncompetitive way," Shernoff notes. "But they also have to overcome challenges that straight men don't have to think about. For one thing, gay men bring to the table their own unresolved homophobia, to whatever degree it exists."

Shernoff identifies three categories of chronically single men. The first group are those "who can't even get to first base," he notes. They are men who usually express difficulty in meeting people to date. These men usually have a long list of requirements a potential mate must fulfill, a list so complex that it effectively keeps them from meeting anyone. Shernoff calls it a "detailed shopping list . . . specifying such categories as race, religion, ethnicity, body type, age, hair color, quantity or absence of body hair, type of work, and geographic location."

The second group are men who do meet lots of men and date quite often but never see their dates move on to become relationships. This group gets past the laundry list of attributes, accepting someone outside their fantasy, but then, overcome with a fear of intimacy, they zero in on one attribute that they don't like in the potential mate—an unappealing body odor, a different taste in music—that makes them drop the person before the relationship can develop.

The third group is able to get to the one-year mark in a relationship, Shernoff says, but then sees the relationship abruptly end, acrimoniously. This group, much like the second group, channels the fear of intimacy into one specific activity or quality about the partner they don't like, and often blows it into something big, creating tension and division in the relationship and ultimately ending it.

"We can't talk about men and relationships without talking about intimacy," Shernoff says. "My own clinical practice indicates that, in general, men have a difficult time identifying their own need for emotional intimacy. . . . The presence of strong sexual passion is often confused with emotional intimacy. . . . I spend a lot of time explaining to clients that if they are to meet someone who will be a companion, or friend, as well as a lover, they will need to base the relationship on a lot more than the fact that the two of them have great sexual chemistry."

Deprogramming then is about cultivating real intimacy rather than allowing the cult of masculinity to seduce us into thinking that the superficial, often competitive liaisons it offers, as well as their powerful and overwhelming sexual energy, is intimacy. Real intimacy requires hard work: It means being honest with others and ourselves. For some of us it means going into therapy, for others it means having the fortitude to be truthful with ourselves on our own.

Deprogramming means learning how to be intimate by relating to one another off the dance floor and out of the sex clubs.

Deprogramming means shedding armor and beginning to see for ourselves beyond the cult of masculinity.

3. Mentor and Get Involved.

Getting beyond the cult and relating to men beyond the cult's trappings means getting involved in new and different and stimulating ventures that shake up your life. Deprogramming is in fact about getting involved in *more* activities, rather than restraining yourself from certain activities. It means broadening the people in your life to include men of different generations, different races, different occupation, and different interests.

For some this might mean getting involved in the usual activities that many men donate their time to, and thus meeting new and different men outside the cult: working in local politics, for a gay-friendly campaign; donating some of your time to AIDS service organizations; or joining an employee gay and lesbian group at your company, or an industry group—gay journalists, gay cops, gay doctors, etc.

But the greater challenge for all of us is to become mentors to others of all ages. That means beginning the process of mentoring in the way that Gregory Hutchings, the Washington AIDS counselor, so eloquently put: mentoring within our own generations as well as reaching out to others.

Visit a gay youth group and talk to young gay men. Go to a gay seniors group and befriend older gay men. Become a bridge between the generations. Challenge friends within your own generation to do the same. Don't accept people's immediate refusal to get involved with younger people—or older people—based on their own stereotypes and fears. Break the cycle that keeps us all apart.

Mentoring not only offers some rewards and bonds for yourself but also begins to open the eyes of others whom you come in contact with, and gradually helps us all break down the stereotypes that keep us chained to the cult.

In this way, deprogramming is about getting involved. Deprogramming is about seeing your life expand and grow and move beyond the cult and seeing the same thing happen to others of generations before you and after you.

4. Take Charge of Safer Sex.

All too often we defer to AIDS groups as the final word on what is safe and what is not safe, and yet AIDS groups have very different ideas about safer sex. Each seems intent on steering us in a particular direction, one that that group truly believes is right, but which might not necessarily be so. Deprogramming is about taking charge of your life, including decisions about safer sex.

Taking charge of safer sex means looking at your individual situation and assessing your needs based on your own sexual behavior. An AIDS organization should only be one among several sources—including respected AIDS reporters, epidemiologists, substance abuse counselors, and other experts—to look to for advice and counseling on safer sex. Ultimately your decisions should be based not on listening to whatever an AIDS organization tells you but on your own independent research, and your own behavior. Couples, for example, might want to consider negotiated safety (see Appendix II).

For those of us who are single who have found it difficult to keep safe during anal sex all of the time—and judging from studies, that appears to be a large percentage of us, perhaps a majority—we should think about lowering our partners and our number of sexual encounters, while at the same time not letting our guard down about using condoms. That is true whether we're negative and trying to keep ourselves from becoming infected, or positive and trying to prevent others from becoming infected.

We must apply some commonsense logic: If we're having trouble using "a condom every time" during anal sex, one way of lowering our odds of becoming infected or infecting others is to limit our numbers of partners and sexual encounters, particularly when we are compromised by drugs or alcohol. We are, after all, only human and are prone to slipping up. But as with anything else, our chances of slipping up—and of becoming infected if we are HIV-negative—will decrease the more we decrease the opportunities that allow it to happen. Though the advice of some AIDS prevention groups, which tell us to go out and have as much sex as we want as long as we use "a condom every time," might be seductive, we should resist being dictated to by blanket urgings.

Taking charge of safer sex means understanding your own problems and needs, learning all that you can about HIV transmission and safer sex, and making your decisions about safer sex in a logical and rational way based on your own situation.

This is particularly true when making decisions in areas of safer sex where there is the most disagreement among professionals. Regarding unprotected oral sex, for example, AIDS groups often differ greatly, and many try to influence gay men in one direction rather than simply give them the facts and let them decide for themselves. While it is perhaps true that the numbers of people who have been infected with HIV through unprotected oral sex are greatly lower than the numbers who have been infected through unprotected anal sex, several studies have shown that HIV transmission does occur through oral sex, however infrequently. There are also enough case reports and there is enough anecdotal information—many of us know someone who believes he was infected through oral sex—to be concerned about the risks of oral sex.

Decisions on oral sex should in fact be made by each individual based on the reality that oral sex does carry some risk of HIV infection. Some HIV-negative men might decide that, based on the facts, they're willing to take the risk that unprotected oral sex carries, deciding for themselves that that risk is relatively low. They may, however, decide to limit their number of partners and sexual encounters. Other men might decide to have unprotected oral sex only with partners they know well, partners whom they know are HIV-negative. Still other men might decide to take precautions, and thus use condoms, every time they have oral sex, or they might decide not to have oral sex at all.

But some AIDS groups are apparently convinced that gay men cannot make these decisions for themselves and seem to want to steer them in a particular direction. Gay Men's Health Crisis, for example, released a report in 1996 concluding that, "unprotected oral sex is classifiable as safer sex or as safe compared to safest. (Safest can refer to completely non-insertive forms of sex, such as masturbation and frottage.)" Try telling the many men who appear to have been infected through oral sex, however, the difference between safest, safer, and safe. One young gay man who became infected through oral sex told the *Village Voice* in 1996, "Before I got infected, safe and safer sounded very similar. Now, having this virus in my body, the gap between them seems a lot wider."

Indeed, for many gay men, safer means *okay* and safe means *totally okay*. Rather than putting these ambiguous and often misleading labels on the risks of oral sex, AIDS prevention groups should simply discuss the risks in relation to studies, and let gay men make their own decisions.

Taking charge of safer sex for yourself therefore means getting the facts and not allowing AIDS organizations' plays on words to rule your own decisions about what is or is not safe for you.

5. Demand Real Harm Reduction.

Deprogramming also means facing the truth about ourselves and others. We must break from our denial. The gay male community is reeling under an epidemic of substance abuse, one that is fueling the AIDS epidemic, contributing to unsafe sex. Drug abuse programs and alcohol abuse programs within the gay and lesbian community are probably among the most effective and most visible. But many of our community groups — and particularly AIDS groups — have refused to take a proactive approach when it comes to dealing with drugs in the gay world, sometimes even turning a blind eye for fear of stigmatization of gay men.

Rather than enable many gay men to continue in sometimes destructive behaviors, we need to seriously implement more of what is known as *harm reduction*: Educating people about the various drugs and their dangers; if they are going to use specific drugs, telling them how to use them with minimal harm; and encouraging them to deal with their problems. Some groups claim that they do implement harm reduction, but their efforts are still rather cautious. Fearing offending people, they don't offer the full range of dangers to drug users and often *only* help show them how to use the drugs safely—and even that information is sometimes sketchy. That, coupled with their sponsorship of drug-fueled circuit events, often makes it appear that they are promoting drug use.

A more comprehensive understanding of harm reduction has as its goal a desire to thoroughly educate people about specific drugs and their effects—not just tell them to make sure to "drink water" if they are using drugs, as some AIDS agencies advise at their circuit events—and to greatly encourage those who might have a problem with alcohol and drug use to seek help.

"For many people, substance use is an integrated and non-problematic part of their life, [however] for some people, substance use becomes a concern as it adversely affects other parts of their life," the Libra Project, a British substance use counseling group notes in a discussion of harm reduction and substance use on its website (http://www.brookes.ac.uk/health/index.html). The Libra Project offers in-depth harm reduction information on many drugs used by gay men, from cocaine to GHB, and also discusses the dangers of these drugs with regard to HIV infection and safer sex.

"Any substance use carries risk," the Libra Project notes in discussing harm reduction and its goals. "By establishing what risks you are engaging in (through self-assessment) and finding areas where risk can be reduced, you can minimize the likelihood of harm. The only way to ensure that you engage in no risk at all is of course not to use any substance." Among the group's aims are:

- "to help those people who choose to use substances to become informed about the substances involved. It's difficult (and potentially dangerous) to make choices without knowledge; finding out about a substance and acting on information about the risks involved can reduce the likelihood of harm."

- "to help those for whom substance use has become problematic to find the support they need. Often counseling, therapy, conventional western medicine and complimentary therapies can all help an individual to regain control of their lives."

Some of our AIDS organizations might say they have similar goals. However, those goals are not evident in their actions. AIDS organizations and HIV-prevention groups should certainly be present at circuit events, dispensing highly detailed information about drug use and unsafe sex associated with it, including the various short- and long-term effects of the drugs. The groups should not, however, be sponsoring or benefiting from such events, thereby being construed as promoting drug use to gay men, or at best looking the other way from it. And we, individually and as a community, must demand no less from them.

6. Get Beyond the Urban Gay Scene.

This is a two-part project. For many of us, getting beyond the scene means developing friendships outside the ghetto, in the gay community and outside as well. It means realizing that the world is a lot bigger than just gay men and the cult. We could do well to involve lesbians in our lives and learn a lot from how they construct their relationships and their families and how they deal with such issues as homophobia. Similarly, not only should we stop cutting off those straight people who were part of our lives previously and still want to be in our lives, but we should cultivate new straight friends as well. Not only does this influence them, making them more understanding of what gay men go through, but it also influences *us*, lets us see that not all heterosexuals are the bogeymen we sometimes make them out to be, and that we can often even learn from them as well.

For others, getting beyond the scene means coming out *for real*: Lesbian and gay activists and therapists have said for decades that living our lives in the closet keeps us from growing; it makes us feel that our lives and our relationships are dirty secrets, things we can't possibly share with family and friends. The urban ghettos can be comfortable refuges for many gay men, places where they can find people like themselves. But they can also prevent us from fully coming out to the people who were most important to us as we grew up: our family. And by not coming out to our families, even though they live far away, we keep reinforcing to ourselves that we are not equal to them and that our homosexuality is a bad thing; internalized homophobia in turn wreaks havoc on our self-esteem, affecting all of our interpersonal relationships and allowing the cult of masculinity to exploit our insecurities.

Those gay men who escape to the ghetto as a way of finding community but also as a way of avoiding their past and everyone where they grew up lock themselves in an eternal adolescence, not moving forward from the "secret" life that teenagers live. And that closet gives us an excuse for not moving on.

Similarly, those who live in the urban centers but often stay closeted even there, to co-workers (even though they could come out) and sometimes even neighbors and friends, again reinforce to themselves that their lives are a secret.

Deprogramming is about coming out beyond just our friends on the urban gay scene, to co-workers who are actively in our lives as well as to family back home who may be less active in our lives today but who are no less important.

Deprogramming means taking control of our lives and not allowing the cult of masculinity to define for us, and for everyone else, what it means to be gay or what it means to be a man.

APPENDIX II

NEGOTIATED SAFETY

Negotiated safety is one option available to gay couples who are deciding upon safer sex guidelines together. Couples need to discuss issues of safer sex together and come to conclusions they are both conformable with (see pages 252-259). If, for example, both members of a couple believe unprotected oral sex is a risk worth taking, find that anal sex without condoms is important to them, and are able to be completely honest with one another, then negotiated safety may be something for them to consider. The rules of negotiated safety that appear below are adapted from Australia's Victorian AIDS Council/Gay Men's Health Centre.

1. Talk with each other about how important it really is to have anal sex together without condoms. If it's not such a big deal to either of you, keep using condoms.

2. Presuming that you are negative simply because you'd tested negative once before—or because you've never tested

but you believe you have not been unsafe — is not a wise presumption and can put your partner at risk. If you'd both really like to engage in anal sex without condoms, each of you should take an HIV test together, be completely honest about the results, and preferably collect the results together.

3. Keep using condoms every time you have anal sex for at least three months after you've tested or perhaps for up to six months just to be sure. It can take up to three months for HIV antibodies to show up on a test.

4. After the time period that you have decided upon has elapsed, get tested together again.

5. If you're both negative, promise each other that you won't engage in anal sex outside the relationship, or that if either of you has anal sex outside the relationship, condoms will always be used.

6. Talk openly with each other and promise each other that if either of you slips up or has an accident (a condom breaks, for example) with regard to safer sex outside the relationship, you will tell your partner immediately and go back to protected sex until you've both been tested again twice, three months apart. Or …

7. Agree that either partner can at any time insist that both of you begin using condoms again.

8. Discuss with one another that accidents might happen, that either of you can at any time slip up, and that it won't mean the end of your relationship. Promise that you won't punish each other or resent each other for being honest, and make sure you can keep to this promise. If it feels like too much to expect from you, then continue to use condoms, always.

9. If you both have HIV, before deciding to stop using con-

doms you should discuss with your doctor the realities of becoming infected with another strain of HIV and of protecting yourself from other sexually transmitted diseases.

10. If one of you has HIV and the other is negative, keep using condoms, always.